T

CW00541451

The Bible after Babel

Historical Criticism in a Postmodern Age

John J. Collins

William B. Eerdmans Publishing Company
Grand Rapids, Michigan / Cambridge, U.K.

© 2005 Wm. B. Eerdmans Publishing Co.
All rights reserved

Wm. B. Eerdmans Publishing Co.
255 Jefferson Ave. S.E., Grand Rapids, Michigan 49503 /
P.O. Box 163, Cambridge CB3 9PU U.K.
www.eerdmans.com

Printed in the United States of America

10 09 08 07 06 05   7 6 5 4 3 2 1

ISBN-10: 0-8028-2892-2
ISBN-13: 978-0-8028-2892-7

Contents

Preface

The six chapters that make up this book were delivered as the Gunning lectures at the School of Divinity of the University of Edinburgh between November 1 and 12, 2004. I would like to thank the Edinburgh faculty for extraordinary hospitality and stimulating discussion. In the first place, my thanks are due to Timothy Lim, who initiated the invitation, suggested the topic, and served as my primary host. Others who deserve special thanks include David Ferguson, Graeme Auld, Nicolas Wyatt, Larry Hurtado, Marcella Althaus-Reid, and Nicholas Adams.

The topic proposed to me for the lectures was "The Bible at the Beginning of the Twenty-first Century." What I have written might be characterized more aptly as an account of some of the main changes in the study of the Hebrew Bible or the Old Testament in the last third of the 20th century. This account is not exhaustive. Many other topics might in principle be treated. Perhaps the most obvious omission is the ongoing debate about the origin of the Pentateuch. Insofar as that debate entails the erosion of the certainties of an earlier generation, it would offer one more instance of the general pattern described in this book. But I trust that the issues I have chosen are adequately representative of the major trends in scholarship of this period. These are also issues where there has been extensive debate and where retrospective assessment is now possible. I have not seriously engaged newer, cutting-edge developments, such as Third World scholarship or Queer Theory. No doubt, these developments will be important as the

21st century develops, but they are only beginning to make an impression in biblical scholarship, and an assessment at this time would be premature.

Several people read parts of this book in manuscript and made helpful suggestions. I would like to thank specifically Adela Yarbro Collins, Christl Maier, Saul Olyan, Yvonne Sherwood, Rebecca Raphael, and Ron Hendel.

Last, but not least, my thanks are due to Michael Thomson of Wm. B. Eerdmans Publishing Company, who solicited the manuscript and guided it through the publication process.

Abbreviations

ABD	*The Anchor Bible Dictionary,* ed. David Noel Freedman
AJA	*American Journal of Archaeology*
AOAT	Alter Orient und Altes Testament
BA	*Biblical Archaeologist*
BAR	*Biblical Archaeology Review*
BASOR	*Bulletin of the American Schools of Oriental Research*
BEvT	Beiträge zur evangelischen Theologie
BibInt	*Biblical Interpretation*
BJS	Brown Judaic Studies
BTB	*Biblical Theology Bulletin*
BZAW	Beihefte zur Zeitschrift für die alttestamentliche Wissenschaft
CBQ	*Catholic Biblical Quarterly*
CC	Continental Commentaries
CHANE	Culture and History of the Ancient Near East
ConBOT	Coniectanea biblica: Old Testament Series
CurBS	*Currents in Research: Biblical Studies*
DDD	*Dictionary of Deities and Demons in the Bible,* ed. Karel van der Toorn, Bob Becking, and Pieter W. van der Horst, 2nd ed.
ErIsr	*Eretz-Israel*
GBS	Guides to Biblical Scholarship
HBT	*Horizons in Biblical Theology*
HSM	Harvard Semitic Monographs
HSS	Harvard Semitic Studies

ABBREVIATIONS

HTR	*Harvard Theological Review*
HUCA	*Hebrew Union College Annual*
IDB	*Interpreter's Dictionary of the Bible*
IEJ	*Israel Exploration Journal*
Int	*Interpretation*
JAAR	*Journal of the American Academy of Religion*
JANER	*Journal of Ancient Near Eastern Religions*
JAOS	*Journal of the American Oriental Society*
JBL	*Journal of Biblical Literature*
JBTh	*Jahrbuch für biblische Theologie*
JES	*Journal of Ecumenical Studies*
JR	*Journal of Religion*
JSJSup	Supplements to the Journal for the Study of Judaism
JSNTSup	Journal for the Study of the New Testament: Supplement Series
JSOT	*Journal for the Study of the Old Testament*
JSOTSup	Journal for the Study of the Old Testament: Supplement Series
JSPSup	Journal for the Study of the Pseudepigrapha: Supplement Series
NEA	*Near Eastern Archaeology*
NIB	*The New Interpreter's Bible*
OBO	Orbis biblicus et orientalis
OBT	Overtures to Biblical Theology
OTL	Old Testament Library
RB	*Revue biblique*
SBL	Society of Biblical Literature
SBLBSNA	Society of Biblical Literature Biblical Scholarship in North America
SBLDS	Society of Biblical Literature Dissertation Series
SBLMS	Society of Biblical Literature Monograph Series
SBLSymS	Society of Biblical Literature Symposium Series
SBT	Studies in Biblical Theology
SHANE	Studies in the History of the Ancient Near East
SJOT	*Scandinavian Journal of the Old Testament*
SJT	*Scottish Journal of Theology*
ThB	*Theologische Bücherei*
ThLZ	*Theologische Literaturzeitung*
VT	*Vetus Testamentum*
VTSup	*Supplements to Vetus Testamentum*
WMANT	Wissenschaftliche Monographien zum Alten und Neuen Testament
WUNT	Wissenschaftliche Untersuchungen zum Neuen Testament
ZAW	*Zeitschrift für die alttestamentliche Wissenschaft*

Historical Criticism and
Its Postmodern Critics

The story of the tower of Babel is told briefly and enigmatically in Gen 11:1-9, at the end of the Primeval History in the J (Yahwist) source. In the beginning, people had one language and the same words throughout the earth. They attracted the attention of the Lord, however, by building a city and a tower, with its top in the heavens, to make a name for themselves. The Lord figured that this was only the beginning of what they would do and, since they were one people with one language, nothing would be impossible to them. To prevent further developments, the Lord went down and confused their language and scattered them abroad over the face of the earth. Therefore the city was called "Babel," because there the Lord confused the language of all the earth.

This intriguing little story has received more than its share of scholarly attention.[1] Commentators have noted that there seem to be two distinct themes in the story: the attempt to build the city and tower and the confusion of language, and, inevitably, source critics have tried to separate the two. On one level, at least, the story is an etiology for the diversity of languages. On another level, it recapitulates a recurring theme in the primeval history — the futile attempts to bridge heaven and earth, whether by hu-

---

1. Claus Westermann, *Genesis 1-11*. CC (Minneapolis: Augsburg, 1984), 531-57; Ellen von Wolde, "The Tower of Babel as Lookout over Genesis 1-11," in *Words Become Worlds: Semantic Studies of Genesis 11:1-9*. Biblical Interpretation 6 (Leiden: Brill, 1994), 84-109.

man beings becoming like God or by "sons of God" becoming human. As the story stands, the confusion of languages seems to be a punishment for human hybris, or at least an attempt by a defensive God to protect his realm from human encroachment. Neither the building nor the confusion of languages is viewed positively. Rather, the story seems to be a final episode in the gradual fall of humanity from the pristine glory of Eden to the postlapsarian condition of human history.

In recent years, this story has received new attention, even attracting notice from one of the icons of postmodernism, Jacques Derrida.[2] The distinctive postmodern take on the story, however, reverses the traditional evaluation. The enterprise of building the tower is still viewed negatively, but the confusion of languages is celebrated as liberation. On the one hand, some critics, especially from the Third World, see the city and tower as symbols of dominion and oppression.[3] This reading acquires credibility from the historical relation between Babylon and Israel and the obvious taunting of Babel in the perverse explanation of the name,[4] even if there is nothing explicit about oppression in the biblical text.[5] The confusion of languages, then, bespeaks political liberation, insofar as each people is freed to pursue its own identity. On the other hand, from a more philosophical perspective, the tower has been taken as a symbol of the aspiration to total, comprehensive, and unitary interpretation, and the con-

2. Jacques Derrida, "Des Tours de Babel," in *Poststructuralism as Exegesis,* ed. David Jobling and Stephen D. Moore. Semeia 54 (1992), 3-34. According to Derrida, "the 'tower of Babel' does not merely figure the irreducible multiplicity of tongues; it exhibits an incompletion, the impossibility of finishing, of totalizing, of saturating, of completing something of the order of edification, architectural construction, system and architectonics. . . . It would be easy and up to a certain point justified to see there the translation of a system in deconstruction" (3-4).

3. See the reflections on "Genesis 11:1-9: A Latin-American Perspective," by José Míguez Bonino, Solomon Avotri, and Choan-Seng Song, in *Return to Babel: Global Perspectives on the Bible,* ed. Priscilla Pope-Levison and John R. Levison (Louisville: Westminster John Knox, 1999), 13-33; and Danna Nolan Fewell, "Building Babel," in *Postmodern Interpretations of the Bible: A Reader,* ed. A. K. M. Adam (St. Louis: Chalice, 2001), 1-15.

4. The etymology is based on the Hebrew root *bll,* which in Westermann's judgment has "only a slight resemblance to Babel" (553). The Akkadian understanding of the name is "gate of God." The inaccuracy of the etymology was noted by Voltaire, who thought that the name signified "city of God." See Derrida, 4.

5. The etymology could easily be viewed as a secondary addition to the story. As Westermann remarks, it is "quite independent and the narrative is complete without it" (553).

fusion of languages has come to symbolize the celebration of diversity. In the context of biblical studies, historical criticism, or the dominant mode of biblical criticism for the last two centuries or so, has been cast as the tower, and the confusion of languages is taken as the joyful eruption of a chatter of new approaches. The issue, of course, is not what the biblical text of Genesis 11 "really meant." Some postmodern critics would deny that a text has any "real meaning" at all. The story simply provides familiar imagery that can serve to visualize the situation in which biblical criticism, and perhaps academia in general, finds itself at the beginning of the 21st century.[6]

It is not the case that the postmodernists have captured the field. Far from it. Diversity of approaches is at best a mixed blessing, and sometimes threatens to become a curse. But neither is traditional historical criticism accurately described as the totalitarian monolith that some of its critics make it out to be. I will begin by reflecting on the character of historical criticism as I understand it. I will then consider some of the distinctive features of postmodern approaches and consider the application of some of them in biblical studies.

I should say at the outset that by training and temperament I am on the modern side of the modern/postmodern debate. My brain has not incubated in the languages of Jacques Derrida, Michel Foucault, or Stanley Fish (if indeed incubation is what happens to a brain in these environments). But it also seems to me that there are some valid concerns and significant insights in the welter of new approaches. Historical criticism has always been a process rather than a technical method, and if it can be said to construct a tower, it has always been a work in progress, whose design and orientation are constantly subject to change. I do not think it either likely or desirable that God's gym and God's beauty parlor will become the twin towers of biblical interpretation in the coming century,[7] but it would be naive to think that scholarship a century from now will look much like it does today, whatever form it may take.

---

6. For Babel as metaphor for the situation in the field of ethics: Jeffrey Stout, *Ethics after Babel: The Languages of Morals and Their Discontents* (Boston: Beacon, 1988).

7. Cf. S. D. Moore, *God's Gym: Divine Male Bodies of the Bible* (New York: Routledge, 1996); *God's Beauty Parlor and Other Queer Spaces in and around the Bible* (Stanford: Stanford University Press, 2001). Moore, to his credit, has no evident hegemonic intentions.

The Character of Historical Criticism

"Historical Criticism" is the label usually applied to what might be termed "mainline" biblical scholarship over the last two centuries or so. As James Barr has insisted, historical criticism is not strictly a method, but a loose umbrella that covers a range of methods (source criticism, form criticism, sociological criticism, etc.) that may sometimes be at odds with each other.[8] In fact, it is not unusual to narrate the history of biblical scholarship as a succession of methods, each of which initially exhibited its anxiety of influence by attempting to kill its father, and whose fathers sometimes disowned the offspring.[9] What these methods have in common is a general agreement that texts should be interpreted in their historical contexts, in light of the literary and cultural conventions of their time. There is also a general assumption that the meaning of a text can be established in an objective manner, but this assumption is more complicated than it may seem. The meaning intended by an ancient author can, at best, only be reconstructed tentatively, and few historical critics would deny that a text may take on new meanings in changing circumstances. (This is in fact the *raison d'être* of redaction criticism.) But historical critics usually assume a hierarchy of meanings and regard the historical context as basic or primary.

Historical criticism of the Bible developed primarily as an enterprise of Protestant Christianity, within the context of the Christian churches.[10] While the Reformation encouraged Christians to read the Bible for themselves, and used it as a counterweight to Catholic tradition, it was not until the 18th century and the Enlightenment that biblical criticism began to emerge in its modern form, and it developed hand in hand with critical

8. James Barr, *History and Ideology in the Old Testament* (Oxford: Oxford University Press, 2000), 32-58.

9. For a survey of these methods, see Steven L. McKenzie and Stephen R. Haynes, eds., *To Each Its Own Meaning: An Introduction to Biblical Criticisms and Their Application* (Louisville: Westminster John Knox, 1993), esp. 11-99.

10. Emil G. Kraeling, *The Old Testament since the Reformation* (New York: Harper, 1955). On Jewish reactions to "higher criticism," see Alan Cooper, "Biblical Studies and Jewish Studies," in *The Oxford Handbook of Jewish Studies*, ed. Martin Goodman (Oxford: Oxford University Press, 2002), 14-35. On the development of Catholic scholarship, see Gerald P. Fogarty, S.J., *American Catholic Biblical Scholarship: A History from the Early Republic to Vatican II* (San Francisco: Harper & Row, 1989).

historiography in the 19th.[11] The principles that guided this criticism were articulated most insightfully by the German theologian and sociologist of religion Ernst Troeltsch, whose views were later reformulated lucidly by Van Harvey.[12]

These principles included the *autonomy* of the historian. This principle is associated with the Enlightenment and especially with Immanuel Kant, although he certainly was not the first to conceive of it.[13] As Harvey has well described it, autonomy represented a change in what may be called the morality of knowledge. Where medieval culture had celebrated belief as a virtue and regarded doubt as sin, the modern critical mentality regards doubt as a necessary step in the testing of knowledge and the will to believe as a threat to rational thought. In the context of biblical studies, autonomy meant first of all freedom from ecclesiastical authorities and heresy trials. In that narrow sense, the need for autonomy can hardly be questioned. But it also represented an ideal of judgment. In the words of the historian R. G. Collingwood, "so far from relying on an authority other than himself, to whose statements his thought must conform, the historian is his own authority."[14] In this sense, autonomy is opposed not only to ecclesiastical interference but also to undue deference to received opinion. Biblical scholarship has not always been characterized by autonomy in the latter sense, although I doubt that many historical critics would dispute the principle!

A second principle of historical criticism is the *principle of analogy*.[15] To understand the ancient context of a text requires some sympathetic

11. Robert Morgan, with John Barton, *Biblical Interpretation* (Oxford: Oxford University Press, 1988), 40-92. An account of these developments with a New Testament focus, from a conservative Christian perspective, can be found in Roy A. Harrisville and Walter Sundberg, *The Bible in Modern Culture: From Baruch Spinoza to Brevard Childs*, 2nd ed. (Grand Rapids: Wm. B. Eerdmans, 2002), 10-168.

12. Ernst Troeltsch, "Ueber historische und dogmatische Methode in der Theologie," *Gesammelte Schriften* (Tübingen: Mohr, 1913), 2:729-53; "Historiography," in *Encyclopedia of Religion and Ethics*, ed. James Hastings (New York: Scribner, 1914), 6:716-23; Van A. Harvey, *The Historian and the Believer* (New York: Macmillan, 1966); Edgar Krentz, *The Historical-Critical Method* (Philadelphia: Fortress, 1975).

13. Immanuel Kant, "What Is Enlightenment?" in *Critique of Practical Reason and Other Writings in Moral Philosophy*, ed. Lewis White Beck (Chicago: University of Chicago Press, 1949), 286-92. See Harvey, 39-42.

14. R. G. Collingwood, *The Idea of History* (Oxford: Oxford University Press, 1946), 236.

15. Harvey, 14-15; Krentz, 55-72.

analogy between ancient and modern situations. Indeed, one of the assumptions of historical criticism is that texts are human products and that human nature has not changed beyond recognition over the centuries. We can assess what is plausible in an ancient situation because we know what human beings are capable of. This principle gave rise to problems with regard to the miraculous aspects of the biblical stories, but it also provided a way of bringing the text to life by analogy with modern experiences.

A third principle of historical criticism is the *principle of criticism*.[16] Scholarship is an ongoing process; its results are always provisional and never final. This is perhaps especially obvious in historical scholarship, where new evidence is constantly coming to light. The historian tries to establish the most probable account of the past, but absolute certainty is never available. Today's results may be overturned by tomorrow's excavation. This element of uncertainty in biblical scholarship has always been especially unsettling for church authorities and for traditional theologians, more so even than heretical conclusions, because it implies that anything we believe may be subject to revision in light of new evidence and undercuts any idea of unchangeable revealed truth.[17]

The original impact of historical criticism in the predominantly Christian contexts of Europe and North America was revolutionary. Robert Morgan has referred to "the death of Scripture" in this context, although the death throes continue to the present day.[18] The impact was felt mainly in connection with the historical reliability of the biblical text. For many Christians, the belief that the text is inspired entailed a belief in its historical accuracy, and that belief is so deeply ingrained that the debate lingers on in various forms after two hundred years of historical criticism. Julius Wellhausen felt obliged to resign from a theological faculty.[19] Scholars like W. Robertson Smith and Charles A. Briggs were subjected to

16. Harvey, 14-15.
17. See the summary and assessment of Troeltsch by Harrisville and Sundberg, 146-68.
18. Morgan, 44-61.
19. See Rudolf Smend, "Julius Wellhausen and His *Prolegomena to the History of Israel*," *Semeia* 25 (1982): 1-20. On 5 April 1882, he wrote to the Prussian Minister of Culture: "I became a theologian because the scientific treatment of the Bible interested me; only gradually did I come to understand that a professor of theology also has the practical task of preparing the students for service in the Protestant Church, and that I am not adequate to this practical task, but that instead despite all caution on my own part I make my hearers unfit for their office" (6).

6

heresy trials.[20] In the United States, the Fundamentalist movement was in large part a reaction against historical criticism and the relativism that it implied.[21] In the Roman Catholic Church, the Modernist movement embraced historical criticism but was condemned by the papacy.[22] Nonetheless, by the early 20th century the point had been made, at least in the so-called mainline churches, that biblical texts did not necessarily always report historical events, or do so in ways that would satisfy modern criteria. The growing appreciation of literary genre and the publication of cognate literature from the ancient Near East were crucial factors in this development.[23] Christian theology, at least in its more liberal forms, reached an accommodation with historical criticism that acknowledged its validity, even if only within certain limits.

Conversely, biblical scholars often sought to reconcile their findings with traditional faith. This tendency was most obvious in the subfield of biblical theology and especially in the so-called biblical theology movement.[24] In the arena of history, this tendency can be seen in the enormously influential *A History of Israel* by John Bright, which scarcely questions the reliability of the biblical record, while buttressing it with a richly informative account of ancient Near Eastern history.[25] There were, of

20. On Robertson Smith see John W. Rogerson, "Smith, William Robertson (1846-94)," in *Dictionary of Biblical Interpretation*, ed. John H. Hayes (Nashville: Abingdon, 1999), 2:477-78; *The Bible and Criticism in Victorian Britain: Profiles of F. D. Maurice and William Robertson Smith*. JSOTSup 201 (Sheffield: Sheffield Academic, 1995). On C. A. Briggs, see Max G. Rogers, "Briggs, Charles Augustus (1841-1913)," in Hayes, 1:138-39.

21. See George M. Marsden, *Fundamentalism and American Culture: The Shaping of Twentieth-Century Evangelicalism, 1870-1925* (New York: Oxford University Press, 1980); and, with a focus on the interpretation of Daniel, Adela Yarbro Collins and John J. Collins, "The Book of Truth: Daniel as Reliable Witness to Past and Future in the United States of America," in *Europa, Tausendjähriges Reich und Neue Welt: Zwei Jahrtausende Geschichte und Utopie in der Rezeption des Danielbuches*, ed. Mariano Delgado, Klaus Koch, and Edgar Marsch (Freiburg: Universitätsverlag, and Stuttgart: Kohlhammer, 2003), 385-404, esp. 395-400.

22. See Fogarty, 78-119.

23. In the Catholic Church, the encyclical of Pius XII, *Divino Afflante Spiritu* (1943), was a landmark in this respect. See C. Louis, O.S.B., ed., *Rome and the Study of the Scriptures: A Collection of Papal Enactments on the Study of Holy Scripture together with the Decisions of the Biblical Commission*, 7th ed. (St. Meinrad: Grail, 1962), 80-107.

24. See the classic account of Brevard S. Childs, *Biblical Theology in Crisis* (Philadelphia: Westminster, 1970), 13-87.

25. 4th ed., with an Introduction and Appendix by William P. Brown (Louisville: Westminster John Knox, 2000); originally published in 1959.

course, profound differences between the American biblical theology movement represented by people like George Ernest Wright, and the more subtle European "history of traditions" approach of Gerhard von Rad,[26] but the common ground was considerable. The Old Testament was viewed from a distinctly Christian perspective. The biblical history was affirmed as a history of salvation, even when its historical facticity was admitted to be in doubt. Ancient Israel was thought to be decisively different from its ancient Near Eastern environment, although that environment provided an essential context for interpretation. In this regard, biblical theology stood in sharp contrast to the history of religions approach of the "Myth and Ritual school."[27] But the dominant voices in biblical scholarship for much of the 20th century were generally subservient to the dominant voices in the biblical text. While historical details might be questioned, and great energy was expended on reconstructing the history of the biblical text, most biblical scholarship took place within the interpretive framework of Christian theology.

In the last quarter of the 20th century, however, that framework became increasingly problematic. We have witnessed what Leo Perdue has called "the collapse of history."[28] Even the assured results of earlier generations, such as the documentary hypothesis in Pentateuchal studies, are under fire.[29] New methods and approaches are sprouting up everywhere. The changes in the character of biblical studies were driven by two factors. On the one hand, there is what the archaeologist William Dever has called "the steady accumulation of empirical data."[30] Beginning in the 19th century, knowledge of the historical context of ancient Israel was transformed by the discovery of Akkadian and Egyptian texts. In the 20th century, the Ugaritic texts found at Ras Shamra in 1929 and the Dead Sea Scrolls have

26. Gerhard von Rad, *Old Testament Theology*, 2 vols. (New York: Harper & Row, 1962-65).

27. The "Myth and Ritual" school was a broad movement in the study of religion. See the anthology, Robert A. Segal, ed., *The Myth and Ritual Theory* (Oxford: Blackwell, 1998). The application of this theory to biblical studies is illustrated by the contributions of S. H. Hooke (83-92) and Ivan Engnell (136-40).

28. Leo G. Perdue, *The Collapse of History*. OBT (Minneapolis: Fortress, 1994).

29. See Ernest W. Nicholson, *The Pentateuch in the Twentieth Century: The Legacy of Julius Wellhausen* (Oxford: Clarendon, 1998).

30. William G. Dever, "What Did the Biblical Writers Know, and When Did They Know It?" in *Hesed ve-Emet: Studies in Honor of Ernest S. Frerichs*, ed. Jodi Magness and Seymour Gitin. BJS 320 (Atlanta: Scholars, 1998), 241-53 (249).

had a major impact on biblical interpretation. While the relevance of the nonbiblical material was obscured in the heyday of biblical theology, it could not be ignored forever, and neither could the sharp differentiation of Israel from its Near Eastern environment be maintained. More recently, archaeology has forced a serious revision of the received account of the origins of Israel. Of course, the new evidence is always subject to interpretation, and its interpretation is never final. But it is no longer possible to claim that independent, objective research supports the basic historicity of the biblical text. Whether archaeological research can be regarded as objective is another matter, but at least the foundations of biblical reliability can no longer be shored up from that quarter.

The existence and importance of empirical data can not be denied, but this is not the major factor in the changing face of biblical studies. Far more important is the changing demography of the field. Up to the 1960s, biblical studies was largely the preserve of white male Christian professors, largely Protestant. The *Sitz-im-Leben* was primarily the seminary or department of theology, or alternatively departments of Near Eastern studies. Beginning in the 1960s, this situation began to change. Catholics began to attain some prominence, and women entered the field in increasing numbers. Jewish scholars sought their training in secular or Christian universities. Racial and ethnic minorities became visible, even if not well represented. Many scholars found themselves teaching in departments of religious studies, with no confessional allegiance. All of these changes had an impact on the way biblical criticism was done. Feminist scholars pointed out the pervasive patriarchy in biblical texts. Jewish scholars uncovered Christian bias in supposedly objective scholarship. And some scholars found their closest colleagues in departments of literature or sociology rather than in theology or Near Eastern studies. It is in light of this new situation that the plethora of new approaches has arisen in biblical studies.

In light of this situation, we may well ask what two hundred years of historical criticism has achieved. We certainly have a lot of new evidence that improves our understanding of life in the ancient world,[31] but the progress of the field as a whole can hardly be characterized as "the steady accumulation of empirical data." It is at least as much a matter of the pro-

---

31. See, e.g., Philip J. King and Lawrence E. Stager, *Life in Biblical Israel* (Louisville: Westminster John Knox, 2001).

9

gressive shedding of certitude. This is perhaps most obvious in the area of history, but it is operative in other areas too. Ongoing criticism has tended to highlight the tensions and differences within the biblical texts. Consequently, it is difficult to regard the Bible, or just the Hebrew Bible, as a whole, as a coherent guide to life. Most fundamentally, cracks have begun to appear in the ethical values of the Bible, and questions are raised about the God that it portrays. All of this might be said to be entailed already in the morality of knowledge that underlies the discipline, which celebrates doubt as virtue and regards faith, in the sense of belief, with suspicion.[32] Historical criticism has seldom, if ever, pushed its principles to their logical conclusion. But in view of the corrosive effect of Troeltsch's "principle of criticism," it is ironic that some recent writers have characterized historical criticism as a quest for "some kind of absolute truth."[33] Nothing could be further from the case.

There is another aspect of historical criticism that I should like to emphasize, and that seems to me to have been quite successful. It has created an arena where people with different faith commitments can work together and have meaningful conversations. The historical focus has been a way of getting distance from a text, of respecting its otherness. The neutrality and objectivity at which the discipline has aimed has allowed Jews and Christians to work together and has allowed feminists to make their case in ways that initially unsympathetic scholars have found compelling. The objectivity in question is not a matter of absolute truth. Rather, it is a matter of making an argument by appeal to assumptions and knowledge shared by the participants in a particular conversation, a quest for what might be called a "regional" truth. What historical criticism does is set limits to the conversation, by saying what a given text could or could not mean in the ancient context.[34] A text may have more than one possible meaning, but it cannot mean just anything at all. So, for example, the meaning of the Hebrew word 'almah in Isaiah 7 is a question of Hebrew lexicography, to be settled by appeal not only to the literary context but to the use of the word in other settings. If Christians want to read the word as "virgin," and see the

32. Cf. the comments of F. W. Dobbs-Allsopp, "Rethinking Historical Criticism," BibInt 7 (1999): 235-71, on the "historicist core" of historical criticism (245).

33. David M. Gunn and Danna Nolan Fewell, Narrative in the Hebrew Bible (Oxford: Oxford University Press, 1993), 7. See the comments of Barr, 32-40.

34. Cf. John Barton, "Historical-critical Approaches," in The Cambridge Companion to Biblical Interpretation (Cambridge: Cambridge University Press, 1998), 9-20 (17).

passage as a prophecy of Christ, they must at least recognize that this is a secondary meaning, which Jewish interpreters cannot be expected to share. The assumptions governing the conversation may change, and have demonstrably changed over the last two generations, as the circle of participants has widened. In this context, the truth claims of the discipline are relative. Assured results are those on which most people, for the moment, agree.[35] Scholarship is a conversation, in which the participants try to persuade each other by appeal to evidence and criteria that are in principle acceptable to the other participants.[36] This model of conversation has served the academy well and is not something that should be lightly abandoned.

Postmodernism

It is precisely this qualified objectivity, however, with its attempt to distance the text from the reader, that is called into question by some postmodern approaches to interpretation. Postmodernism, it should be said, is an even larger umbrella term than historical criticism, and it encompasses a wide range of approaches and methods that are not necessarily compatible with each other.[37] It has been said to cover everything "from punk rock to the death of metanarrative."[38] But like historical-critical approaches, postmodernist ones have a family resemblance. They rely heavily on a few poststructuralist French critics, such as Jacques Derrida and

35. Cf. Jürgen Habermas's ideal of rational society as "the communication community *[Kommunikationsgemeinschaft]* of those affected, who as participants in a practical discourse test the validity claims of norms and, to the extent that they accept them with reasons, arrive at the conviction that in the given circumstances the proposed norms are 'right'"; *Legitimation Crisis* (Boston: Beacon, 1975), 105. Cf. also the "practical realism" endorsed by Joyce Appleby, Lynn Hunt and Margaret Jacob, *Telling the Truth about History* (New York: Norton, 1994), 285: "its notion of truth emerges from a consensus of practitioners."

36. Cf. the comments of Dobbs-Allsopp, 260-61, on the need to persuade.

37. See George Aichele et al. (The Bible and Culture Collective), *The Postmodern Bible* (New Haven: Yale University Press, 1995); A. K. M. Adam, *What Is Postmodern Biblical Criticism?* GBS (Minneapolis: Fortress, 1995); "Post-modern Biblical Interpretation," in Hayes, *Dictionary of Biblical Interpretation* 2:305-9; ed., *Handbook of Postmodern Biblical Interpretation* (St. Louis: Chalice, 2000); *Postmodern Interpretations of the Bible.* On the diversity within postmodernism, note the caution of Herman Rapaport, *The Theory Mess: Deconstruction in Eclipse* (New York: Columbia University Press, 2001), XI.

38. Terry Eagleton, *The Illusions of Postmodernism* (Oxford: Blackwell, 1997), 21.

Michel Foucault, and some American literary critics such as Stanley Fish.[39] The following statement by Terry Eagleton provides, I think, a serviceable sketch of the phenomenon:

> By "postmodern," I mean, roughly speaking, the contemporary movement of thought which rejects totalities, universal values, grand historical narratives, solid foundations to human existence and the possibility of objective knowledge. Postmodernism is sceptical of truth, unity and progress, opposes what it sees as elitism in culture, tends towards cultural relativism, and celebrates pluralism, discontinuity and heterogeneity.[40]

Perhaps the most widely shared assumption of postmodernists is a rejection of "objectivity," or of the distinction between the subjective and the objective.[41] In the Foucaultian strand of postmodernism, objectivity is no more than a pretense that masks the vested interests of the interpreter, and this view is also articulated very forcefully by Stanley Fish.[42] If this is correct, and everyone has a power-seeking agenda, then it is better to have these agendas out in the open. Typically, postmodernists also deny that they are claiming absolute truth for their own positions, although in some cases this claim is difficult to reconcile with the vehemence of their rhetoric.[43] They are also suspicious of consensus, on the grounds that it suppresses minority views. Jean-François Lyotard, who adopts Wittgenstein's theory of language-games, calls for "a theory of games which accepts agonistics as a founding principle"[44] and objects that "consensus does vio-

---

39. See, e.g., Stephen D. Moore, *Poststructuralism and the New Testament: Derrida and Foucault at the Foot of the Cross* (Minneapolis: Fortress, 1994). Derrida and Foucault should not necessarily be held responsible for everyone who invokes their names. See the cautions of Yvonne Sherwood, "Introduction: Derrida's Bible," in *Derrida's Bible* (New York: Palgrave Macmillan, 2004), 8-9: "Biblical Studies and Theology has its own supply of Derrida cartoons and pseudo-Derrida clones."

40. Terry Eagleton, *After Theory* (New York: Basic Books, 2003), 13.

41. Adam, "Post-modern Biblical Interpretation," 306.

42. Stanley Fish, *The Trouble with Principle* (Cambridge, Mass.: Harvard University Press, 1999). For a recent example in biblical studies, see George Aichele, *Sign, Text, Scripture: Semiotics and the Bible.* Interventions 1 (Sheffield: Sheffield Academic, 1997), 40.

43. Eagleton, *The Illusions of Postmodernism*, 26: "For all its vaunted openness to the Other, postmodernism can be quite as exclusive and censorious as the orthodoxies it opposes." See also the nicely ironic comments of Robert P. Carroll, "Poststructuralist Approaches: New Historicism and Postmodernism," in Barton, 58-59, on *The Postmodern Bible*.

44. Jean-François Lyotard, *The Postmodern Condition: A Report on Knowledge.* Theory

lence to the heterogeneity of language games. And invention is always born of dissension."[45] A similar Hobbesian, or even Machiavellian, philosophy is propounded by Fish[46] and advocated for biblical studies by David Clines.[47] Not all postmodernists are necessarily so agonistic, but much of this literature is characterized by what Yvonne Sherwood has called "the promotion of idiosyncrasy over communication,"[48] and this too militates against the quest for consensus.

Another common postmodernist assumption is that there is no univocal, unambiguous meaning. Any text is open to multiple interpretations. On the one hand, reader response critics are wont to deny that a text has any meaning apart from the reader who "constructs" it.[49] On the other hand, Derrida's theory of deconstruction is text-based, but holds that every text contains elements that can undermine its meaning, like loose threads to be pulled by the deconstructionist critic.[50] To deconstruct a text is "to show how it undermines the philosophy it asserts, or the hierarchical oppositions on which it relies."[51] Deconstruction, then, tends towards in-

----

and History of Literature 10 (Minneapolis: University of Minnesota Press, 1984), 160. See also the preface to this volume by Frederic Jameson, which contrasts Lyotard's views with those of Habermas.

45. Lyotard, xxv.

46. See, e.g., *The Trouble with Principle*, 13.

47. David J. A. Clines, *Interested Parties: The Ideology of Writers and Readers of the Hebrew Bible*. JSOTSup 205 (Sheffield: Sheffield Academic, 1995), 92-93: "It must be, once we admit that we are not all engaged in some objective quest for determinate meanings, and that our ideologies, our locations, our interests and our personalities determine our scholarship — and separate us from one another. . . there is a lot we don't like, don't approve of, and will not stand for, in our colleagues, a lot that has yet to be brought into the light, taken the measure of, and fought over."

48. Yvonne Sherwood, *The Prostitute and the Prophet: Hosea's Marriage in Literary-Theoretical Perspective*. JSOTSup 212 (Sheffield: Sheffield Academic, 1996), 163: "For many readers the promotion of idiosyncrasy over communication renders the 'classic' texts of deconstruction almost perversely inaccessible and ensures that they receive only limited circulation."

49. See *The Postmodern Bible*, 20-69.

50. A brief but helpful introduction to Derridean deconstruction can be found in Sherwood, *The Prostitute and the Prophet*, 150-202. See also Richard Kearney, *Dialogues with Contemporary Continental Thinkers* (Manchester: University of Manchester Press, 1984), 105-26.

51. Jonathan D. Culler, *On Deconstruction: Theory and Criticism after Structuralism* (Ithaca: Cornell University Press, 1982), 86.

determinacy of meaning.[52] Historical critics may also appreciate ambiguity in texts, but often argue that one meaning is primary — either the author's intention or what the text would have meant in its original setting. Thorough-going postmodernists, in contrast, deny that there is any one primary meaning. In the words of A. K. M. Adam, they "suspect that any univocity is the product of an interpretive violence that suppresses ambiguity by a will to unity."[53]

There is some range of attitudes among postmodern critics as to whether the text can be said to set limits to valid interpretation. Daniel Patte, in his book on *The Ethics of Biblical Interpretation*, advocates a "multidimensional exegesis" which apparently regards all interpretations, scholarly and popular, as equally valid, so long as they are not absolutized.[54] *The Postmodern Bible*, in the chapter on reader response criticism, correctly characterizes the typical historical-critical view as one that holds that a text has a determinate core of meaning, but not necessarily only one correct meaning. In the view of the authors, however, the determinate core is itself determined by the critic's reading strategy. Yet in the same essay we read that "deconstructive reading relies necessarily on traditional historical criticism as 'an indispensable guardrail' or 'safeguard' for reading. If it were not so, Derrida cautions, 'one could say just anything at all.'"[55] Sherwood finds it impossible to dispense with some construct of text and author, because of "the sheer impossibility of telling a story of reading using the reader as the only protagonist."[56] Mieke Bal denies that interpretation can be text-based, but continues:

52. This tendency is often subject to criticism. See the scathing remarks of feminist critic Somer Brodribb, *Nothing Mat(t)ers: A Feminist Critique of Postmodernism* (North Melbourne: Spinifex, 1992), 8: "Deconstruction is a certain masturbation with the text, playing with the terms at hand. Derrida demonstrates the careful, contingent manipulation of meanings and the endless deferral of sense." Obviously, deconstruction also admits of a more sympathetic description, as a careful and patient examination of the possibilities of a text.

53. Adam, "Post-modern Biblical Interpretation," 306.

54. Daniel Patte, *The Ethics of Biblical Interpretation: A Reevaluation* (Louisville: Westminster John Knox, 1995). See the review by William Schweiker in *JR* 76 (1996): 355-57.

55. *The Postmodern Bible*, 64, with reference to Jacques Derrida, *Limited Inc.* (Evanston: Northwestern University Press, 1988), 141.

56. Sherwood, *The Prostitute and the Prophet*, 28. Cf. *A Biblical Text and Its Afterlives: The Survival of Jonah in Western Culture* (Cambridge: Cambridge University Press, 2000), 212-13.

14

The text is not an object upon which we can operate; it is another subject that speaks to us. We can listen, and just as in real life, we will hear our own voice reflected; yet we cannot attribute just anything to the other speaker. If we shout too loud, so that the other is reduced to silence, we will lack arguments to make our case. This is the point of rational argumentation, of the attempt to give evidence in the text while we do not believe interpretations can ever be truly based on it. It is not a matter of empirical proof; it is a matter of plausible interaction.[57]

"The notion of Otherness," write "New Historicist" critics Jeffrey N. Cox and Larry J. Reynolds, "is essential to historicism, for the historical imagination exists only when one can conceive of a time, a place, a people, a culture different from ours, only when the past becomes something other than a mirror image of our concerns and interests."[58]

Yet another assertion of at least some postmodernist critics is that time is not an essential consideration in meaning.[59] The fact that texts were composed long ago and in another place is not necessarily significant. Accordingly, postmodernists do not share the historical critic's dread of anachronism. Stephen Moore confesses, with disarming understatement, that "the avoidance of anachronism is not, perhaps, my strong suit as an exegete" as he proceeds to apply analogies from body-building to the biblical God.[60] Yvonne Sherwood speaks of "hurling all kinds of contemporary idioms/preoccupations — all kinds of ropes of analogy — out to the shores of the ancient text in the hope that they will form some kind of attachment and in the process rearrange and reanimate the over-familiarised text."[61] Whether one finds these far-flung analogies illuminating, entertaining, annoying, or infuriating, depends, I suppose, on where one's brain has incubated or been pickled. Historical critics should have no objection in principle to analogies from any source. The question is how the analogies are used and what the issue is that is under consideration. Anachro-

57. Mieke Bal, *Death and Dissymmetry: The Politics of Coherence in the Book of Judges* (Chicago: University of Chicago Press, 1988), 240.

58. Jeffrey N. Cox and Larry J. Reynolds, "The Historicist Enterprise," in *New Historical Literary Study: Essays on Reproducing Texts, Representing History* (Princeton: Princeton University Press, 1993), 3-38 (15). See further Dobbs-Allsopp, 265-66, who speaks of respect for the otherness of the text or of history as an ethical issue.

59. Adam, *What Is Postmodern Biblical Criticism?* 305.

60. Moore, *God's Gym*, 123.

61. Sherwood, *A Biblical Text and Its Afterlives*, 291.

nism becomes a problem only in questions of historical meaning, and even then anachronistic analogies can still have heuristic value.

Some formulations of postmodernism are evidently more congenial to historical criticism than others.[62] The kind of limitless possibilities envisioned by Patte's *The Ethics of Biblical Interpretation* lead one to wonder why one should bother with criticism at all. As Robert Morgan put it, "A Bible that can mean anything means nothing."[63] Even if determinate meanings are determined by the critic's reading strategy, for meaningful communication to occur there is need of some basic consensus on the limits of valid interpretation, some shared sense of the text that constrains the free play of imagination. And, as Robert Alter has insisted, "The words of the text afford us at least a narrow strip of solid ground in the quagmire of indeterminacy, because the words a writer uses, despite the margin of ambiguity of some of them, have definite meanings, and no critic is free to invent meanings in order to sustain a reading."[64] A good deal of postmodernist commentary on the Bible seems to me to fall outside the range of what might reasonably be called exegesis, or to forgo concern for "plausible interaction" with the text. Virginia Burrus and Stephen Moore argue that Song 5:7, where the speaker reports that she was beaten by the sentinels, can validly be read as a sado-masochistic fantasy,[65] but they seem closer to the mark when they describe such an interpretation as "a blissful act of willful misreading."[66] Such writing may still be entertaining, stimu-

62. See the remarks of Fred W. Burnett, "Postmodern Biblical Exegesis: The Eve of Historical Criticism," *Semeia* 51 (1990): 51-80.

63. Morgan, 13. Cf. the objection of John Barton to "what looks like a refusal to accept that [the text] *constrains* the interpreter"; "Beliebigkeit," in Sherwood, *Derrida's Bible*, 301. Sherwood insists that the reading of Derrida as promoting free play with the text is an "institutionalized misreading" which is "no less than catastrophic" (7).

64. Robert Alter, *The Pleasures of Reading in an Ideological Age* (New York: Simon and Schuster, 1989), 224.

65. Virginia Burrus and Stephen D. Moore, "Unsafe Sex: Feminism, Pornography, and the Song of Songs," *BibInt* 11 (2003): 24-52 (49). There are many interesting and valid insights in this article into the interpretation of the Song, both ancient and modern. See also Moore, *God's Beauty Parlor*, 21-89.

66. Burrus and Moore, *BibInt* 11 (2003): 44. They adduce no hint from the text that the beating is perceived as pleasurable. The sexual interpretation of Burrus and Moore is mild compared to that of Roland Boer, "Night Sprinkle(s): Pornography and the Song of Songs," in *Knockin' on Heaven's Door: The Bible and Popular Culture* (New York: Routledge, 1999), 53-70; and "The Second Coming: Repetition and Insatiable Desire in the Song of Songs," *BibInt* 8 (2000): 276-301.

lating, and illuminating, but its concerns and objectives are different from those of exegetical scholarship, even on the broadest definition of the latter. "Texts trigger readings," writes Mieke Bal; "That is what they are: the occasion of a reaction."[67] But not every reaction triggered by a text can be regarded as a valid meaning or interpretation.

Again, to say that critics have agendas is hardly news. This is precisely why we need critical method, to arbitrate between them. The conflict of approaches may be viewed in ethical, or even political, terms. *The Postmodern Bible* correctly describes historical criticism, and most of First World academia, as a form of democratic pluralism that tries to regulate debate to resolve, or at least mitigate, conflicts of interpretation.[68] The postmodern vision of Lyotard or Fish, in contrast, posits irreconcilable language games, where the protagonists pursue their own interests in agonistic fashion. Personally, I would rather live in the pluralistic democracy, but admittedly the democracy works well only if due account is taken of the voices from the margins.

From the perspective of a democratic pluralist, however, there are still things to be learned from postmodern exegesis. Even when postmodern critics play by the rules of the game, so to speak, they often push the questions farther than traditional historical critics have been inclined to do. Broadly speaking, these questions are of two types. Deconstructive questions, in the spirit of Derrida, tend to undermine the truth claims of the biblical text, while ideological criticism, in the spirit of Foucault, raises problems about its moral status.

Deconstructive Reading

As an example of explicitly deconstructionist reading, we may consider the discussion of Hosea by Yvonne Sherwood.[69] I choose this example, from her dissertation, because of its methodological explicitness and clarity, although these very features make it somewhat atypical of the genre. Much of the better deconstructionist writing, including Sherwood's later work, is

67. Mieke Bal, *Lethal Love: Feminist Literary Readings of Biblical Love Stories* (Bloomington: Indiana University Press, 1987), 132.

68. Cf. Appleby, Hunt, and Jacob, 285: "pragmatism only works if democratic institutions are strong and functioning daily."

69. Sherwood, *The Prostitute and the Prophet*, 203-53.

17

more complex and enriched by intertextual allusions.[70] But this simpler example may illustrate the basic method more effectively for introductory purposes.

According to Sherwood, the rhetorical strategy of Hosea 1-2 can be reduced to three essential premises: 1. Israel was initially pure. 2. She betrayed YHWH by pursuit of Baal. 3. YHWH threatened Israel with rejection, but ultimately restored her to favor. In each of these premises "there is an implicit violent hierarchy, in which the first term is promoted as stronger, prior, superior and triumphant: 1. Innocence-Deviance (the pattern of 'The Fall'). 2. Yhwh-Baal. 3. Love-Hate (Acceptance-Rejection)." Sherwood claims that "traditionally, each hierarchy has been affirmed not only by the text but by the critical tradition that seeks to uphold it." She, in contrast, seeks to show how the hierarchies inevitably deconstruct, "because in this, as in all texts, what the author sees is systematically related to what he does not see."[71]

In Sherwood's reading, "the idea of a pure origin becomes the linchpin of the text's rhetoric."[72] In Hos 2:5(3), "Yhwh equates the woman Israel with a naked baby and infantile innocence," and in 2:16-17(14-15) he talks of a future when Israel will respond "as in the days of her youth." This motif of original innocence appears again in Hosea 11, a text that Sherwood does not discuss. Yet, she claims, this argument is subverted by the imagery of Hosea's marriage, "for if Yhwh is claiming that Israel loved him and then betrayed him, this logical sequence is subverted by a metaphor in which the wife is already harlotrous at the point of marriage."[73] So, Yhwh's marriage metaphor, which is presumably designed to reinforce his position, also works against him. The marriage is contaminated by promiscuity from the beginning and there is no virgin bride.

I do not find this reading entirely convincing. One could, after all, take the "woman of harlotry" whom Hosea marries as one who is recognized as such in hindsight, or even if one supposes that she was already a prostitute

70. See, e.g., her essay with John D. Caputo, "Otobiographies, Or How a Torn and Disembodied Ear Hears a Promise of Death (A Prearranged Meeting between Yvonne Sherwood and John D. Caputo and the Book of Amos and Jacques Derrida)," in *Derrida and Religion: Other Testaments*, ed. Sherwood and Kevin Hart (New York: Routledge, 2004), 209-39. Several good examples of Derridean readings can be found in Sherwood, *Derrida's Bible*.
71. Sherwood, *The Prostitute and the Prophet*, 207.
72. Sherwood, *The Prostitute and the Prophet*, 208.
73. Sherwood, *The Prostitute and the Prophet*, 210.

the symbolism need not be pressed to demand perfect correspondence. Neither, I think, is the argument of the text necessarily deconstructed by the inherent ambiguity of the imagery of the wilderness, which is at once a place of death and new beginning. It is precisely this ambiguity that gives this text its poetic richness. The idea that rebirth comes only through purging and destruction is inherent in the prophet's message.[74] This imagery is not "undecideable" in the sense of offering an impossible choice between two interpretations; both interpretations must clearly be held in tension. In this case, then, the deconstructive reading seems to me somewhat willful.[75]

Sherwood is more successful, however, in her deconstruction of the other binary oppositions. The text presents a clear hierarchical contrast between Yahweh and Baal, and this hierarchy has often been endorsed, quite uncritically, by biblical scholarship. Our concern, for the present, is not whether this contrast does justice to Canaanite religion, but whether it is an adequate reading of Hosea. The seeds of deconstruction here lie in the fact that Yahweh and Baal seem to be perceived in very similar terms, as the lover who provides Israel with grain, wine, and oil. The question seems to be, which is the true fertility god? Many critics concede that Hosea is here "participating in Canaanizing in a certain sense."[76] It will not do to assert that "the Canaanite myth. . . is affirmed and dissolved at the same time."[77] It leaves an imprint on the portrayal of Yahweh that belies the stark contrast on which the prophet insists. Now it should be said that chapter 2 is not Hosea's last word on Yahweh. We get a rather fuller picture, for example, in chapter 4, where the people are indicted for swearing, lying and murder, stealing, adultery and bloodshed. Baal was not, to our knowl-

74. See the more traditional literary reading of Hosea 2 by Shemaryahu Talmon, "The 'Desert Motif' in the Bible and in Qumran Literature," in *Biblical Motifs*, ed. Alexander Altmann (Cambridge, Mass.: Harvard University Press, 1966), 31-63.

75. Similarly, the argument of Clines, 67, that the oracle on Zerubbabel in Hag 2:20-23, in a book primarily concerned with the rebuilding of the temple, has a deconstructive effect, since "the reader experiences an aporia over what should be designated the overall theme of the work," seems to me to create an artificial problem.

76. Anton Wessels, "Biblical Presuppositions for and against Syncretism," in *Dialogue and Syncretism: An Interdisciplinary Approach,* ed. Jerold Gort, Hendrik Vroom, Rein Ferhout, and Wessels. Currents of Encounter (Grand Rapids: Wm. B. Eerdmans, 1989), 52-65 (60).

77. Harold Fisch, "Hosea: A Poetics of Violence," in *Poetry with a Purpose: Biblical Poetics and Interpretation* (Bloomington: Indiana University Press, 1988), 136-57 (148).

edge, a god who made moral demands of his worshippers, although we should not be too quick to suppose that they, or any other ancient people, condoned murder and stealing. Nonetheless, it seems to me that Sherwood makes a valuable point here, that historical critics should be, and increasingly are, ready to grant. Yahweh and Baal are not as sharply different as traditional readings of Hosea have often implied. She also makes a valuable point in highlighting the tendency of many historical critics to defend the values of the biblical text.[78] This latter tendency, it seems to me, does not arise from historical criticism as such, but rather from the residual piety of its practitioners, who can sometimes be accused, like the friends of Job, of "speaking falsely for God" (Job 13:7). (Incidentally, this tendency is by no means peculiar to historical critics. Derrida waxes romantic about Abraham's willingness to sacrifice his son as "the absolute religious experience, if there is such a thing: the pure act of faith, the asymmetrical obedience to an absurd order, an unintelligible order, an order that is beyond ethics and knowledge," although he recognizes that Abraham's action is criminal in ethical terms.[79] The actions of the terrorists on September 11, 2001, were equally acts of obedience to an order beyond ethics and knowledge, and who is to say that they were not acts of faith? But the case of Abraham is treated differently because of its biblical status.[80])

Deconstructionist reading is also successful in casting the renewal of the relationship between Yahweh and Baal in a new light. Two of Hosea's children are given the incredibly harsh names of Lo-ruhamah ("not pitied," or even "unloved"), and Lo-ammi ("not my people"). At the end of chapter 2, however, Yahweh says, "I will have pity on Lo-ruhamah, and I will say to Lo-ammi, 'you are my people.'" Harold Fisch argues that each name contained from the beginning the "trace" of its opposite, so that the negative names are unstable from the beginning.[81] Sherwood astutely ob-

78. This tendency is repeatedly criticized by Clines, *Interested Parties*.

79. Jacques Derrida in "Epochē and Faith: An Interview with Jacques Derrida," in Sherwood and Hart, 27-50 (35). Derrida reflects on the story of Abraham at greater length (in a Kierkegaardian vein) in *The Gift of Death* (Chicago: University of Chicago Press, 1995).

80. See my essay, "Faith Without Works: Biblical Ethics and the Sacrifice of Isaac," in *Recht und Ethos im Alten Testament: Gestalt und Wirkung*. Festschrift Horst Seebass, ed. Stefan Beyerle, Günther Mayer, and Hans Strauss (Neukirchen-Vluyn: Neukirchener, 1999), 115-31.

81. So Sherwood, *The Prostitute and the Prophet*, 239. She does not specify the reference.

serves that each positive name, no less than the negative, is "haunted by its contrary."[82] Israel may reasonably wonder whether its restoration is in any way definitive. We may compare the restoration of Job, who seems to get back everything he had lost and more, but who must live henceforth with the knowledge that everything could be wiped out again in one bad day. Moreover, the fragile, unstable nature of the restoration is not just a product of the postmodern imagination. Sherwood cites the *Pesikta of Rab Kahana*, which juxtaposes Hos 14:6(Eng. 5) ("henceforth I will be as the dew to Israel") and 9:16 ("Ephraim is smitten, their root is dried up") and asks,"which words am I to believe, yesterday's or today's?"[83] Or again in Hos 11:8-9, Yahweh declares passionately that his compassion grows warm and tender and so he will not again destroy Ephraim, for he is "God and not man," only to declare two chapters later that "compassion is hid from my eyes" and that "Samaria shall bear her guilt" (13:14, 16). If one believes in revelation in history, it would seem that the latter sentiment prevailed. Sherwood accuses modern critics of repeating one of the faults of which Israel is accused: "the complacent assumption that the people of God are loved."[84]

One can cavil with some aspects of Sherwood's analysis. Her eagerness to deconstruct occasionally leads to a forced or unreasonable reading of the text. She also dallies with the temptation to portray Hosea as a deconstructionist.[85] Nonetheless, I feel that my own reading of the opening chapters of Hosea is sharpened and enriched by Sherwood's discussion.[86] Insofar as her deconstructionist interpretation consists of a close reading of the text, with an eye for its inner tensions and contradictions, I do not see why any historical critic should object to it.[87] In fact, historical

82. Sherwood, *The Prostitute and the Prophet,* 239.

83. *Pesikta de-Rab Kahana* (Philadelphia: Jewish Publication Society of America, 1975), 295, cited by Sherwood, *The Prostitute and the Prophet,* 240.

84. Sherwood, *The Prostitute and the Prophet,* 241.

85. This tendency is also in evidence in Sherwood and Caputo, 211, with reference to Amos.

86. Similarly, David J. A. Clines makes some valuable observations in his essay on "Haggai's Temple, Constructed, Deconstructed, and Reconstructed," in *Interested Parties,* 46-75. There are tensions in the text as to whether the rebuilding of the temple is sufficient to bring about the return of the divine glory, and as to whether a people whose works are impure can properly build the temple.

87. The affinities of Derridean deconstruction with rabbinic midrash were noted already by Susan A. Handelman, *The Slayers of Moses: The Emergence of Rabbinic Interpreta-*

criticism arose to a great extent through precisely such readings. For a long time the tendency of historical critics was to resolve the tensions of the text with a redactional scalpel. I think source criticism is a necessary tool in the critic's toolbox, but most biblical scholars nowadays would agree that it has been used far too hastily in the past. We are all slowly learning to respect the fact that ancient authors did not necessarily see contradictions where we do, and that tensions and contradictions can be found in the writings of most authors, ancient and modern.

Sherwood's analysis, of course, is not just a close reading in the "new critical" sense. She is specifically looking for things that go against the grain of the usual interpretation of the text and that resist our impulse to harmonize and make coherent.[88] Sometimes she strains in this effort, but on the whole it is enlightening. Hosea, after all, was not a "logocentric" systematic theologian, but a prophet, who said one thing one day and something else the next. Coherence was not his biggest concern, and despite the best efforts of some canon-oriented interpreters, it does not seem to have been a major concern of the editors either. Consequently, when we look at this text from a distance it is inevitable that we see things of which the ancient authors were not aware.

The cases where Sherwood's interpretation seems most sharply disjunctive from older scholarship are those that involve theological judgments. The great bulk of historical critics have affirmed the prophet's denunciations of Baal and accepted his assurances of restoration without question. These judgments do not follow from any principles of historical criticism. Arguably, they represent failure to apply the principles of historical criticism consistently. There is something to be said, then, for Stephen Moore's characterization of postmodern exegesis as the "id" of historical criticism, the probing of its darker implications that traditional historical critics have preferred to avoid.[89]

Perhaps the most fundamental challenge posed by deconstruction to traditional biblical exegesis, however, is expressed by Sherwood in a summary comment on Derrida's essay on the tower of Babel: "Derrida treats

---

tion in Modern Literary Theory (Albany: State University of New York Press, 1982), 163-78 ("Reb Derrida's Scripture").

88. Cf. the methodological remarks of Mieke Bal in Death and Dissymmetry, 16-18, on "reading with a 'countercoherence'": "A countercoherence relates the 'official' reading to what it leaves out. . . . It relates everything that is denied importance to the motivations for such denials."

89. Moore, Poststructuralism and the New Testament, 117.

Yhwh, as most literary critics do, not as an entity but as a construct of the text."[90] Again, there is no reason why a historical critic should object. The whole drift of historical criticism has been away from the view that the Bible is a timeless revelation of God, and an insistence that its writings are time-conditioned products of human authors, and that its wisdom, to adapt a phrase of Stanley Fish, is "of an age and not for all time," at least not in all cases.[91] But the authoritative claims of biblical revelation are hard to resist. Sherwood herself continues, with obvious approval, to declare that Derrida's Yahweh is God of Babel, master of dispersal and confusion, resistant to univocality and union.[92] Should we infer that this is, after all, the true God, and that we should make our pilgrimages to the shrine of St. Jacques[93] (de Paris, not Compostela)?[94] Or should we draw the more radical conclusion that the God of the Bible is not only not the God of the philosophers but is not necessarily a reliable representation of ultimate reality at all?

90. Sherwood, *The Prostitute and the Prophet*, 200.

91. Fish, 46. Fish would not, I think, accept the qualification, "not in all cases."

92. Derrida famously declared that he does "quite rightly pass for an atheist," in "Circumfession: Fifty-nine Periods and Periphrases," in *Jacques Derrida*, ed. Geoffrey Bennington and Derrida (Chicago: University of Chicago Press, 1993), 155-56, but later said, in an interview with John Caputo, "I know that I've given a number of signs of my being a nonbeliever in God in a certain way, of being an atheist. Nevertheless, although I confirm that it is right to say that I am an atheist, I can't say, myself, 'I am an atheist'. . . . I wouldn't say, 'I am an atheist' and I wouldn't say, 'I am a believer,' either" (Sherwood and Hart, 47). In the same interview, he says that "God could not be the omnipotent first cause, the prime mover, absolute being, or absolute presence. . . . God is far beyond any given existence; he has transcended any form of being. . . . On the other hand, God has an essential link to being named, being called, being addressed. When I use the word 'God,' I mention it. It is a word that I receive as a word with no visible experience or referent" (37). There have been many attempts to view Derrida as a proponent of "negative theology." See esp. John D. Caputo, *The Prayers and Tears of Jacques Derrida* (Bloomington: Indiana University Press, 1997). Richard Kearney, in contrast, argues that "in the heel of the hunt, [Derrida] prefers ghosts to gods. He prefers, as is his wont and right, to leave matters open"; "Deconstruction, God and the Possible," in Sherwood and Hart, 304. See further the detailed study of Hent de Vries, *Philosophy and the Turn to Religion* (Baltimore: Johns Hopkins University Press, 1999). According to de Vries, "Derrida's writings exhibit the paradox of a nontheological, and, it would seem, even nonreligious, concern with religion" (i-ix).

93. Sherwood is careful to insist that she is not "absurdly proclaiming Derrida as Messiah"; *Derrida's Bible*, 1.

94. The opening of Hosea is evoked in the film, "The Milky Way," by Luis Bunuel (1967), when a beggar on his way to Compostela encounters a mysterious man who tells him to "take unto thyself a wife of harlotry."

Ideological Criticism

As an example of ideological criticism, we may consider David Clines's book, *Interested Parties*, and specifically his essay, "Metacommentating Amos."[95] Like Sherwood, Clines reads against the grain of the text, a procedure that he describes as "reading from left to right" (whereas Hebrew is read from right to left).[96] Clines, however, has a more distinctly ethical focus, and is concerned with ideology as "the kind of large-scale ideas that influence and determine the whole outlook of groups of people."[97] It is not unusual, of course, to find critiques of the ideology of some parts of the biblical corpus in historical-critical scholarship. The royal ideology has often come in for criticism by liberal or leftist critics. Nowadays there is increased sensitivity to the ideology of the conquest narratives. But nearly all biblical scholars find some parts of the canonical corpus to be morally above criticism. The Ten Commandments are one such segment, and the book of Amos is another. In good postmodern fashion, Clines pushes the critique in precisely these areas.[98] In the case of the Ten Commandments, he disputes the common assumption that these are timeless ethical maxims and asks repeatedly whose interests are being served. The presumed addressees are married male Israelite property-owners.[99] Women are not addressed. The people whose interests are served by having "a text telling these pillars of society what they should and shouldn't do, in the name of Yahweh" are "the fathers of those addressed, that is, the old men of the society, . . . whose interests are represented in every one of the commandments."[100] Whether or not one agrees with that analysis, Clines's main point is that the commandments do not serve the interests of all members of a society equally.

In the case of Amos, Clines's critique has more substantive bite. With regard to the prophet's scathing critique of the rich in Amos 6:4-7, he asks: "Is there some sin in having expensive ivory inlays on your bedframe? . . . And as for singing idle songs, who among the readers of Amos can cast a stone? Has karaoke suddenly become a sin, as well as a social disease?"[101]

95. Pp. 76-93.
96. Clines, *Interested Parties*, 20.
97. Clines, *Interested Parties*, 11.
98. Clines, *Interested Parties*, 26-45 (the Ten Commandments), 76-93 (Amos).
99. Clines, *Interested Parties*, 33.
100. Clines, *Interested Parties*, 35.
101. Clines, "Metacommentating Amos," 78-79.

Above all, are we really to accept the prophet's claim that the destruction of Israel was fit punishment for social inequities and reflected the will of Yahweh rather than the contingencies of the balance of power in the ancient Near East? Commentators, says Clines, fail to notice the injustice of the indiscriminate punishment inflicted by Amos's God, or "that Yahweh can't be very compassionate to the poor if he intends them to be carried into exile because of the wrongdoing of their leaders, or that the prophet's demand for justice does not seem to apply to the deity."[102]

All of this, it seems to me, can be construed as pushing historical criticism to its logical conclusions, in a way that historical critics have traditionally failed to do. The skepticism and suspicion that Clines directs towards the biblical text are the analogue of the suspicion of contemporary philosophers towards Enlightenment ideals, or towards any ideals for that matter.[103] Because of its canonical status, the Bible has often enjoyed a presumption of transcendent value, even if that value is not distributed equally in all its parts. Clines is surely right that such a presumption has no place in critical scholarship. This is not to endorse the opposite assumption, that the Bible has no enduring value, but to hold biblical scholars responsible for the ethical implications of their interpretation. As he asks in another essay, "What ethical responsibility do I carry if I go on helping this text to stay alive?"[104]

But radical relativism also has its dangers. At the end of his essay on the Ten Commandments, Clines asks facetiously, "Is there a chance that an analysis like the present one, that focuses on the sectional interests they support, will demythologize them — without at the same time bringing western civilization tumbling?"[105] But such a critique does in fact raise fundamental questions about the foundations (if any) of morality and the continued viability of any biblical theology. We shall return to these questions in the final chapter of this book after we have examined some developments in recent biblical criticism in more detail.

102. Clines, "Metacommentating Amos," 91.
103. E.g., Alasdair MacIntyre, *Whose Justice? Which Rationality?* (Notre Dame: University of Notre Dame Press, 1988).
104. Clines, "The Postmodern Adventure in Biblical Studies," in *Auguries: The Jubilee Volume of the Sheffield Department of Biblical Studies,* ed. Clines and Stephen D. Moore. JSOTSup 269 (Sheffield: Sheffield Academic, 1998), 286.
105. Clines, *Interested Parties,* 44-45.

The Crisis in Historiography

The field of historiography, like many others and more than most, has been subject to postmodernist critiques in recent years. More than 30 years ago, Hayden White drew attention to the creative story-shaping character of historiography and argued that historians do not accumulate objective knowledge, but "generate a discourse about the past."[1] The content of this discourse is "as much invented/imagined as found."[2] Historiography is "the attempted imposition of meaningful form on to a meaningless past."[3] Whereas history writing had been conceived in the 19th century as "heroic science," the possibility of neutral, objective, knowledge of the past is now widely questioned.[4]

1. Hayden White, *Metahistory: The Historical Imagination in Nineteenth-Century Europe* (Baltimore: Johns Hopkins University Press, 1973); *Tropics of Discourse* (Baltimore: Johns Hopkins University Press, 1978). The quotation is from Joyce Appleby, Lynn Hunt, and Margaret Jacob, *Telling the Truth about History,* 245.

2. This is the formulation of Keith Jenkins, *On "What Is History?" From Carr and Elton to Rorty and White* (London: Routledge, 1995), 145, with reference to White. Cf. the similar views of Richard Rorty, *Consequences of Pragmatism* (Minneapolis: University of Minnesota Press, 1982), and the discussion in Jenkins, 97-133.

3. Jenkins, 137.

4. See, e.g., Peter Novick, *That Noble Dream: The "Objectivity Question" and the American Historical Profession* (Cambridge: Cambridge University Press, 1988), 415-629; Appleby, Hunt, and Jacob, 129-237; and for a more popular treatment, Norman J. Wilson, *History in Crisis? Recent Directions in Historiography* (Upper Saddle River: Prentice Hall, 1999).

In part, the skepticism arises from the fact that the past no longer exists, and so is accessible "only by way of its prior textualizations."[5] Consequently, there seems to be an unbridgeable gap between historiographical literature and the actual events of the past. In the words of Peter Munz, "We cannot glimpse at history. We can only compare one book with another book."[6] In part, the skepticism arises from the inevitable contamination of any reconstruction by the interests and prejudices of the interpreter. In a postmodernist assessment of historiography, Robert F. Berkhofer writes, "Under such conditions the very definition of history must take on a more reflexive meaning, one that shows its socially constructed nature, its self-consciousness of its own creation, and the social conditions that allow such a practice."[7]

Postmodernist critics are especially critical of meta-narratives that provide grand schemas for organizing the writing and interpretation of history, such as the model of progress or Marxism.[8] In the formulation of Terry Eagleton, "postmodernism . . is wary of History but enthusiastic on the whole about history."[9] Grand schemas are inherently ideological, and inevitably privilege some perspectives to the exclusion of others. Taken to an extreme, such criticisms can lead to a view of history as an "interminable pattern without meaning."[10] Even in a more moderate form, they cast severe doubt on any attempt to view history-writing as the simple accu-

---

5. Hayden White, "New Historicism: A Comment," in *The New Historicism*, ed. H. Aram Veeser (London: Routledge, 1989), 293-302 (297), citing Fredric Jameson. Cf. the comments of Ernst Axel Knauf, "From History to Interpretation," in *The Fabric of History*, ed. Diana Vikander Edelman. JSOTSup 127 (Sheffield: JSOT, 1991), 26-64.

6. Peter Munz, *The Shapes of Time: A New Look at the Philosophy of History* (Middletown: Wesleyan University, 1977), cited by Michael Bentley, *Modern Historiography: An Introduction* (London: Routledge, 1999), 143.

7. Robert F. Berkhofer, *Beyond the Great Story* (Cambridge, Mass.: Harvard University Press, 1995), 7-8.

8. See esp. Berkhofer. Jean Lyotard, *The Postmodern Condition*, xxiv, argued that postmodernism entailed "incredulity toward metanarratives." See Bentley, 143.

9. Terry Eagleton, *The Illusions of Postmodernism*, 32.

10. Appleby, Hunt, and Jacob, 233, citing Elizabeth Deeds Ermarth, *Sequel to History: Postmodernism and the Crisis of Representational Time* (Princeton: Princeton University Press, 1992), 212. See the critical comments of Eagleton, 34. Note also the ironic comment of Peter Osborne, *The Politics of Time* (London: Verso, 1995), 157, that "the narrative of the death of metanarrative is itself grander than most of the narratives it would consign to oblivion."

mulation of empirical facts, or as the record of "how it really happened," in the famous phrase of Leopold von Ranke.[11] Needless to say, postmodern skepticism has not put an end to the writing of history. Traditional realists have objected vehemently to the "descent into discourse," to use the title of a book by a Marxist critic.[12] Even scholars who are somewhat sympathetic to the issues raised by postmodernists rightly insist that a convincing case can be made for "qualified objectivity" that comes to terms with "the undeniable elements of subjectivity, artificiality and language dependence in historical writing."[13] Rhetoric is not incompatible with the pursuit of truth, although it can obviously be used for other purposes.[14] In fact, history writing "lays claim, both rhetorically and actually, to a validity of correspondence to the public processes of the real world."[15] Arnaldo Momigliano has rightly insisted that "what has come to distinguish historical writing from any other type of literature is its being submitted as a whole to the control of evidence."[16] It is a common experience in history writing that stubborn facts resist and subvert the metanarratives of the historian. The paradigm shifts that occur with some regularity in the field testify not only to the changing interests of historians, but also, at least sometimes, to data that cannot be accommodated in the old paradigm. Nonetheless, it is fair to say that the old model of historiography as "heroic science," dispassionate, disinterested, and value-free, is now viewed as rather ironic, if it is not entirely defunct.

11. Von Ranke may not have been as positivistic as he is often assumed to be. In a letter to his brother in 1838, he wrote of his desire "to root tradition in our knowledge of actual existence and in our insight into its essence." See Bentley, 36-42. Novick (27) describes him as "a thoroughgoing philosophical idealist" whose goal was to penetrate to the essence of history.

12. Bryan D. Palmer, *Descent into Discourse: The Reification of Language and the Writing of Social History* (Philadelphia: Temple University Press, 1990).

13. So Appleby, Hunt, and Jacob, 259. See also R. J. Evans, *In Defence of History* (London: Granta, 1997), and the "critical historicism" advocated by F. W. Dobbs-Allsopp, *BibInt* 7 (1999): 235-71.

14. So esp. Carlo Ginzburg, *History, Rhetoric, and Proof.* The Menahem Stern Jerusalem Lectures (Hanover, N.H.: University Press of New England, 1999).

15. Albert Cook, *History/Writing* (Cambridge: Cambridge University Press, 1988), 1.

16. Arnaldo Momigliano, "The Rhetoric of History and the History of Rhetoric: On Hayden White's Tropes," in *Sèttimo Contributo alla Storia degli Studi Classici e del Mondo Antico.* Storia e Letteratura: Raccòlta di Studi e Tèsti 161 (Rome: Edizioni di Storia e Letteratura, 1984), 49-59 (51). Cf. also his essay in the same volume, "Considerations on History in an Age of Ideologies," 253-69; and Carlo Ginzburg, "Clues: Roots of an Evidential Paradigm," in *Clues, Myths, and the Historical Method* (Baltimore: Johns Hopkins University Press, 1989), 96-125.

The Crisis in Historiography in Biblical Studies

The last quarter of the 20th century has also seen the development of a crisis in the historiography of ancient Israel, which shows no sign of abating
in the early years of the 21st. This crisis takes the form of a progressive loss
of confidence in the historical value of the biblical narratives. In the middle of the 20th century, English language scholarship on ancient Israel was
dominated by the Albright school, which placed great confidence in archaeology as a means by which to affirm the essential reliability of the biblical text, beginning in the time of Abraham. This approach found its classic expression in John Bright's *History of Israel*, an impressive attempt to
contextualize the biblical story by interweaving it with what we know of
ancient Near Eastern history.[17] Even when Bright wrote, a more skeptical
view prevailed in German scholarship, at least with regard to the early
books of the Bible.[18] But the scene has changed drastically in the last quarter century. In a book originally published in 1992, Philip Davies claimed
that "biblical scholars actually know — and write — that most of the 'biblical period' consists not only of unhistorical persons and events, but even
of tracts of time *that do not belong in history at all!*"[19] Davies offered the
Patriarchal period (the stories of Abraham, Isaac, and Jacob in the book of
Genesis) as an obvious example, and the point has been widely conceded
since the ground-breaking 1974 monograph, *The Historicity of the Patriarchal Narratives*, by Thomas L. Thompson.[20] Davies continued. "The same
is widely acknowledged, if by a slightly lesser majority, of the 'Exodus' and
the 'wilderness period' and a still substantial majority of scholars would
probably accept as much for most, if not all, of the 'period' of the
'judges.'"[21] He went on to argue that it will not do to truncate the history of
Israel by starting with David, or Omri, or some later point. The biblical account of Israel has its own integrity, and it is different from any modern
reconstruction: "By starting at the moment in history that we do, we are
abandoning the literary Israel of the Bible, and commencing to write the

17. 4th ed., 2000.

18. The classic formulation is that of Martin Noth, *Geschichte Israels* (Göttingen:
Vandenhoeck & Ruprecht, 1950); Eng. trans., *The History of Israel* (New York: Harper & Row,
1960).

19. Philip R. Davies, *In Search of "Ancient Israel."* JSOTSup 148 (Sheffield: JSOT, 1992), 26.

20. BZAW 133 (Berlin: de Gruyter, 1974).

21. Davies, *In Search of "Ancient Israel,"* 27.

history of another society."[22] It should be clear that Davies here is offering a metanarrative of his own that privileges the views of a rather small group of skeptical scholars, of whom the most prominent are Thompson and Niels Peter Lemche, both of the University of Copenhagen.[23] In subsequent years this group proceeded to question the historical value of most of the biblical corpus, and the focus of debate has shifted to the existence of a united monarchy, and even to the construction of the Babylonian exile as a myth of origin in the Persian period.[24] Thompson and Lemche have argued that the Bible should be a regarded as "a Hellenistic book."[25]

William G. Dever has made a spirited argument that the skeptical, revisionist approach to the history of Israel is informed by "the postmodern agenda." He provides his own sweeping account of that agenda, listing nine "main features":

(1) rebellion against all authority; (2) distrust of all universal, "totalizing" discourse; (3) the assumption that "social constructs" determine all knowledge; (4) it is only "discourse" and "realms of discourse" that matter; (5) all truth is relative; (6) there is no intrinsic "meaning,"

22. Davies, *In Search of "Ancient Israel,"* 28.

23. See Thomas L. Thompson, *Early History of the Israelite People from the Written and Archaeological Sources.* SHANE 4 (Leiden: Brill, 1992); *The Mythic Past: Biblical Archaeology and the Myth of Israel* (New York: Basic Books, 1999); Niels Peter Lemche, *The Israelites in History and Tradition* (Louisville: Westminster, 1998). Note also Gösta W. Ahlström, *The History of Ancient Palestine from the Palaeolithic Period to Alexander's Conquest* JSOTSup 146 (Sheffield: Sheffield Academic, 1993); Giovanni Garbini, *History and Ideology in Ancient Israel* (New York: Crossroad, 1988); and Keith W. Whitelam, *The Invention of Ancient Israel* (London: Routledge, 1996). See also the essays in Edelman, *The Fabric of History; The Origins of the Ancient Israelite States,* ed. Volkmar Fritz and Philip R. Davies. JSOTSup 228 (Sheffield: Sheffield Academic, 1996); and *Can a "History of Israel" Be Written?* ed. Lester L. Grabbe. JSOTSup 245 (Sheffield: Sheffield Academic, 1997). A skeptical approach to the early history of Israel is also found in Israel Finkelstein and Neil Asher Silberman, *The Bible Unearthed: Archaeology's New Vision of Ancient Israel and the Origin of Its Sacred Texts* (New York: Free Press, 2001).

24. See the essays in *Leading Captivity Captive: "The Exile" as History and Ideology,* ed. Lester L. Grabbe. JSOTSup 278 (Sheffield: Sheffield Academic, 1998).

25. See the debate in *Did Moses Speak Attic? Jewish Historiography and Scripture in the Hellenistic Period,* ed. Lester L. Grabbe. JSOTSup 317 (Sheffield: Sheffield Academic, 2001). Note esp. the vigorous refutation of the late dating by Rainer Albertz, "An End to the Confusion? Why the Old Testament Cannot Be a Hellenistic Book!" 30-46. There are responses by Thompson and Lemche.

only that which we supply; (7) there is no operative "consensus" view, so that everything becomes ideology, ultimately politics; (8) one ideology is as appropriate as another (sometimes the more "radical" the better); (9) ideological discourse need not be rational or systematic, but may be intuitive or even eccentric, representing the neglected "peripheries" of society rather than the "center."[26]

This account of postmodernism is obviously polemical, but several features are familiar from other discussions of the topic: distrust of master paradigms, attention to the peripheries, and the insistence that meaning is constructed rather than inherent in data.

The so-called "revisionists," primarily Davies, Thompson, Lemche, and Keith Whitelam, are not necessarily all in agreement on everything. Some are more influenced by postmodern ideas than others. Whitelam's controversial book on *The Invention of Ancient Israel* is, I think, the most clearly postmodern work of any of these scholars. Davies likes to highlight the interested, ideological character of other people's scholarly theories — Whose history? Whose Israel? Whose Bible?[27] His sharp distinction between the literary construct of ancient Israel in the Bible and the Israel of history bears a *prima facie* resemblance to the insistence of Hayden White on the literary character of all historiography. But Davies seems to think that the situation of the Hebrew Bible is exceptional, because of its theological character, and seems to imagine that an objective "history of Palestine" could be written.[28] The scholars in this group who have written the most extensive histories, Thompson and Lemche, seem to me to be quite old-fashioned, empirical historians.[29] Lemche speaks explicitly of "playing the von Ranke game" by distinguishing carefully between primary documents and later sources.[30] To

26. William G. Dever, *What Did the Biblical Writers Know and When Did They Know It?* (Grand Rapids: Wm. B. Eerdmans, 2001), 25.

27. Philip R. Davies, "Whose History? Whose Israel? Whose Bible? Biblical Histories, Ancient and Modern," in Grabbe, *Can a "History of Israel" Be Written?* 104-22. Cf. his book *Whose Bible Is It Anyway?* JSOT 204 (Sheffield: Sheffield Academic, 1995). Davies is less than forthcoming about his own ideological agenda.

28. Davies, *In Search of "Ancient Israel,"* 42-46. See the criticism of Davies in this respect by Iain W. Provan, "Ideologies, Literary and Critical: Reflections on Recent Writing on the History of Israel," *JBL* 114 (1995): 585-606, esp. 599.

29. Provan, 602, labels the revisionists "positivist," but the label is pejorative and best avoided. See the comments of James Barr, *History and Ideology in the Old Testament*, 68-69.

30. Lemche, *The Israelites in History and Tradition*, 22-34. On the importance of the dis-

be sure, his treatment of some documents seems unduly skeptical. When an inscription was found at Tel Dan in 1993 mentioning "the house of David", Thompson, Lemche, and Davies resorted to rather desperate arguments to deny the reference,[31] although Lemche rightly noted that a 9th-century inscription would not count as primary evidence for the historical David in any case.[32] The suggestion that the entire Hebrew Bible is a Hellenistic book ignores the development of genres and language and cannot be taken seriously.[33] But virtually all "mainline" scholars date the finalization of the Torah, prophets, and historical books no earlier than the Persian period, and Lemche's insistence that "the Old Testament is not a primary source for the history of Israel" is unimpeachable.[34] It is precisely the lack of primary documents attesting key episodes in the history of Israel that gives rise to the skepticism of Lemche and Thompson.

As many critics have noted, the "minimalists" go to extremes in refusing to take the biblical text into account in reconstructing the history of Israel,[35] and they are sometimes too hasty in drawing negative conclusions from the absence of archaeological evidence (e.g., in the case of David and Solomon). It may be true, as Dever suggests, that there is an element of rebellion against religious authority in this discussion. It does not seem to me, however, that either Lemche or Thompson has an evident postmodern agenda. The crisis in historiography in the study of ancient Israel does not

---

tinction between primary and secondary sources, see Moses I. Finley, *Ancient History: Evidence and Models* (London: Chatto and Windus, 1985), 7-46. Finley notes that documents ask no questions, although they sometimes provide answers (46).

31. Thomas L. Thompson, "'House of David': An Eponymic Referent to Yahweh as Godfather," *SJOT* 9 (1995): 59-74; Lemche, 43; Philip R. Davies, "'House of David' Built on Sand: The Sins of the Biblical Maximizers," *BAR* 20/4 (1994): 54-55. See the rejoinders to Davies by Anson Rainey, "The 'House of David' and the House of the Deconstructionists," *BAR* 20/6 (1994): 47; and David Noel Freedman and Jeffrey C. Geoghegan, "'House of David' Is There," *BAR* 21 (1995): 78-79. For the inscription: Avraham Biran and Joseph Naveh, "The Tel Dan Inscription: A New Fragment," *IEJ* 45 (1995): 1-18; André Lemaire, "The Tel Dan Stela as a Piece of Royal Historiography," *JSOT* 81 (1998): 3-14.

32. Lemche, *The Israelites in History and Tradition*, 24.

33. Albertz, 30-46. See also Avi Hurvitz, "The Historical Quest for 'Ancient Israel' and the Linguistic Evidence of the Hebrew Bible," *VT* 47 (1997): 307-15.

34. Lemche, *The Israelites in History and Tradition*, 24.

35. Hans M. Barstad speaks appropriately of "The Strange Fear of the Bible: Some Reflections on the 'Bibliophobia' in Recent Ancient Israelite Historiography," in Grabbe, *Leading Captivity Captive*, 120-27. See also his balanced essay, "History and the Hebrew Bible," in Grabbe, *Can a "History of Israel" Be Written?* 37-64.

arise from philosophical predispositions but from the limitations of the available evidence.

The more extreme theses of Thompson and Lemche, such as the claim that the Bible is a Hellenistic book, do not seem to me to warrant discussion. Instead, I will focus primarily on the early history of Israel, which has been the arena of the most intense debates. In the minds of most students of the Bible, whether professional or lay, special importance attaches to the question of the origins of Israel. This may be an example of what the historian Marc Bloch called "the idol of origins,"[36] but it engages popular interest nonetheless, especially for people with religious commitments. In the words of William Dever: "Anyone even remotely acquainted with Jewish and Christian traditions instinctively grasps that these are fundamental issues, as they have to do with the *origins,* as well as the distinctive nature, of the people of the Bible. People rightly ask, 'If the story of the Exodus from Egypt is all a myth, what *can* we believe?'"[37]

Salvaging the Biblical Tradition

Inevitably, the broadside attacks of the so-called "minimalists" have provoked responses from more conservative scholars. These responses are of different types.

At one end of the spectrum is a substantial tome, *On the Reliability of the Old Testament,* by the Egyptologist Kenneth Kitchen.[38] This is a richly documented collection of data from the ancient Near East that might possibly illustrate or support the historicity of the biblical narratives. But it is ultimately a work of apologetics. The embarrassing archaeological finding of Kathleen Kenyon that Jericho was not occupied in the 13th century when Joshua was supposed to have destroyed it, is explained blithely by appeal to "erosion."[39] In the case of Ai, which was also deserted at that time, Kitchen assures us that, while the site that has been excavated "does not (yet?) have the requisite archaeological profile" to support the conquest story, "there might well be another site of a similar kind that does, yet to be

36. Marc Bloch, *The Historian's Craft* (New York: Knopf, 1953), 29.
37. William G. Dever, *Who Were the Early Israelites and Where Did They Come From?* (Grand Rapids: Wm. B. Eerdmans, 2003), 3.
38. (Grand Rapids: Wm. B. Eerdmans, 2003).
39. Kitchen, 187.

found."[40] One is reminded of the comments of U.S. Vice President Dick Cheney on the search for weapons of mass destruction in Iraq. The historian must work with evidence that is available, not with hypothetical evidence that may (or may not) be found in the future. Kitchen admits that there is no evidence directly supporting the exodus and that "nowhere in Sinai has a body of Late Bronze Age people passing through left explicit traces."[41] But he tries to make a circumstantial case, arguing that "exoduses happened in the second millennium" and that quail do migrate via Sinai, and so forth.[42] Besides, "as for no clues in Sinai, it is silly to expect to find traces of everybody who ever passed through the various routes in that peninsula."[43] The patriarchal stories "give a picture of real human life as lived by West Semitic pastoralists," etc.[44] In light of this relaxed standard of evidence, it is surprising that Kitchen gives up so easily on the historicity of Genesis 1-11. These stories, we are told, share a literary pattern with a small group of related compositions from early Mesopotamia. But we are assured that nobody composed such stories afresh after about 1500 B.C.E.,[45] although the Enuma Elish is commonly dated several centuries later by Assyriologists.[46] For Kitchen, the biblical story (at least from the time of Abraham) is true until proven otherwise. Needless to say, he is not troubled by postmodernism or deconstruction, which he dubs "the crown of all follies."[47] His critiques of Lemche, Thompson, and others are not without substance, but his own views are too blatantly apologetic to warrant serious consideration as historiography.

More sophisticated, but ultimately equally apologetic, is another volume published in 2003, by Iain Provan, V. Phillips Long, and Tremper Longman III, entitled provocatively, *A Biblical History of Israel.*[48] Provan had garnered some attention a decade ago by jousting with Thompson and

40. Kitchen, 189. Contrast the refreshing honesty of Joseph Callaway, the Southern Baptist professor who excavated the site, recounted by Dever, *Who Were the Early Israelites,* 47-48.

41. Kitchen, 310.

42. Kitchen, 311.

43. Kitchen, 467.

44. Kitchen, 365.

45. Kitchen, 447.

46. Benjamin R. Foster, *From Distant Days: Myths, Tales, and Poetry of Ancient Mesopotamia* (Bethesda: CDL, 1995), 9.

47. Kitchen, 469.

48. (Louisville: Westminster John Knox, 2003).

Davies, in an exchange that generated considerably more heat than light.[49] Unlike Kitchen, Provan and friends pay considerable attention to issues of historiography and the philosophy of history. They recognize that Thompson and Lemche differ from earlier critical scholars only in the degree of their distrust of the biblical text. The real problem, from their perspective, lies in the ideal of scientific historiography fostered in the 19th century, with its distrust of tradition. They welcome the critiques of Rankean historiography by postmodernists and others, but they are far from embracing the postmodernist response, which renders all historical knowledge problematic. Instead, they invoke the category of "testimony": "What is commonly referred to as 'knowledge of the past' is more accurately described as 'faith in the testimony,' in the interpretations of the past, offered by other people."[50] They specifically take issue with the ideal of autonomy, advocated by such theoreticians as Ernst Troeltsch and R. G. Collingwood, who insisted that the critical historian must not defer to authority.[51] They acknowledge, briefly, that testimony may be untrustworthy, and that critical thinking is necessary: "We are by no means advocating . . . a *blind faith* in testimony, whether it concerns present or past reality. Given the mixed nature of testimony, this approach would be far from rational. Some *kind* of autonomy in respect of testimony, of the sort after which Collingwood is grasping, is clearly necessary if the individual is to have any possibility of differentiating falsehood from truth." "Yet," they add, "just as autonomous agency in normal adult life life does not necessitate the renunciation of dependence on others, so autonomous *thinking* is entirely compatible with fundamental reliance on the word of others as a path to knowledge."[52] In fact, it becomes clear that Provan and his collaborators regard the biblical stories as fundamentally reliable history and that the nod to critical thinking is perfunctory.

49. Provan, *JBL* 114 (1995): 585-606; Thomas L. Thompson, "A Neo-Albrightean School in History and Biblical Scholarship?" *JBL* 114 (1995): 683-98; Philip R. Davies, "Method and Madness: Some Remarks on Doing History with the Bible," *JBL* 114 (1995): 699-705; Provan, "In the Stable with the Dwarves: Testimony, Interpretation, Faith and the History of Israel," in *Congress Volume, Oslo,* ed. André Lemaire and Magne Saebø. *VTSup* 80 (Leiden: Brill, 2000), 281-319; repr. in *Windows into Old Testament History,* ed. V. Philips Long, David W. Baker, and Gordon J. Wenham (Grand Rapids: Wm. B. Eerdmans, 2002), 161-97. See also the comments of Barr, 59-101.
50. Provan, Long, and Longman, 37.
51. Provan, Long, and Longman, 46.
52. Provan, Long, and Longman, 48.

To their credit, Provan and his colleagues are forthright about their methodological assumptions. "Why," they ask, "should verification be a prerequisite for our acceptance of a tradition as valuable in respect of historical reality? Why should not ancient historical texts rather be given the benefit of the doubt in regard to their statements about the past unless good reasons exist to consider them unreliable in these statements? . . . Why should we adopt a verification instead of a falsification principle?"[53] They also reject the standard historical distinction between primary and secondary sources, and insist that texts written centuries after the events they report may be none the less reliable for that. Finally, they reject the principle of analogy with modern experience as a guide to the credible. Such indeed are the principles that are necessary if one wants to keep open the possibility of accepting everything recorded in the Bible as historically valid. But this "epistemological openness" is purchased at the price of forgoing common ground with anyone who does not approach the Bible with an equally trusting attitude. In giving the Bible the benefit of the doubt, Provan and his colleagues merely assume what needs to be demonstrated or supported by evidence and argument.

In light of their "falsification" principle, Provan and company proceed very much in the manner of Kitchen, whom they frequently cite. They acknowledge that some alleged parallels to patriarchal customs in the Nuzi texts are not valid, but they defend a 2nd-millennium date for the patriarchs on the grounds that some of their conduct, both sexual and cultic, is condemned in Exodus and Deuteronomy.[54] The force of the argument depends, of course on the date of the laws in Exodus and Deuteronomy, a subject they do not discuss. On the problem of Jericho, they dwell at some length on the attempt of Bryant Wood to date the destruction of Jericho to the Late Bronze Age (ca. 1400), when it could be associated with Joshua. They admit that Wood "has not succeeded in getting a large scholarly following,"[55] but conclude that "the jury is still out."[56] The site of Ai may be misidentified, as Kitchen suggests. The widely shared view of archaeologists such as Israel Finkelstein and William Dever that the settlers in the central highlands were indigenous is questioned because of the absence of

---

53. Provan, Long, and Longman, 55.
54. Provan, Long, and Longman, 115.
55. Provan, Long, and Longman, 176.
56. Provan, Long, and Longman, 190.

pig-bones,[57] although it is not apparent why abstinence from pork should require an exodus from Egypt. In all of this, the assumption is that the "testimony" of the biblical texts should be accepted unless it is conclusively proven to be false. There is nothing critical about this assumption. It only shows that those who have a prior commitment to biblical historicity are not easily dissuaded by evidence to the contrary.

I have spent some time on the "histories" of Kitchen and Provan because they are as extreme at one end of the spectrum as those of Thompson and Davies are at the other. Provan and his collaborators are quite right to protest against the attempt of the minimalists to exclude the biblical text from discussions of the history. When our evidence is so scanty, it is obvious folly to exclude anything that has *prima facie* relevance. But the argument that this "testimony" should be given the benefit of the doubt is credible only to committed believers. They are also right to insist that nonbiblical and archaeological evidence is not "objective fact" but requires critical interpretation. Archaeological data become meaningful only when they are fitted into some larger story. But some data cannot be fitted into some stories. The archaeological evidence for the land west of the Jordan in the Late Bronze and Early Iron ages can be construed so as to support more than one historical reconstruction. But it cannot, on the basis of the evidence now available, be made to support the account of conquest presented in the book of Joshua.

Finally, neither the minimalists nor the maximalists have much sensitivity for literary genre. Provan and his colleagues argue that Genesis is "a project in history writing" because "one cannot conceive of the original audience as thinking of Abraham as other than a real person."[58] This is to confuse descriptive realism with historiographic intention. Indeed, the criterion of intentionality, proposed by Baruch Halpern as a way of distinguishing between history writing and fiction,[59] has been widely recognized to be unworkable.[60] The authors and compilers of Genesis may have had various intentions; it is not apparent that providing an accurate record of the past ranked high among them. On the "minimalist" side, the same tin ear is evident in Davies's argument that one cannot distinguish between

57. Provan, Long, and Longman, 188.
58. Provan, Long, and Longman, 111.
59. Baruch Halpern, *The First Historians* (San Francisco: Harper & Row, 1988), 7-8.
60. See Susan Niditch, "Historiography, 'Hazards,' and the Study of Ancient Israel," *Int* 57 (2003): 138-50, esp. 140.

the different biblical books in the matter of historical reliability.[61] There are obvious differences in genre between the more chronistic parts of Kings, for example, and the miraculous stories of Exodus and Joshua. Sweeping assumptions about the reliability of the biblical text, whether positive or negative, are not very helpful. Each book, or even each passage, must be examined in its own right, both with regard to its literary character and to its potential historical value, regardless of the fact that it is now integrated into the "metahistory" of the Bible.

Dever and Finkelstein

After considering Thompson and Lemche on the one hand and Kitchen and Provan on the other, the work of Israel Finkelstein and William Dever seems refreshingly moderate and centrist.[62] While the two have sparred over various issues, such as the origin of the settlers in the hill country and the evidence for the 10th century,[63] there is a broad area of agreement in their views on early Israel.[64] Both are archaeologists, and they agree on several key interpretations of the archaeological record:

1. There is no evidence of a mass exodus of Israelites from Egypt; there is no evidence of violent conquest of the land west of the Jordan by invaders from outside.
2. There is, however, evidence of extensive new settlements in the central highlands that were later the heartland of Israel, in the 13th century

---

61. Thompson, *The Mythic Past*, 62-81, makes much of the fictional character of biblical narrative, but does not show much nuance with regard to the ways that historical information may be conveyed even in sources that are in some respects legendary or mythical. For a defense of the historiographical character (not necessarily the historical reliability) of some biblical books, primarily those in the so-called Deuteronomistic history, see Halpern, *The First Historians;* Marc Zvi Brettler, *The Creation of History in Ancient Israel* (London: Routledge, 1995); Cook, 139-58. Brettler takes Chronicles as a model for biblical history.

62. Finkelstein presents his own position as centrist: "Archaeology and Text in the Third Millennium: A View from the Center," in *Congress Volume, Basel*, ed. André Lemaire. *VTSup* 92 (Leiden: Brill, 2002), 323-42.

63. Their disagreements have become increasingly acrimonious. See Hershel Shanks, "In This Corner: William Dever and Israel Finkelstein Debate the Early History of Israel," *BAR* 30/6 (2004): 42-45.

64. See Dever, *Who Were the Early Israelites*, 153-54.

B.C.E. The archaeological evidence indicates that the settlers were indigenous Canaanites, rather than immigrants from another cultural area. Since this area is later associated with Israel, and since the stela of Merneptah mentions a people called Israel somewhere in this area at the end of the 13th century,[65] it is reasonable to assume that the settlers in the 13th century were, or at least included, the forefathers of the Israelites.[66] In his early work, Finkelstein readily identified these settlements as Israelite. He is now more hesitant than Dever in this regard.

The two archaeologists also have different theories about the provenance of the settlers, Finkelstein regarding them as nomads who settled down, Dever as people displaced from the lowlands. Nonetheless, the two archaeologists are in substantial agreement about the archaeological data.[67]

Finkelstein's treatment of the biblical texts is flawed by an obsessive tendency to date all the biblical sources to the 7th century B.C.E., but this has little bearing on his assessment of the early history of Israel. Here I will focus on Dever's presentation, as he is engaged more directly in the debate with the so-called minimalists, and his work represents an interesting case study in current scholarly rhetoric on the subject of Israelite historiography.

Dever presents the "minimalists," or "nihilists" as he sometimes calls them, as a threat to the foundations of Western civilization:

But what if ancient Israel was "invented" by Jews living much later, and the biblical literature is therefore nothing but pious propaganda? If that is the case, as some revisionist historians now loudly proclaim, then there was no ancient Israel. . . . The story of Israel in the Hebrew Bible would have to be considered a monstrous literary hoax, one that has cruelly deceived countless millions of people until its recent exposure by a few courageous scholars. And now, at last, thanks to these social revolutionaries, we sophisticated modern secularists can be "liberated" from

65. See J. Maxwell Miller and John H. Hayes, *A History of Ancient Israel and Judah* (Philadelphia: Westminster, 1986), 68-69.

66. In contrast, Thompson, *The Mythic Past*, 79, denies that the Israel of Merneptah is at all related to the Israel of the Bible!

67. See also Lawrence E. Stager, "Forging an Identity: The Emergence of Ancient Israel," in *The Oxford History of the Biblical World*, ed. Michael D. Coogan (New York: Oxford University Press, 1998), 123-75.

the biblical myths, free to venture into a Brave New World unencumbered by the biblical baggage with which we grew up.[68]

In light of this rousing opening, the reader expects an equally rousing affirmation of biblical historicity, and the same seems to be promised by the title of the concluding chapter: "Salvaging the Biblical Tradition: History or Myth?"

But Dever is no Kenneth Kitchen or Iain Provan. He is a professional archaeologist who respects archaeological evidence and is not willing to explain it away. Citing an article from *The New York Times* entitled "The Bible, as History, Flunks New Archaeological Tests," he asks: "but does it?"[69] His answer is hardly the ringing denial that we might have been led to expect. "Perhaps the books of Exodus and Numbers do, because as we have seen their accounts of escape from Egypt, of wandering in the wilderness, and of massive conquests in Transjordan are overwhelmingly contradicted by the archaeological evidence. That may make many uncomfortable, but it is a fact, one from which no open-minded person can escape."[70] Moreover, "there is little that we can salvage from Joshua's stories of the rapid, wholesale destruction of Canaanite cities and the annihilation of the local population. It simply did not happen; the archaeological evidence is indisputable."[71] Needless to say, Genesis is of no help to the historian. This does not seem to be salvaging much of the biblical tradition. But salvation comes from an unlikely source, the book of Judges. This, we are told, "fits astonishingly well with the current archaeological facts on the ground."[72] But what in the stories of Judges has been verified by archaeology? Has someone found a bloodstained jawbone of an ass, beside a pile of Philistine skulls? What Dever apparently means is that there is nothing in Judges that is falsified by the archaeological record. For the scholar who wants to salvage something of the biblical record, this is such a relief, after the negative results in Exodus and Joshua, that it seems like astonishing vindication.[73]

---

68. Dever, *Who Were the Early Israelites,* ix. For the view that biblical history was invented in the Hellenistic period, see Thompson, *The Mythic Past,* 200-25.

69. Dever, *Who Were the Early Israelites,* 227, The article in *The New York Times* was dated July 19, 2000.

70. Dever, *Who Were the Early Israelites,* 227.

71. Dever, *Who Were the Early Israelites,* 227-28.

72. Dever, *Who Were the Early Israelites,* 228.

73. Contrast the nuanced view of Judges as traditional literature in Niditch, 144-50.

Provan and his collaborators would surely object that archaeological findings are scholarly constructs and that Dever is being positivistic in his reliance on them. But the point is not whether Dever's interpretation of the archaeology is objective fact. It surely is not. The point is, rather, whether the findings of archaeology, as they exist in their present provisional state, can be reconciled with the biblical master narrative. And as Dever acknowledges, with refreshing honesty, they can not.

What is more puzzling, in light of Dever's assessment of the archaeological evidence, is why he fulminates so fiercely against the "minimalists." There is, of course, some difference between their positions. Dever remains confident that "the Iron I colonists in the central hill country of Canaan may be tentatively identified as proto-Israelites, that is, as the initial settlers in the area whose culture evolved by the 10th century B.C. into the Israel of the Monarchy, if not the ideal Israel of the Hebrew Bible."[74] The minimalists are more skeptical about the continuity and, in any case, point out, quite rightly, that there is no evidence that these "proto-Israelites" correspond to anything described in the Bible. The differences between Dever and his adversaries become more pronounced in the period of the monarchy. But with regard to the admittedly foundational stories of the exodus and conquest, their positions on the historicity of the Bible are hardly distinguishable at all. Dever concludes that, "rather than attempt to defend the factual historicity of the Exodus traditions, I suggest that we must understand the Exodus story precisely as a myth, specifically as a 'metaphor for liberation.' Instead of demanding to know 'what really happened' that might have given rise to the story. . ., we need to ask what the story meant in ancient times, and what it can mean today."[75] And yet "the mythic past" has a different ring to it when Thompson uses it as the title of one of his books.

In a perceptive commentary on an exchange between Lemche and Dever, Norman Gottwald suggests that the real differences between them are on the level of ideology.[76] For Gottwald, this is not necessarily a bad

74. Dever, *Who Were the Early Israelites*, 218.
75. Dever, *Who Were the Early Israelites*, 233.
76. Norman K. Gottwald, "Triumphalist versus Anti-Triumphalist Versions of Early Israel," *CurBS* 5 (1997): 15-42. Cf. Niels Peter Lemche, "Early Israel Revisited," *CurBS* 4 (1996): 9-34; Dever, "Revisionist Israel Revisited: A Rejoinder to Niels Peter Lemche," *CurBS* 4 (1996): 35-50; Lemche, "Response to William G. Dever, 'Revisionist Israel Revisited,'" *CurBS* 5 (1997): 9-14.

thing. Everyone has an ideology, although some scholars are oblivious to their own while acutely conscious of everyone else's. In Gottwald's view, Dever is a "triumphalist," while Lemche is an "anti-triumphalist": "Dever, I would judge, stands in continuity with the mainstream of biblical interpretation accustomed to tracing a single teleological line of development from tribal and monarchic Israel onward to later Judaism and Christianity, and in the process passing rather quickly over all the ancient peoples who were not 'caught up' in the forward movement of biblical Israel, except as they were Israel's antagonists."[77] The revisionist agenda is "in stark opposition to the dominant *triumphalist* ideology in biblical scholarship." From this perspective, scholarly views of both Israel's relation to other peoples and its own internal society have been over-determined by a teleological reading of ancient Israel based on subsequent Jewish and Christian religious and political developments.[78] Gottwald quite rightly notes that the revisionist agenda is complex, and that all its proponents do not necessarily agree with each other. To characterize it as "anti-triumphalist" may attribute to it a disinterested character that is implausible, even on the assumptions of its practitioners. The negative claims of Thompson and Davies seem to me to be just as imperialistic and totalizing as anything Albright ever wrote, and in fact to be quite triumphalist in their undermining of traditional beliefs. But Gottwald is, I think, on track when he suggests that the differences are ideological, even political, rather than simply a matter of scholarly argument. Dever approaches the material with an evident desire to uphold the biblical tradition, even while recognizing that much of it cannot be salvaged. Davies and Thompson operate with an equally obvious delight in undermining the tradition wherever possible.

Ethnicity in Early Israel

One of the foci of debate about the archaeological evidence for early Israel has been the question of ethnicity. Older scholarship frequently singled out some archaeological features as distinctively Israelite — the four-room house, collar-rimmed jars. Recently the absence of pig-bones in the central highlands has attracted much attention. None of these features was unique

77. Gottwald, *CurBS* 5 (1997): 28.
78. Gottwald, *CurBS* 5 (1997): 30.

to this area, however. As Elizabeth Bloch-Smith shows in a recent overview, "the distribution of pillared houses and store jars and the absence of pork in the diet. . . both temporally and spatially. . . exceed the parameters of early Israel."[79] But the attempt to define ethnicity in terms of the presence or absence of specific features is flawed in any case. As Fredrik Barth argued several decades ago, the crucial question concerns the boundary markers that people in a given group considered significant.[80] Bloch-Smith concedes, in another article, that "without written evidence indicating a group's affiliation, or clarifying how, for example, others regarded it, it is very difficult to establish ethnic identity."[81] She proposes a "Tell-Tale" approach that relies on correspondences between the archaeological record and biblical traditions. By this means, she attempts to identify "significant Israelite ethnic traits vis-à-vis the Philistines." For this purpose it is not necessary to find features that were unique to Israel, just features that distinguished them from the neighbors in the coastal plain. She argues that "circumcision, sporting a short beard rather than a clean-shaven face, and abstaining from eating pork, none of which may have been exclusive to Israel, differentiated Israelites from Philistines and so likely functioned as circumstantial ethnic markers. Each of these traits was given significance and, by a later time, codified into law."[82] But of these, only circumcision is noted as a distinguishing trait in the biblical stories about the Philistines (1 Sam 18:25-27; 31:4; 2 Sam 3:14), and I am not aware of relevant archaeological evidence. For evidence for biblical traditions about beards and pork, one must turn to Leviticus and Deuteronomy, both compiled several centuries after the period under discussion. Even then, Leviticus does not specify that beards must be short; it only prohibits trimming the edges (Lev 19:27). Pork is prohibited, but in a list that includes the meat of the camel and the rock-badger, and it is not singled out

79. Elizabeth Bloch-Smith, "Israelite Ethnicity in Iron I: Archaeology Preserves What Is Remembered and What Is Forgotten in Israel's History," *JBL* 122 (2003): 401-25 (407). In contrast, Finkelstein and Silberman, 119, and Mark G. Brett, "Israel's Indigenous Origins: Cultural Hybridity and the Formation of Israelite Ethnicity," *BibInt* 11 (2003): 400-12, still maintain the distinctiveness of the absence of pork.

80. Fredrik Barth, "Introduction," in *Ethnic Groups and Boundaries: The Social Organization of Cultural Difference* (Boston: Little, Brown, 1969), 14-15.

81. Elizabeth Bloch-Smith and Beth Alpert Nakhai, "A Landscape Comes to Life," *NEA* 62 (1999): 62-92, 101-27 (63).

82. Bloch-Smith, *JBL* 122 (2003): 422. She also notes that the Israelites perceived themselves as militarily inferior, because of their lack of iron weapons (415; 1 Sam 13:19).

for special significance. Bloch-Smith may be right that these features distinguished Israelites from Philistines already in the 11th century, but we do not in fact have evidence that Israelites at that time regarded these features, other than circumcision, as boundary markers.[83] Since ethnic identity depends heavily on self-understanding and the perceptions of others, any discussion of ethnicity depends inevitably on verbal, and in the case of antiquity written, evidence. When the written sources are admitted to come from a time several centuries later, the discussion becomes very difficult, and it is not possible to have much confidence in the conclusions.

Bloch-Smith feels that she can use texts of postexilic date as sources for early Israel because she regards them as depositories of the collective memory of the Israelite people.[84] There is certainly some justification for this view. Much of the Bible, especially in the early part, is traditional literature that took shape gradually over the centuries, and contains material that is much older than the final redaction. Collective memory has come into vogue somewhat in biblical studies in recent years, in part because of the influential work of Jan Assman, *Moses the Egyptian*.[85] Some scholars have tried to salvage a measure of historicity from the Exodus story in this way. Ronald Hendel argues that "certain actions and policies of the Egyptian empire in Canaan may be discerned in the portrait of the Egyptian oppression. A devastating epidemic in the late fourteenth century, interpreted as an act of divine punishment, may be distantly recalled in the story of the Egyptian plagues. A historical figure named Moses may have been transformed into the savior and mediator of all Israel, perhaps generalized from the memory of a smaller group."[86] Baruch Halpern finds echoes of the Hyksos in the

---

83. Contrast the more cautious approach of Brian Hesse and Paula Wapnish, "Can Pig Remains Be Used for Ethnic Diagnosis in the Ancient Near East?" in *Archaeology of Israel: Constructing the Past*, ed. Neil A. Silberman and David B. Small. JSOTSup 237 (Sheffield: Sheffield Academic, 1997), 238-70 (261-63). They argue for a postexilic date for the biblical ban on pork. Brett, 404, admits that to speak of a pig taboo in Iron I goes beyond the evidence, but nonetheless finds it to be a plausible inference.

84. Bloch-Smith, *JBL* 122 (2003): 422.

85. Jan Assman, *Moses the Egyptian: The Memory of Egypt in Western Monotheism* (Cambridge, Mass.: Harvard University Press, 1997). See Mark S. Smith, "Remembering God: Collective Memory in Israelite Religion," *CBQ* 64 (2002): 631-51 and the bibliog. there cited, notably Jacques LeGoff, *History and Memory* (New York: Columbia University Press, 1992).

86. Ronald Hendel, "The Exodus in Biblical Memory," *JBL* 120 (2001): 601-22 (621). See now also Hendel, *Remembering Abraham: Culture, Memory, and History in the Hebrew Bible* (Oxford: Oxford University Press, 2005).

story of the descent into Egypt, and notes that the brickmaking described in Exodus "reflects close knowledge of conditions under the XIXth Dynasty."[87] But as Hendel readily admits, "historical events are the most difficult to isolate."[88] "Each aspect of this complex tale may contain traces of historical events and persons, mingled together with mythic motifs, themes, and structures — the stuff that makes the past truly memorable."[89] Halpern speaks of the exodus as a national myth and compares it to the *Odyssey*. Collective memory can be a highly creative process, and in many cases we can speak just as well of the invention of tradition.[90] Collective memory is ultimately a better guide to what the remembering community regarded as important than to the events of the past in any objective sense.

There is then a remarkable consensus, to which all but conservative apologists such as Kitchen and Provan would subscribe, that the foundation stories of exodus and conquest are best understood as myths. There is considerable disagreement as to when these myths became current and when they attained their present form, but they cannot be taken as history in any positivistic sense. Thus far, at least, the sweeping claims made by Davies in 1992 are justified, and indeed, this situation was recognized already in the mid-1980's in the "Histories of Israel" by J. Alberto Soggin and by Miller and Hayes.[91]

The Later History of Israel

I have confined my attention to the early, premonarchic history of Israel, in part because this is an area where polemical rhetoric often masks substantial agreement and in part because these stories are foundational for

87. Baruch Halpern, "The Exodus from Egypt: Myth or Reality?" in Hershel Shanks et al., *The Rise of Ancient Israel* (Washington: Biblical Archaeology Society, 1992), 87-113 (101).

88. Hendel, *JBL* 120 (2001): 621.

89. Hendel, *JBL* 120 (2001): 620-21.

90. See the work of Eric Hobsbawm and Terence Ranger, eds., *The Invention of Tradition* (Cambridge: Cambridge University Press, 1983); and, with reference to the exodus, Karel van der Toorn, "The Exodus as Charter Myth," in *Religious Identity and the Invention of Tradition*, ed. Jan Willem van Henten and Anton Houtepen (Assen: van Gorcum, 2001), 113-27; John J. Collins, "The Development of the Exodus Tradition," in van Henten and Houtepen, 144-55.

91. Davies, *In Search of "Ancient Israel,"* 26; J. Alberto Soggin, *A History of "Ancient Israel"* (Philadelphia: Westminster, 1985); Miller and Hayes (1986).

both Jewish identity and Christian theology. What is true of this early material is not necessarily true of the later books. Despite the iconoclastic claims of Philip Davies, the Bible is not all of one piece with respect to history. There are obvious differences in literary genre between the legendary, miracle-filled book of Exodus, the sober prose fiction of 1 and 2 Samuel, and some rather annalistic passages in the books of Kings. Of course, to say that a story is "historylike" is not to say that it necessarily reflects historical events accurately. Unless we are willing to make a Provan-style leap of faith and trust the "testimony" of the biblical books, we are dependent on outside sources for confirmation.

In the much disputed case of the united monarchy, such confirmation is not available. No extant nonbiblical texts mention David or his kingdom, except for the indirect reference to the "house of David" in the Tel Dan inscription. For Solomon, we have to wait until one Menander of Ephesus, if we credit the testimony of Josephus.[92] The absence of Akkadian corroboration is not especially surprising, as Assyrian power was in abeyance at the time. But it is remarkable that there are no Egyptian inscriptions mentioning Israel or Judah, Solomon or Rehoboam. This does not necessarily mean that the stories of David and Solomon have no historical basis. Baruch Halpern has made an ingenious case for a plausible historical reading of the career of David, arguing that the books of Samuel, like ancient Near Eastern inscriptions, may exaggerate the significance of events and actions, but not invent them out of whole cloth.[93] But without confirming evidence the argument remains in the realm of the possible. Archaeologists have long claimed to find some confirmation of the reign of Solomon at the sites of Megiddo, Gezer, and Hazor, which he built up, according to 1 Kgs 9:15. At each of these sites a six-chambered gate was found, attached to a casemate fortification, and this was taken as confirmation of Solomon's building activity by the excavator of Megiddo, Yigael Yadin.[94] But this evidence is now in dispute. Finkelstein and David Ussishkin, who

92. Josephus *Ag. Ap.* 1.116-25; *Ant.* 8.144; Ahlström, 541.

93. Baruch Halpern, *David's Secret Demons: Messiah, Murderer, Traitor, King.* The Bible in Its World (Grand Rapids: Wm. B. Eerdmans, 2001). Halpern invokes "the principle of minimal interpretation," asking, "what is the minimum the king might have done to lay claim to the achievements he publishes?" (126).

94. Yigael Yadin, "Hazor, Gezer and Megiddo in Solomon's Time," in *The Kingdoms of Israel and Judah*, ed. Abraham Malamat (Jerusalem: Israel Exploration Society, 1961), 66-109. See Halpern, *David's Secret Demons,* 433-37.

led the most recent excavation at Megiddo, have argued that these structures do not date to the time of Solomon at all. According to Finkelstein, "essentially, archaeology misdated both 'Davidic' and 'Solomonic' remains by a full century. The finds dated to the time just before David in the late eleventh century belonged in the mid-tenth century and those dated to the time of Solomon belonged in the early ninth century BCE. The new dates place the appearance of monumental structures, fortifications, and other signs of full statehood precisely at the time of their first appearance in the rest of the Levant."[95] Thompson, as might be expected, uses this finding as an occasion to hold forth on the perils of interpreting archaeological discoveries by reference to the Bible.[96] But the revisionist dating has not gone unchallenged, and indeed so far has not persuaded the majority of archaeologists of ancient Israel.[97]

Even if the structures at Megiddo and elsewhere are dated to the time of Solomon, however, this would by no means corroborate the full biblical story.[98] Even defenders of the tradition, such as Halpern, readily grant that the biblical account gives a misleading impression of the glory of Solomon's empire.[99] The story of David is artfully fashioned, and much of it has historical verisimilitude. While it has the character of a historical novel, it is not correct to say that it is not about history at all.[100] Unlike the stories of the exodus and conquest, this story does not admit of archaeological verification or refutation. But whether the events it reports are

95. Finkelstein and Silberman, 142.
96. Thompson, *The Mythic Past*, 202-3.
97. Hershel Shanks, "Where Is the Tenth Century?" *BAR* 24/2 (1998): 56-61. See the detailed refutation of the revisionist dating by Halpern, *David's Secret Demons*, 427-78; "The Gate of Megiddo and the Debate on the 10th Century," in Lemaire and Saebø, 79-121.
98. Archeological investigation of Jerusalem in the 10th century is impeded by the impossibility of excavating under the Temple Mount. See the debate in *BAR* 24/4 (1998), with contributions by Margreet Steiner (26-32, 62-63), who argues that the lack of archaeological remains shows that there was no significant city, and Jane Cahill (34-41, 63) and Nadav Na'aman (42-44), who argue that the evidence supports its existence. See also Na'aman, "Cow Town or Royal Capital? Evidence for Iron Age Jerusalem," *BAR* 23/4 (1997): 43-47, 67.
99. Halpern, *David's Secret Demons*, 478: "The state was far from impressive, but it was real." Na'aman, *BAR* 23/4 (1997): 47, agrees that Judah was a chiefdom in the 10th and 9th centuries and that it did not become a state until the 8th century.
100. *Pace* Thompson, *The Mythic Past*, 206. Contrast the discussion of the historical value of Gustave Flaubert's novel, *L'Éducation Sentimentale*, by Ginzburg, *History, Rhetoric, and Proof*, 92-110.

based on fact or are pure fiction, we ultimately do not know. The denials of
the minimalists are no more warranted than the uncritical acceptance of
the "biblical historians."

In the case of the books of Kings, we have at least several reference
points, where figures or events are also attested in nonbiblical sources. This
is acknowledged by both Halpern and Lemche in their diverse ways.[101]
Even Davies admits, in the case of the siege of Jerusalem by Sennacherib,
that "there is an historical event lurking here" and that both biblical and
Assyrian accounts refer to it in some way.[102] To be sure, the biblical account has a theological agenda and cannot be accepted at face value, but
the Assyrian account is no less ideological and propagandistic.[103] Nonetheless, in cases such as this it is possible to see what the biblical and
nonbiblical accounts have in common, and so the biblical story has some
evidentiary value, in a way that the stories of the patriarchs or the exodus
do not.

The same is true of the accounts of the exile and the Persian period, although these too are ideological documents. The attempt of Thompson to
deny continuity between those who were deported from Jerusalem by the
Babylonians and those who were restored under the Persians seems to me
extremely farfetched, although the continuities between preexilic and
postexilic Judah could certainly be construed differently from what we
find in the book of Ezra.[104] But, again, our understanding of the Persian
period, including the careers of Ezra and Nehemiah, suffers from lack of
corroboration from external sources. This does not warrant the conclu-

101. Baruch Halpern, "Erasing History: The Minimalist Assault on Ancient Israel," in
Israel's Past in Present Research: Essays on Ancient Israelite Historiography, ed. V. Philips Long.
Sources for Biblical and Theological Study 7 (Winona Lake: Eisenbrauns, 1999), 415-26;
Lemche, *The Israelites in History and Tradition,* 35-64. See also the maximalist account of
Kitchen, 7-64.

102. Davies, *In Search of Ancient Israel,* 33. See the essays in *"Like a Bird in a Cage": The
Invasion of Sennacherib in 701 BCE,* ed. Lester L. Grabbe. JSOTSup 363 (Sheffield: Sheffield
Academic, 2003).

103. The role of theological claims in Akkadian documents has been emphasized help-
fully by Rainer Albertz, "Die Exilszeit als Ernstfall für eine historische Rekonstruktion ohne
biblische Texte: Die neubabylonischen Königsinschriften als 'Primärquelle,'" in Grabbe,
Leading Captivity Captive, 22-39.

104. Thompson, *The Mythic Past,* 214. See the debate in Grabbe, *Leading Captivity Captive,* and esp. the balanced treatment by Rainer Albertz, *Israel in Exile: The History and Literature of the Sixth Century B.C.E.* (Atlanta: SBL, 2003).

sion that the books of Ezra and Nehemiah are entirely fictional, but it does call for some reservations in their use as historical sources.[105]

Conclusion

The current turmoil regarding the history of ancient Israel has various causes. Most basic, perhaps, is the fact that the subject has been bound up for so long with issues of religious belief, leading to what George Ernest Wright called a "projection of faith into facts."[106] The distorting effect of the will to believe can still be seen in the case of some very learned scholars whose learning is harnessed for apologetic goals. At the other end of the spectrum, some of the more skeptical historians seem on occasion to have a real animus against religious belief, which leads to obsessive negativity.[107] In the case of early Israel, however, the so-called "collapse of history" is simply a reflection of the nature of the evidence and results from the quite conventional work of archaeologists and historical critics. It is not helpful, in my view, to lump all the "minimalists" together as postmodernists, as Dever does. Some of them, in fact, appear to have a quite positivistic faith in archaeological fact.

In one respect, however, the rise in skepticism with regard to the history of Israel is quite postmodern. Most biblical scholars in the past have accepted the broad biblical outline of Israel's history without question. The so-called "minimalists," in contrast, are distinguished precisely by their refusal to subscribe to, or "buy into," this master narrative. This fundamental orientation is, I think, the major factor that separates a critical historian like Dever from Lemche and Thompson, with respect to Israel in the early Iron Age. As Thompson remarks with regard to the exile, "the problem is not whether there was ever a historical exile. . . . The historical problems arise with the question of continuity: the continuity of people,

105. The historicity of Ezra is denied by Garbini, 151-69. See the discussion by Robert North, "Ezra," *ABD* 2:726-28, who concludes that "the claim of having proved that 'Ezra never existed,' when looked at more closely turns out to mean rather that hagiographic and ideological features are attached to an individual who may have existed in some much humbler fashion" (727).

106. George Ernest Wright, *God Who Acts: Biblical Theology as Recital.* SBT 8 (London: SCM, 1952), 117.

107. The reaction to the Tel Dan inscription is a case in point.

of their culture and their traditions."[108] For Thompson, people "created continuity and coherence because of and out of the discontinuities of . . . experience."[109] Other constructions of continuity were always possible. For example, one could consider the rise of Israel from the perspective of the Canaanites or the Philistines; or the people who remained in the land at the time of the exile might have been regarded as the primary carriers of the tradition rather than those who returned from Babylon.

In his book, *History and Ideology in the Old Testament,* James Barr writes, "it seems to me that the cutting of the link of continuity presents a threat to religion of a kind and magnitude quite different from what happened when various books or strata came to be dated 'late.' If it should be proved to be historically correct, then theology would have to consider how it should be met. For the present, I suggest that it is sufficient to deny its historical seriousness."[110] But this is too facile. The problem of continuity arises from the possibility of different viewpoints and is a perfectly serious issue. The political and ethical implications of this issue will come to the fore in the next chapter, in which we consider the story of Israel as a paradigm of liberation and the critique of that paradigm in light of postcolonial discourse.

108. Thompson, "The Exile in History and Myth," in Grabbe, *Leading Captivity Captive,* 101-18 (110).

109. Thompson, "The Exile in History and Myth," 110.

110. Barr, 100.

3

Exodus and Liberation
in Postcolonial Perspective

Regardless of its historicity, the story of the exodus is one of the great stories of Western culture. Its enduring appeal is shown by the way it has been appropriated again and again over the centuries, by Puritans and Boers, Zionists and black South Africans. In recent decades, the story has been associated especially with liberation theology, a movement that originated in South America but was taken up in other parts of the world and enjoyed broad sympathy in Europe and North America in the last quarter of the 20th century.[1] This theological movement is primarily concerned with the plight of the poor and has the practical goal of transforming society.[2] In the present context, we are not concerned with the overall assessment of the movement, but only with its use of the Bible and primarily of the Exodus story.[3]

1. For a good history of the movement, see David Tombs, *Latin American Liberation Theology* (Leiden: Brill, 2002). For South African perspectives, see Gerald O. West, *Biblical Hermeneutics of Liberation: Modes of Reading the Bible in the South African Context*, 2nd ed. (Maryknoll; Orbis, 1991); Itumeleng J. Mosala, *Biblical Hermeneutics and Black Theology in South Africa* (Grand Rapids: Wm. B. Eerdmans, 1989). A wider range of perspectives is represented in Joerg Rieger, ed., *Opting for the Margins: Postmodernity and Liberation in Christian Theology* (Oxford: Oxford University Press, 2003).

2. See, e.g., the works of Leonardo and Clodovis Boff, *Salvation and Liberation: In Search of a Balance between Faith and Politics* (Maryknoll: Orbis, 1984); and *Liberation Theology: From Confrontation to Dialogue* (San Francisco: Harper & Row, 1986), or Gustavo Gutiérrez, "The Situation and Tasks of Liberation Theology Today," in Rieger, 89-104.

3. Leo G. Perdue, *Reconstructing Old Testament Theology After the Collapse of His-*

The Exodus in Liberation Theology

While the appeal to the exodus is ubiquitous in liberation theology, it is not usually grounded in detailed exegesis.[4] Gustavo Gutiérrez, arguably the most influential liberation theologian, devotes only a few pages to the exodus in his *A Theology of Liberation,* but he articulates some basic principles of liberationist exegesis. First, he insists that creation, not the exodus, is the first salvific act in the Bible. The exodus of the particular people, Israel, must be understood in the context of the creation of all humanity. Second, the exodus must be viewed as a social and political event: "The Exodus is the long march towards the promised land in which Israel can establish a society free from misery and alienation. Throughout the whole process, the religious event is not set apart." Thirdly, "the Exodus experience is paradigmatic. It remains vital and contemporary due to similar historical experiences which the People of God undergo."[5] Granted that the story is told in the Bible of one particular people, Israel, liberation theology depends on the validity of analogy and on the belief that other people, in other times and places, may qualify as "the people of God." The primacy of creation is invoked to provide a theological basis for this belief.

In a similar vein, J. Severino Croatto, the Latin American theologian who has worked most extensively on the exodus, interprets it as a socio-political event that remains revelatory for contemporary Latin America, just as it was for ancient Israel: "We are enjoined to prolong the Exodus event because it was not an event solely for the Hebrews but rather the manifestation of a liberative plan of God for all peoples. According to a hermeneutical line of thinking it is perfectly possible that we might understand ourselves from the perspective of the biblical Exodus and, above all, that we might understand the Exodus from the vantage point of our situation as peoples in economic, political, social, or cultural 'bondage.'"[6]

---

tory. OBT (Minneapolis: Fortress, 2005), 76-101, provides a broader survey with attention to African-American scholarship and some New Testament material.

4. See Enrique Dussel, "Exodus as a Paradigm in Liberation Theology," in *Exodus: A Lasting Paradigm,* ed. Bas van Iersel and Anton Weiler (Edinburgh: T. & T. Clark, 1987), 83-92. The volume contains a good sampling of the uses of the exodus in liberation theology.

5. Gustavo Gutiérrez, *A Theology of Liberation* (Maryknoll: Orbis, 1973), 157-59.

6. J. Severino Croatto, *Exodus: A Hermeneutics of Freedom* (Maryknoll: Orbis, 1978), 15.

Croatto bases his hermeneutic on Paul Ricoeur's theory of a "surplus of meaning."[7] The biblical text of the exodus is already an interpretation, at some distance from the original event. New layers of meaning in this story emerge in light of later events, such as the crossing of the Jordan and the return from Babylon. Croatto is also aware that texts are polysemous and can disclose different meanings when they are interpreted from different standpoints and in different circumstances.

The most distinguished biblical scholar to address the role of the exodus in liberation theology is Norbert Lohfink.[8] Lohfink explains that his concern is not with the critical reconstruction of the underlying historical events but with the "canonical shape" of exodus theology. So he follows Gerhard von Rad in finding "the classic formulation of the Exodus-credo" in Deut 26:5-10, although, unlike von Rad, he considers this to be a relatively late Deuteronomic formulation, not an ancient cultic recitation.[9] He regards this passage as "the quintessence of Israel's faith,"[10] but also argues, against von Rad, that it requires the revelation at Sinai for its completion: "The canonical form of the Pentateuch demands the constitution of a new society at Sinai as an essential step between the departure from Egypt and the entry into the land flowing with milk and honey."[11] This new society "is not only in contrast to the Egyptian society they have left behind, but beyond that it is in contrast to all other existing societies in their world. Deuteronomy makes this explicit by saying that this new society finally embodies what all human societies long and strive for, but never really attain."[12] When Lohfink ventures behind the "canonical form" of the text to speak about Israel's historical beginnings, he seems to subscribe to a view similar to that of Norman Gottwald. So he speaks of a variety of groups, immigrants from Mesopotamia, border nomads, socially homeless groups of Habiru and rural Canaanites who withdrew from the control of the city-states. All of these, we are told, accepted the story of those who had actually come out

7. J. Severino Croatto, *Biblical Hermeneutics: Toward a Theory of Reading as the Production of Meaning* (Maryknoll: Orbis, 1987), esp. 17.

8. Norbert F. Lohfink, S.J., *Option for the Poor: The Basic Principle of Liberation Theology in the Light of the Bible* (Berkeley: BIBAL, 1987).

9. Lohfink, 34; cf. Gerhard von Rad, *Old Testament Theology*, 1:121-28.

10. Lohfink, 36.

11. Lohfink, 44.

12. Lohfink, 45.

of Egypt as their own. What bound these groups together was the ideal of an egalitarian society.[13]

It should be said that Lohfink's book was written in the mid-1980s, before the work of Israel Finkelstein and the latest round of debates about the origin of Israel. I do not know whether Lohfink has changed his views in the meantime. Gottwald has certainly modified his. While he still maintains that "the biblical traditions about prestate Israel provide 'glimpses' and 'echoes' of a people among whom social power was broadly distributed in local settings," Gottwald now emphasizes the lack of social information about early Israel and acknowledges that early Israel may not have been entirely egalitarian but rather a "heterarchy" in which some regions were more centralized than others.[14] But Lohfink's 1987 book is fairly typical of the understanding of the exodus in liberation theology's classic phase. While the focus is on the canonical story, it is assumed that the story has historical underpinnings, even if these do not correspond exactly to the biblical account. While the primacy of the Hebrew slaves in Egypt is assumed, the Exodus story is not viewed as the exclusive story of one ethnic group, but as one that from the beginning could be appropriated also by other groups, as a paradigm of deliverance from oppression.

Lohfink rightly acknowledges that concepts of righteousness and justice, manifested in concern for the poor and defenseless, were inculcated in the ancient Near East for more than a millennium before the rise of Israel.[15] The main novelty of the Hebrew Bible in its ancient Near Eastern setting is the way that these concepts are embedded in a story that celebrates the escape of a group of slaves. The Exodus story then provides a context for exhortations to justice: "You shall not oppress a resident alien; you know the heart of an alien, for you were aliens in the land of Egypt" (Exod 23:9). This is essentially a formulation of the Golden Rule, which is not only basic to the teaching of Jesus but is also known to nearly every culture East and West,[16] acquiring specificity in the biblical story of Israel. Liberation theologians echo the Israelite prophets by condemning "as

13. Lohfink, 48-49.

14. Norman K. Gottwald, *The Politics of Ancient Israel* (Louisville: Westminster John Knox, 2001), 170-71.

15. Lohfink, 16-25. See further Moshe Weinfeld, *Social Justice in Ancient Israel and in the Ancient Near East* (Minneapolis: Fortress, 1995).

16. See Hans Dieter Betz, *The Sermon on the Mount*. Hermeneia (Minneapolis: Fortress, 1995), 509-16.

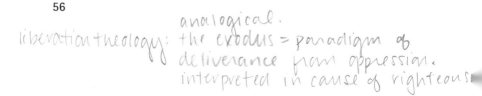

worthless religiosity a concern with offering God worship when we were unmindful of the sociopolitical implications of our religion."[17] The concern for the poor and oppressed also fits well with the postmodern attention to the "margins" and attention to points of view that are often suppressed by master narratives.[18] It is difficult, then, to quarrel with the aims of liberation theology. Here, it would seem, the Bible is interpreted in the cause of righteousness, for the sake of justice.

Criticisms of Liberation Theology

Nonetheless, liberation theology has always had its critics. Many of these, of course, are reactionary conservatives, not only in society at large but also in the Christian churches and in the guild of biblical scholars, Jewish and Christian. Our concern here is only with the critique in the context of biblical studies. Few of the prominent liberation theologians have been biblical scholars, and sometimes their work is open to the charge of naïveté with respect to the historicity of the text. Alternatively, when the liberationist cause is taken up by a sophisticated biblical critic such as Norman Gottwald, the speculative reconstruction of history has been open to criticism. Neither of these criticisms, however, seems to me to go the heart of the liberationist enterprise.[19] The story is compelling regardless of its historicity, and the more speculative reconstructions, such as that of Gottwald, are not, in my view, essential to the liberationist enterprise. Lohfink's book is a good illustration of the latter point; while he evidently subscribes to something like Gottwald's view of Israelite origins, his argument is ultimately based on the canonical text.

From the viewpoint of biblical scholarship, one of the most incisive critiques of liberation theology is that of Jon Levenson, who questions "the categories in which the exodus should be conceived."[20] Like many critics of

17. Desmond Tutu, *The Rainbow People of God: The Making of a Peaceful Revolution* (New York: Doubleday, 1994), 29.

18. Cf. Rieger.

19. For a defense of liberation theology against some of the most typical criticisms, see Christine E. Gudorf, "Liberation Theology's Use of Scripture: A Response to First World Critics," *Int* 41 (1987): 5-18.

20. Jon D. Levenson, *The Hebrew Bible, the Old Testament, and Historical Criticism* (Louisville: Westminster/John Knox, 1993), 127-59 (140). Cf. his essay, "Liberation Theology

liberation theology, Levenson disputes the social and political interpretation of the exodus. "*What for*," we are told, "matters more than *what
from*."[21] Levenson insists that "the Hebrew Bible does not conceive the exodus as a move from slavery to freedom, either freedom in the older, liberal
sense of emancipation from external constraint for the purpose of self-
determination, or freedom in the newer, Marxist sense of liberation from
oppression and alienation for the purpose of equality, solidarity, and community."[22] Exodus is only the prelude to the covenant, and is, in effect, the
substitution of one form of servitude for another: "For it is to me that the
Israelites are servants: they are my servants whom I freed from the land of
Egypt" (Lev 25:55). The Lord instructs Moses to say to Pharaoh, "Let my
people go, so that they may serve me" (Exod 7:16). There is no intrinsic objection to slavery in the biblical text, as can be seen from the Book of the
Covenant, which provides for slavery in its very first law (Exod 21:2-6).

All of this is true, but it does not negate the fact that social and political liberation is a fundamental part of the Exodus story, as Levenson also
admits.[23] The Lord tells Moses at the burning bush: "I have observed the
misery of my people who are in Egypt; I have heard their cry on account of
their taskmasters. Indeed, I know their sufferings, and I have come down
to deliver them from the Egyptians, and to bring them up out of that land
to a good and broad land, a land flowing with milk and honey" (Exod 3:7-
8). Without social and political liberation, the people are not free to serve
their God in the way prescribed. Any interpretation of the Exodus story
that neglects the social aspect is no less a distortion than one that neglects
its religious motivation. The story is first of all about liberation from slavery and oppression. Most, if not all, liberation theologians would agree
that this liberation brings its own new, covenantal obligations, related to

---

and the Exodus," in *Jews, Christians, and the Theology of the Hebrew Scriptures*, ed. Alice
Ogden Bellis and Joel S. Kaminsky. SBLSymS 8 (Atlanta: Society of Biblical Literature, 2000),
215-30. I have discussed Levenson's treatment of liberation theology in "The Exodus and
Biblical Theology," *BTB* 25 (1995): 152-60; repr. in Bellis and Kaminsky, 247-61, with a rejoinder by Levenson, 263-75.

21. Levenson, *The Hebrew Bible, the Old Testament, and Historical Criticism*, 145-46, citing John Howard Yoder, "Probing the Meaning of Liberation," *Sojourners* 5/7 (1976): 26-29
(28).

22. Levenson, *The Hebrew Bible, the Old Testament, and Historical Criticism*, 146.

23. Levenson, *The Hebrew Bible, the Old Testament, and Historical Criticism*, 152-53,
where he cites Exod 2:23-25.

the construction of a just society under God.[24] Lohfink, for example, argues that "the canonical form of the Pentateuch demands the constitution of a new society at Sinai as an essential step between the departure from Egypt and the entry into the land flowing with milk and honey."[25] The liberationists do not deny that the exodus leads to a covenant or that it brings obligations with it, but they see those obligations in social and political terms as "the beginning of the construction of a just and fraternal society."[26]

Levenson insists that "the point is not that it is Israel's *suffering* that brings about the exodus, but that it is *Israel* that suffers."[27] Any analogical use of a biblical text, however, involves some selectivity, and some departure from the frame of reference of the original text. The Exodus story, as found in the Bible, is a highly particularistic story. "The question may be asked," writes Levenson, "whether God would have freed pharaoh's slaves at all if they had not happened to be the descendants of Abraham, Isaac, and Jacob, to whom God had promised a land of their own."[28] Some Christian theologians, no less than Jewish, insist on strict conformity to the biblical text on this point. So the late John Howard Yoder wrote: "To transpose the motif of liberation out of that distinct historical framework and thereby away from the distinct historical identity of the God of Abraham, Isaac, and Jacob, into some kind of general theistic affirmation of liberation, is to separate the biblical message from its foundation."[29] Conversely, Croatto (or Ricoeur) would argue that to confine a text to its original historical framework is to deny its implications and unjustifiably limit its meaning. In fact, the Hebrew prophets who spoke of a new exodus had already loosened the story from its original moorings, even if they did not formulate a general theistic affirmation of liberation.

Even Levenson acknowledges the validity of the analogical use of the Exodus story by Martin Luther King, Jr.[30] He claims, however, that libera-

24. Cf. the comment of Walter Brueggemann, "Pharaoh as Vassal: A Study of a Political Metaphor," *CBQ* 57 (1995): 27-51: "No one I know imagines that the exodus results in autonomous independence" (28).

25. Lohfink, 44.

26. Gutiérrez, *A Theology of Liberation*, 155.

27. Levenson, *The Hebrew Bible, the Old Testament, and Historical Criticism*, 152.

28. Levenson, *The Hebrew Bible, the Old Testament, and Historical Criticism*, 151.

29. Yoder, 28.

30. Levenson, *The Hebrew Bible, the Old Testament, and Historical Criticism*, 156-57.

tion theology, as represented by Jorge Pixley's commentary on Exodus,[31] does not just make an analogy between Israel in Egypt and Latin America, but reconstructs "a past in which the people Israel has been *replaced* by the poor and the oppressed, first by a heterogeneous underclass in Egypt and then by a band of rebellious peasants who, though they came to call themselves 'Israel,' were really Canaanites and linked to each other not by kinship ties but by social class and revolutionary activity."[32] It seems to me, however, that Levenson has greatly exaggerated the contrast between the liberation theologians and King. For better or worse, most liberation theologians accept the divine election of biblical Israel and base themselves on the biblical text rather than the reconstructed history.[33] Pixley's reconstruction of the origin of Israel, which relies heavily on the work of Gottwald, is certainly open to dispute. The essential move of liberation theology, however, is simply to take the biblical text as paradigmatic, so that people in another time and place can identify with the Israelites. As Walter Brueggemann has observed, "perhaps the most convincing warrant for such a usage is the undeniable fact that [the Exodus story] is so used, that its adherents find it to 'work.'"[34]

We shall return to the issues of particularism and universalism at the end of this chapter, in connection with the characteristically postmodern suspicion of universal ideals. For the present, it will suffice to say that there should be no objection to liberation theology on the grounds that its use of the exodus is analogical.

The Promised Land

To say that the Exodus story can be used analogically and that it "works," however, is not necessarily to say that it works in any particular way. Levenson has raised an important point by showing that the implications of the Exodus story (or of any other story) depend to a great degree on how we construe the shape of the story. It makes a great difference whether we stop reading immediately after the crossing of the sea, when Israel has escaped

31. George V. Pixley, *On Exodus: A Liberation Perspective* (Maryknoll: Orbis, 1987).
32. Levenson, *The Hebrew Bible, the Old Testament, and Historical Criticism*, 157.
33. See, e.g., Lohfink, 33.
34. Brueggemann, *CBQ* 57 (1995): 27.

from Egypt, or regard the giving of the Law on Mount Sinai as the culmination of the story. But it also makes a difference whether one reads on and finds the culmination of the story in the conquest of the promised land, the *telos* indicated in the Lord's words to Moses at the burning bush in Exod 3:8, "to bring them up out of that land to a good and broad land, a land flowing with milk and honey, to the country of the Canaanites, the Hittites, the Amorites, the Perizzites, the Hivites, and the Jebusites" (cf. Deut 26:3-10). This land was allegedly promised to the patriarchs, beginning with Abraham in Genesis 15, but it was not without inhabitants, and these were not about to vacate it voluntarily, according to the biblical story. In Deuteronomy 7, Moses spells out what was required for the occupation of the land:

> When the Lord your God brings you into the land that you are about to enter and occupy, and he clears away many nations before you — the Hittites, the Girgashites, the Amorites, the Canaanites, the Perizzites, the Hivites, and the Jebusites, seven nations mightier and more numerous than you — and when the Lord your God gives them over to you and you defeat them, then you must utterly destroy them. Make no covenant with them and show them no mercy. Do not intermarry with them, giving your daughters to their sons or taking their daughters for your sons, for that would turn away your children from following me, to serve other gods. Then the anger of the Lord would be kindled against you, and he would destroy you quickly. But this is how you must deal with them: break down their altars, smash their pillars, hew down their sacred poles, and burn their idols with fire. For you are a people holy to the Lord your God; the Lord your God has chosen you out of all the peoples on earth to be his people, his treasured possession. (Deut 7:1-6)

The execution of this commandment, with some omissions, is described in the book of Joshua.

As we have seen in the previous chapter, all but conservative apologists have now abandoned the historicity of the Conquest story as found in Joshua. Rather, this story served the propagandistic purposes of King Josiah or of later Deuteronomistic editors.[35] There is much to be said for the view that neither Deuteronomy nor Joshua was intended to "incite lit-

---

35. For the range of interpretations of the book of Joshua, see A. Graeme Auld, *Joshua Retold: Synoptic Perspectives* (Edinburgh: T. & T. Clark, 1998), 129-49. Auld expresses skepticism about the existence of a connected Deuteronomistic history.

61

eral violence against ethnic outsiders," but rather was directed against "insiders who pose a threat to the hierarchy being asserted."[36] But this does not relieve the moral problem presented by the story. In the words of James Barr, "the problem is not whether the narratives are fact or fiction, the problem is that, whether fact or fiction, the ritual destruction is *commended*."[37] Taken at face value, the text authorizes one group of people to take the land of others and slaughter the inhabitants, in virtue of a divine command. The land is given to Israel as a grant, and, in the words of Norman Habel, "the ideology of the land as a grant supports the rights of the invading people to occupy the land by divine sanction."[38]

Deuteronomy provides some rationalizing justification for this aggression: In the towns that are near to them, the Israelites "must not let anything that breathes remain alive . . . so that they may not teach you to do all the abhorrent things that they do for their gods, and you thus sin against the Lord your God" (Deut 20:16-18). Ethnic cleansing becomes a means to ensuring cultic purity. Sihon, king of Heshbon, is condemned for his lack of hospitality to the Israelites (Deut 2:26-35). The most practical justification is given in Num 33:55: "But if you do not drive out the inhabitants of the land from before you, then those whom you let remain shall be as barbs in your eyes and thorns in your sides; they shall trouble you in the land where you are settling."

The claim of divine authorization for all of this is not likely to reassure many people in the modern world. The divine commands dovetail too neatly with the interests of one group, and the manipulation of such claims for political ends has a history that is long and well known.[39] Few, I should hope, would dispute the judgment of Barr that "the command of consecration to destruction is morally offensive and has to be faced as such,"[40] and the same must be said of the invasion and occupation of other people's land, whether in ancient or modern times. One of the most troubling aspects of

36. Lori L. Rowlett, *Joshua and the Rhetoric of Violence: A New Historicist Analysis.* JSOTSup 226 (Sheffield: Sheffield Academic, 1996), 12-13.

37. James Barr, *Biblical Faith and Natural Theology* (Oxford: Clarendon, 1993), 209.

38. Norman C. Habel, *The Land Is Mine: Six Biblical Land Ideologies.* OBT (Minneapolis: Fortress, 1995), 50.

39. See further my comments in "The Zeal of Phinehas: The Bible and the Legitimation of Violence," *JBL* 122 (2003): 3-21; repr. as *Does the Bible Justify Violence?* (Minneapolis: Fortress, 2004).

40. Barr, *Biblical Faith and Natural Theology*, 218.

this biblical story is the way it has been used, analogically, over the centuries as a legitimating paradigm of violent conquest — by the Puritans in Ireland and in New England, by the Boers in South Africa, and by right-wing Zionists and their conservative Christian supporters in modern Israel.[41]

The conquest certainly provides a jarring conclusion to the master narrative of liberation theology, which aims at the promotion of social justice and human community. It has been dealt with mainly by either simple omission or by the reconstruction of an underlying history that did not involve large-scale conquest and slaughter (most notably in the work of Gottwald). The glossing over is especially conspicuous in studies of the motif of "the land." So, for example, Habel, in his study of biblical land ideologies, notes that "the rights of the original Canaanite inhabitants are totally dismissed and their culture negated," and that "the Canaanites have no rights to land and apparently no right to justice." He remarks that "this ideology ignores the historical reality that much of Canaan's culture persisted in Israel and that many of the indigenous people of Canaan became part of the Israelite nation," but he does not evaluate or criticize the ideology as such.[42] Other treatments do not acknowledge the problem at all.[43] W. D. Davies excused himself from considering "what happens when the understanding of The Promised Land in Judaism conflicts with the claims of the traditions and occupancy of its other peoples," on the grounds that it would demand another volume.[44] When

41. See further my comments in *Does the Bible Justify Violence?* 17-20. On the political use of the Bible in modern Israel, see the sober comments of Moshe Greenberg, "On the Political Use of the Bible in Modern Israel: An Engaged Critique," in *Pomegranates and Golden Bells: Studies in Biblical, Jewish and Near Eastern Ritual, Law and Literature in Honor of Jacob Milgrom*, ed. David P. Wright, David Noel Freedman, and Avi Hurvitz (Winona Lake: Eisenbrauns, 1995), 461-71.

42. Habel, 50-51. He notes in his conclusion that "the only ideology that reflects any sympathy for the indigenous Canaanites is the immigrant ideology of the Abraham narratives" (147).

43. This was true of Walter Brueggemann's *The Land: Place as Gift, Promise, and Challenge in Biblical Faith*. OBT (Philadelphia: Fortress, 1977), as he himself acknowledges in the preface to the 2002 edition of the book (xiv-xvi).

44. W. D. Davies, *The Territorial Dimension of Judaism, with a Symposium and Further Reflections* (Minneapolis: Fortress, 1991), xiii. He addresses the question of modern Israel in the symposium appended to the book. The moral problem is highlighted in some of the contributions to the symposium, esp. those of Kenneth Cragg (99-102) and J. S. Whale (115-17). See further Michael Prior, *The Bible and Colonialism*. Biblical Seminar 48 (Sheffield: Sheffield Academic, 1997), 253-60.

biblical scholars have addressed the problem, they have most often ech-oed the judgment of the biblical texts on the corrupt nature of the Canaanites. So, for example, George Ernest Wright asserted that "the Canaanite civilization and religion was one of the weakest, most deca-dent, and most immoral cultures of the civilized world at that time."[45] William F. Albright, who, to his credit, reflected on the problem at some length, noted that the actions attributed to the ancient Israelites were no worse than numerous massacres in the history of Christianity, or in mod-ern warfare. And he noted that "we Americans have perhaps less right than most modern nations, in spite of our genuine humanitarianism, to sit in judgement on the Israelites of the thirteenth century B.C., since we have, intentionally or otherwise, exterminated scores of thousands of In-dians." Nonetheless, he concluded that "From the impartial standpoint of a philosopher of history, it often seems necessary that a people of mark-edly inferior type should vanish before a people of superior potentiali-ties."[46] The great majority of biblical scholars, Christian as well as Jewish, identify with Israel in reading the biblical text. The Canaanites, in the phrase of Michael Walzer, are "excluded from the world of moral con-cern."[47] The blindness of biblical scholarship on this issue speaks volumes for the power of the master narrative of exodus and conquest.

The Canaanite Perspective

To my knowledge, the first modern scholar to offer a reading of the Exodus story from a Canaanite perspective was not a biblical scholar at all, but a lit-erary critic, the Palestinian intellectual Edward Said, in a polemical review of Michael Walzer's book, *Exodus and Revolution*.[48] Both Walzer and Said wrote with an eye to the modern Israeli-Palestinian conflict. Walzer, as a Jewish moderate, sought to oppose the politics of messianic zeal in modern

45. G. Ernest Wright, "The Deuteronomic History of Israel in Her Land," in *The Book of the Acts of God: Christian Scholarship Interprets the Bible*, ed. Wright and Reginald H. Fuller (Garden City: Doubleday, 1957), 108.

46. William Foxwell Albright, *From the Stone Age to Christianity: Monotheism and the Historical Process*, 2nd ed. (New York: Doubleday, 1957), 280.

47. Michael Walzer, *Exodus and Revolution* (New York: Basic Books, 1985), 141-43.

48. Edward Said, "Michael Walzer's 'Exodus and Revolution,' A Canaanite Reading," *Grand Street* 5 (Winter 1986): 86-106.

Israel by expounding what he calls "exodus politics," as a form of realism that accepts the necessity of living in an imperfect world. But his book is also an exercise in hermeneutics, with strong apologetic overtones: it is an attempt to retrieve the best sense of a tradition by one who stands within it, and also to glorify Judaism by depicting the Exodus story, somewhat implausibly,[49] as the paradigm of radical social democratic politics.[50] He acknowledges that the Canaanites are excluded from moral concern, but he claims that this "plays only a small part" in exodus politics, and that it "doesn't survive the work of interpretation"[51] (referring, presumably, to rabbinic interpretation). While the rabbis restrict the analogical use of the conquest, however, the story itself retains the status of sacred scripture. Said objects that Walzer refuses to meet the problem head-on. For Said, "there is no Israel without the conquest of Canaan and the expulsion or inferior status of Canaanites — then as now."[52] (The conquest is not an insignificant epilogue to the exodus, but is the goal and culmination of the entire story.)

The modern conflict in Palestine also casts a shadow over the book that has most forcefully brought the dark side of the exodus to the attention of biblical scholars, Keith Whitelam's *The Invention of Ancient Israel*, subtitled *The Silencing of Palestinian History*. Whitelam rightly notes the tendency of modern scholars to identify with the viewpoint of the biblical master narrative. As he comments with reference to Albright: "Israel, as the taproot of Western civilization, represents the rational while 'Canaan', the indigenous Palestinian population, represents the irrational Other which must be replaced in the inexorable progress of divinely guided evolution."[53] The goal of that evolution may be viewed as the rise of Christianity, or it may be viewed as the triumph of enlightened values over backward cultures. In either case, there is a failure to appreciate "the face of the other," in the phrase

---

49. Cf. Said, 92: "It seems unlikely to expect that the kind of secular and decent politics Walzer salvages from Exodus could co-exist with the authority of the sole Divinity plus the derivative but far more actual authority of His designated human representatives."

50. Mark Walhout, "The Intifada of the Intellectuals: An Ecumenical Perspective on the Walzer-Said Exchange," in *Postcolonial Literature and the Biblical Call for Justice*, ed. Susan VanZanten Gallagher (Jackson: University of Mississippi Press, 1994), 198-217. To some degree, Walzer views the exodus through the lens of the English Puritan revolution.

51. Walzer, 141-43.

52. Michael Walzer and Edward W. Said, "An Exchange," *Grand Street* 5 (Summer 1986): 255.

53. Keith Whitelam, *The Invention of Ancient Israel*, 85.

of Emmanuel Lévinas,[54] or to allow the subaltern to speak.[55] The tendency of Western readers, both Jewish and Christian, to identify with the Israel of the biblical story undeniably prejudices attitudes towards the modern Palestinian-Israeli conflict, in a way that is detrimental to the Palestinians.[56]

Whitelam's book has several obvious flaws, which undercut to some degree the valuable point he is making.[57] The Canaanites of the Bronze Age were not "Palestinians." The name Palestine comes from the Philistines, who were no more indigenous than the biblical Israelites (and probably less so than the historical Israelites). The modern Palestinians are descended neither from the Canaanites nor from the Philistines, but are Arabs, who emerged as the people of this land well into the Common Era. To speak of the history of the ancient Canaanites as "Palestinian history," then, is misleading, and offers too facile a continuum between the ancient story and the modern situation.

Neither is it fair to accuse biblical scholarship of silencing Palestinian history, or even Canaanite history. Biblical scholars, by definition, are interested in the Bible, and the Bible is interested in Israel, and only incidentally in the Canaanites. We have regrettably few other sources for any of the peoples in this area in antiquity. Such books as we have on the Canaanites, especially on the Canaanite literature from Ugarit, are largely the work of biblical scholars.[58] Most biblical scholars would agree, I think, that their discipline would

54. See Emmanuel Lévinas, *Alterity and Transcendence* (New York: Columbia University Press, 1999), 23, where he speaks of "the face of the other as being the original locus of the meaningful."

55. The phrase of Gayatri Chakravorty Spivak, "Can the Subaltern Speak?" in *Marxism and the Interpretation of Culture*, ed. Cary Nelson and Lawrence Grossberg (Urbana: University of Illinois Press, 1988), 271-313.

56. Cf. the remarks of Naim Stifan Ateek, *Justice, and Only Justice: A Palestinian Theology of Liberation* (Maryknoll: Orbis, 1989), 74-77. The problematic character of the biblical conquest accounts is also recognized by many Jewish scholars, most prominently Marc H. Ellis, *Toward a Jewish Theology of Liberation*, 3rd ed. (Waco: Baylor University Press, 2004). See the comments of J. David Pleins, *The Social Visions of the Hebrew Bible: A Theological Introduction* (Louisville: Westminster John Knox, 2001), 168-70.

57. For a fuller critique of Whitelam, see my essay, "The Politics of Biblical Interpretation," in *Biblical and Near Eastern Essays: Studies in Honour of Kevin J. Cathcart*, ed. Carmel McCarthy and John F. Healey. JSOTSup 375 (London: T. & T. Clark, 2004), 195-211.

58. I think, e.g., of the contributions of Albright, H. L. Ginsberg, Frank Moore Cross, Marvin Pope, Mark Smith, to mention only some of the most prominent. Note also the sympathetic work of the revisionist historian Niels Peter Lemche, *The Canaanites and Their Land: The Tradition of the Canaanites*. JSOTSup 110 (Sheffield: JSOT, 1991).

be enriched by any light that can be shed on the ancient Canaanites. There is no Zionist plot for the suppression of information about ancient Canaan.

Finally, Whitelam risks reducing his thesis *ad absurdum* when he tries to explain all modern theories of the origin of Israel by Zionist sympathies. Such sympathies can be documented in the case of Albright,[59] but Whitelam also finds that Albrecht Alt's model of "peaceful infiltration" was colored by Zionist settlement in Palestine in the 1920s. Again, Gottwald's view "sounds remarkably like a description of early Zionism where Jews from many different European countries, or more recently from the influx of American, Russian and Ethiopian Jews, among others, 'diverse ethnically and culturally', have been welded together as a modern nation."[60] Israel Finkelstein is accused of "the smuggling into 'objective' historical inquiry of values configured by modern experience and expectation."[61] We should not, of course, be surprised that the work of any historian is colored to some degree by contemporary events and circumstances, but Whitelam's implication of a vast web of Zionist sympathy, embracing everyone from Albright to Finkelstein, smacks of paranoia.

Nonetheless, Whitelam has rendered a valuable service to scholarship in calling attention to the "others" at the margin of the biblical story. The Hebrew Bible is often viewed, with considerable justification, as a great repository of humanistic values, and arguably the strongest voice crying out for justice in Western tradition.[62] But the central biblical doctrine of the divine election of Israel, with its consequent authorization of the chosen people to take the land, and lives, of others, fits uneasily in this humanistic reading of the Bible. The force of the "Canaanite" reading does not depend only on its application to modern Palestine. It is equally relevant to the experience of native Americans, black South Africans, Australian aborigines, or any other people whose lands have been conquered and expropriated. In the words of

---

59. Despite the implicatiøns of anti-Jewish bias in Burke O. Long, *Planting and Reaping Albright: Politics, Ideology, and Interpreting the Bible* (University Park: Penn State University Press, 1997).

60. Whitelam, 113.

61. Whitelam, 13, citing Christopher Edens's review of Robert B. Coote and Keith W. Whitelam, *The Emergence of Early Israel in Historical Perspective*, and Israel Finkelstein, *The Archaeology of the Israelite Settlement*, AJA 93 (1989): 289-92 (292).

62. See e.g., Moshe Weinfeld, *Deuteronomy and the Deuteronomic School* (1972; repr. Winona Lake: Eisenbrauns, 1992), 282-97; and *Social Justice in Ancient Israel and in the Ancient Near East*.

Laura Donaldson, a scholar of Native American background "when we listen to the voices which are silenced by canonical readings of the story, the Exodus loses its appropriateness as a model for human liberation."[63] This is not to say that liberation theology is without biblical foundations. There are many resources in the Hebrew Bible for a theology that emphasizes social justice and national liberation. But, as Jonathan Boyarin has argued, the Exodus narrative does not just "work" autonomously in this way: "it is merely available for effective rhetoric in a wide variety of situations."[64] The Exodus narrative "is susceptible to both colonizing and liberationist readings," and these are often intermingled in the minds of the readers.[65] As Walter Benjamin argued, "there is no cultural document that is not at the same time a record of barbarism."[66] The biblical story has inspired various revolutionary, liberatory movements but it is also implicated in the violent conquests of biblically minded zealots.[67]

In the full biblical story, liberation and colonization are two moments in the same extended process, and another, less political, moment is provided by the giving of the law. One may, as many have, choose to focus on only one of these moments, for the sake of effective rhetoric. But the story as a whole has an inherent ambiguity that gives rise to a plurality of interpretations. In view of the authority traditionally ascribed to the Bible, we need to be aware of the full picture. The Bible does not impose the divine "option for the poor" in the rather simple way that many liberation theologians have assumed.[68] It can just as easily be taken, and unfortunately has often been taken, to authorize

63. Laura E. Donaldson, "Postcolonialism and Biblical Reading: An Introduction," in *Postcolonialism and Scriptural Reading*. Semeia 75 (1996): 1-14 (11). Cf. Robert Allen Warrior, "Canaanites, Cowboys, and Indians: Deliverance, Conquest, and Liberation Theology Today," *Christianity and Crisis* 49 (1989): 261-65.

64. Jonathan Boyarin, "Reading Exodus into History," *New Literary History* 23 (1992): 523-54 (532).

65. Boyarin, 543.

66. Walter Benjamin, *One Way Street, and Other Writings* (London: New Left, 1979), 359.

67. Prior provides chapters on "colonial appropriations of the land tradition in Latin America, South Africa, and Palestine," but surprisingly discusses North America only in passing.

68. The problem of the exodus paradigm in the context of liberation theology is also recognized in *The Postmodern Bible*, 282-90, and by Prior, 278-84. To speak of a new exodus and promised land, however, does not rehabilitate the idea of the exodus quite as easily as Prior supposes.

conquest, subjugation, and slaughter.[69] The South African biblical scholar Itumeleng Mosala argues that "not all of the Bible is on the side of human rights or of oppressed and exploited people."[70] But the problem is not simply one of separating the liberating parts from the oppressive ones. The same story may be liberating or oppressive, depending on the viewpoint from which it is read. The postcolonial critic R. S. Sugirtharajah rightly concludes that "the Bible continues to be an ambivalent and unsafe text."[71] Appeal to biblical authority in ethical matters is a dangerous undertaking.

The Bible and Postcolonialism

As we have noted, the appreciation of the dark side of the Exodus story in recent discussion is due in some part to the "Canaanite" perspective introduced by Edward Said, whose name is associated with the current intellectual movement of "postcolonialism."[72] This movement is not defined by a method as such, scarcely even by a theory, but rather by a perspective and angle of vision. It "deals with the effects of colonization on cultures and societies."[73] Needless to say, there are many points at which this perspective can be applied to biblical studies with illuminating results.[74] While Israel is depicted as the colonizer in the book of Joshua, it was more often the victim of conquest and colonization. Gottwald regards the entire postexilic period as "colonial."[75] Much of the prophetic and apocalyptic literature is con-

---

69. On the moral ambiguity of the Bible, see further Regina M. Schwartz, *The Curse of Cain: The Violent Legacy of Monotheism* (Chicago: University of Chicago Press, 1997).

70. Mosala, 30.

71. R. S. Sugirtharajah, *Postcolonial Criticism and Biblical Interpretation* (Oxford: Oxford University Press, 2002), 119.

72. See esp. Edward W. Said, *Orientalism* (New York: Vintage, 1979); *Culture and Imperialism* (New York: Vintage, 1994). For an historical perspective on postcolonialism, see Robert J. C. Young, *Postcolonialism: An Historical Introduction* (Oxford: Blackwell, 2001). For samplings of postcolonial criticism, see Bill Ashcroft, Gareth Griffiths, and Helen Tiffin, *The Empire Writes Back: Theory and Practice in Post-colonial Literatures*, 2nd ed. (London: Routledge, 2002); *The Post-Colonial Studies Reader*, 2nd ed. (London: Routledge, 2005); also *Key Concepts in Post-Colonial Studies* (London: Routledge, 1998).

73. Ashcroft, Griffiths, and Tiffin, *Key Concepts in Post-Colonial Studies*, 186.

74. See, in general, Sugirtharajah; Donaldson, *Postcolonialism and Scriptural Reading*; Perdue, *Reconstructing Old Testament Theology*, 280-339.

75. Gottwald, *The Politics of Ancient Israel*, 96-112, 235-45.

cerned in one way or another with the encroachments of foreign empires.[76] Relatively little of this literature can be categorized as explicit resistance literature. (Daniel 7-12 is perhaps the most obvious example.) But much, if not all, of it contains "hidden transcripts"[77] that show the various ways in which Judeans and Diaspora communities negotiated their identity under foreign rule. This is a rich area for future exploration, and it is one that is quite congenial to the traditional aims of liberation theology.[78]

I would like to conclude this chapter, however, by reflecting on a different kind of issue raised by postcolonial criticism that has to do with ethnocentrism and the biblical idea of the election of Israel.

In his critique of liberation theology, Levenson insists that "no biblical theology, and certainly no theology of the book of Exodus, can succeed if it fails 'to take account of the tension between "the preferential option for the poor" and the chosenness of Israel.'"[79] The divine election of Israel is certainly affirmed by the biblical text. It also provides the theological underpinning for the gift of the land and the conquest of Canaan, and the commanded slaughter of the Canaanites.[80]

Joel Kaminsky has rightly protested that the election of Israel did not necessarily imply the mistreatment of non-Israelites.[81] The book of Deuteronomy, which contains the most blood-curdling command to annihilate the Canaanites, is nonetheless famously solicitous for the resident alien.[82] Not all Gentiles are classified with the Canaanites and Amalekites as "anti-elect," in Kaminsky's terminology. The great mass of humanity is

76. See my essay, "Temporality and Politics in Jewish Apocalyptic Literature," in *Apocalyptic in History and Tradition*, ed. Christopher Rowland and John Barton. JSPSup 43 (Sheffield: Sheffield Academic, 2002), 26-43.

77. For the phenomenon of "hidden transcripts," see James C. Scott, *Domination and the Arts of Resistance: Hidden Transcripts* (New Haven: Yale University Press, 1990).

78. For an example of this kind of approach, see Daniel L. Smith-Christopher, "The Book of Daniel," *NIB* 7 (1996): 17-151.

79. Jon D. Levenson, "The Perils of Engaged Scholarship: A Rejoinder to Jorge Pixley," in Bellis and Kaminsky, 240.

80. Cf. Gerd Lüdemann, *The Unholy in Scripture: The Dark Side of the Bible* (Louisville: Westminster John Knox, 1997), 55-75: "The Election of Israel and Its Consequences for Others."

81. Joel S. Kaminsky, "Did Election Imply the Mistreatment of Non-Israelites?" *HTR* 96 (2003): 397-425.

82. See Christiana van Houten, *The Alien in Israelite Law.* JSOTSup 107 (Sheffield: JSOT, 1991), 68-108.

merely "non-elect," and Israel relates to it in various ways. Nonetheless, while the idea of divine election is not malignant all the time, its use as a rationale for conquest and slaughter is not incidental. In the words of another critic: "The pressure that builds up naturally in the idea of election is here unleashed, and the idea is given its fullest expression. The Conquest tradition is the primary expression and fulfillment of the idea — the *Urtext*. The biblical idea of election is the ultimate antihumanistic idea."[83] Even if we regard this as something of an overstatement, the implication of the idea of election in the justification of genocide remains troubling.

From the viewpoint of a religious Jew such as Levenson, or indeed of many traditional Christians, the election of Israel is a theological given, however politically incorrect it may be. From the perspective of a "Canaanite" reading of the exodus, divine election "is simply an expression of raw ethnocentrism and thus has no positive role to play in modern theological discourse."[84] But while the dark side of election cannot be glossed over or denied, we must also recognize that Deuteronomy and Joshua are atypical biblical uses of the idea of election, simply because they describe an atypical situation where Israel is in a position of power and, in effect, able to act as colonizer. The resonance of the idea of election is quite different when the chosen people is powerless and trying to maintain its identity.

The latter situation is the more typical one in Israelite and Jewish history, and it has often given rise to cognitive dissonance. The apocalypse of 4 Ezra, written after the destruction of Jerusalem by the Romans but set in the period after the destruction by the Babylonians, expresses well the pathos of "the chosen people":

> All of this I have spoken before thee, O Lord, because thou hast said that it was for us that thou didst create this world. As for the other nations which have descended from Adam, thou hast said that they are nothing, and that they are like spittle, and thou hast compared their abundance to a drop from a bucket. And now, O Lord, behold, these nations, which are reputed as nothing, domineer over us and devour us. But we thy people, whom thou hast called thy firstborn, only begotten . . . and most dear, have been given into their hands. (4 Ezra [2 Esdras] 6:55-58)

83. So Jeremy Cott, "The Biblical Problem of Election," *JES* 21 (1984): 199-228 (204).
84. Kaminsky, 424. Kaminsky attempts to counter this assessment.

The claim of divine election here entails a rather contemptuous view of Gentiles as spittle, but the circumstances mitigate the arrogance of the speaker. After the destruction of Jerusalem, Jews had little to cling to except the counterintuitive belief that they were still uniquely special in the eyes of God. This kind of situation has unfortunately recurred throughout history. Ezra's prayer might well have been spoken in reaction to the Holocaust.

Postmodernism, generally, is suspicious of master narratives and affirmative of minority voices. Postmodern ethicists "have been suspicious of the project of universal commensurability and have argued for a politics of difference."[85] Postcolonialism has its whole *raison d'être* in the affirming of minority identities against the overarching claims of empires. In light of this, many scholars are now more sympathetic to the particularism associated with the idea of election than was the case in the modernist era. Ethnocentrism, we are told, is not universally a vice. It is malign only when it is combined with homogenizing political power, and it can be justifiable in contextual terms. Ethnocentrism, in short, can be redeemed by a postmodern "ethic of difference."[86]

Ethnocentrism is seldom more prominently in evidence than it is in the story of the Judean restoration after the Babylonian exile. Daniel Smith acknowledges that "social boundaries erected as a mechanism for survival led to conflicts upon returning to Palestine."[87] The "sons of the Golah" are said to preserve "the holy seed," and accordingly those who have married foreign wives are obliged to divorce them. Haggai refers to "the remnant of the people," a designation which, like the "holy seed," is as important for whom it excludes as for whom it includes. The returnees formulate "a theology of innocence and purity," in contrast to the defilement of those who had remained behind.[88] But, argues Smith:

> to be troubled by what appears to be "exclusivism" on the part of Haggai, or to feel a need to put an acceptable face on the separation of

---

85. Mark G. Brett, "The Ethics of Postcolonial Criticism," *Semeia* 75 (1996): 219-28 (223), referring to Zygmunt Bauman, *Postmodern Ethics* (Oxford: Blackwell, 1993).

86. Brett, *Semeia* 75 (1996): 222, paraphrasing Daniel Boyarin, *A Radical Jew: Paul and the Politics of Identity* (Berkeley: University of California Press, 1994), 247-50.

87. Daniel L. Smith, "The Politics of Ezra: Sociological Indicators of Postexilic Judaean Society," in *Second Temple Studies, 1: Persian Period*, ed. Philip R. Davies. JSOTSup 117 (Sheffield: JSOT, 1991), 73-97 (97).

88. Daniel L. Smith, 97.

the marriages in Ezra-Nehemiah, is to misunderstand profoundly the nature of group solidarity and survival of minorities. Sociological literature . . . alerts the biblical exegete towards a possibility of a creative response to the threat of domination and minority existence. We are invited to look at Ezra-Nehemiah, Haggai, and others from an "exilic consciousness", from the perspective of their worries and experiences in order to understand fully the "politics of Ezra".[89]

There are, of course, limits to what may be justified in the name of ensuring minority existence, and I for one continue to be troubled by Ezra's dissolution of mixed marriages. As Daniel Boyarin has argued eloquently, "a synthesis must be found, one that will allow for stubborn hanging on to ethnic, cultural specificity but in a context of deeply felt and enacted human solidarity."[90] Boyarin claims that such a synthesis can be found in the history of Diaspora Judaism, where "many Jews discovered that their wellbeing was absolutely dependent on principles of respect for difference. . . . Complete devotion to the maintenance of Jewish culture and the historical memory were not inconsistent with devotion to radical causes of human liberation."[91] The imposition of universal values can be tyrannical if it is coercive to the point of suppressing minority identity, but the imposition of group boundaries in the name of minority survival can be tyrannical too. And some universal values, pertaining to basic rights and "human liberation," are necessary if there is to be any restraint on tribal self-interest. Belief in divine election, or ethnocentricity, can be justified as a strategy of survival and can give needed sustenance to a beleaguered community. But it can also provide justification for oppression when the group in question is in a position to wield power. The idea of divine election, whether of Israel, the church, or any other entity, is not exempt from criticism because it is strongly affirmed in the Bible. Its merit depends on the context in which it occurs and the consequences that are drawn from it.

Conclusion

The story of the exodus remains an inspiring story, and liberation theolo-

89. Daniel L. Smith, 97.
90. Boyarin, *A Radical Jew*, 257.
91. Boyarin, *A Radical Jew*, 257. Boyarin argues for an anti-Zionist model of Judaism.

gians are right to emphasize its potential for giving hope to the oppressed. But as David Tracy has put it, "Exodus is not an innocent text."[92] The "option for the poor" attested in the Bible is selective at best. The Exodus story has been used to justify oppression as well as liberation, and in fact the text provides rhetorical resources to support both positions.

One implication of this discussion is a cautionary one against according intrinsic authority to any story or any text.[93] Attractive though it may be to proclaim the Bible as the Word of God when it advocates justice and freedom and to point to modern analogies, we must remember that it is the same Bible that commands the slaughter of the Canaanites and Amalekites and that it lends itself all too readily to analogical application in those cases too. Liberation in all its forms remains a noble ideal, and there is much in the Bible to support it, but it does not derive its validation merely from the fact that it is affirmed in the Bible. We shall return to this issue in the final chapter.

92. David Tracy, "Exodus: Theological Reflection," in van Iersel and Weiler, 118-24 (120).

93. Cf. Sugirtharajah, 117: "There is a danger in liberation hermeneutics making the Bible the ultimate adjudicator in matters related to morals and theological disputes."

The Impact of Feminist and Gender Studies

4

Of all the voices from the margins that have emerged in biblical scholarship over the last several decades, none is louder, or has commanded more attention, than that of feminist criticism.[1] The goals of this movement are in no way peculiar to biblical studies, and are avowedly political: "to point out and change inequalities between women and men."[2] The existence of such inequalities is omnipresent, in literature as well as history. The only real surprise is that the recognition of gender inequalities has been so belated. In this respect, the field of biblical studies has not been, I think, significantly worse than other branches of the humanities. But it certainly has not been significantly better. Despite the revolutionary implications often imputed to the Bible, it was not biblical study that led to the abolition of slavery, and neither did it contribute much to the rise of feminism. In fact, the Bible occupies a prominent place in the history of

---

1. The integral relationship between feminism, postcolonialism, and other kinds of ideological criticism is emphasized in recent scholarship, e.g., Gale A. Yee, *Poor Banished Children of Eve: Woman as Evil in the Hebrew Bible* (Minneapolis: Fortress, 2003); and Kwok Pui-lan, *Postcolonial Imagination and Feminist Theology* (Louisville: Westminster John Knox, 2005).

2. Joan Wallach Scott, *Gender and the Politics of History* (New York: Columbia University Press, 1988), 3. Cf. Elisabeth Schüssler Fiorenza, "Feminist Hermeneutics," *ABD* 2:783: "The term 'feminist' is commonly used today for describing those who seek to eliminate women's subordination and marginalization."

feminism because the Bible was recognized as a profoundly patriarchal book that gave religious legitimation to the subordination of women in Western society.[3]

In general feminist studies of the late 20th century, it is possible to distinguish two distinct phases. In the first phase, the focus was on gathering information about women and bringing female characters and authors to the center of attention.[4] This enterprise has often been dubbed "her-story." This kind of research attempted to refute the claim that women had no history or no significant place in literature. It often carried the corollary that the kind of personal, private experience associated with women should be valued just as much as the public, political events that are usually taken to make up the stuff of history. It tended, however, to isolate women's history as a special and separate topic and thereby to reinforce, unwittingly, some of the stereotypical distinctions between male and female. In the words of Joan Scott: "Women's history written from this position, and the politics that follow from it, end up endorsing the ideas of unalterable sexual difference that are used to justify discrimination."[5] Accordingly, there has been a shift away from "women's history" (although that is still a thriving enterprise) to a focus on the criticism of ideology and rhetoric, to "asking questions about *how* hierarchies such as those of gender are constructed or legitimized."[6] In the discourse of this kind of scholarship, the word "gender" assumes great prominence. "Gender" is a way of denoting social or cultural constructions, the social roles assigned to women and men, on the assumption that these are not simply "natural" but are precisely social constructions.[7] Moreover, "gender is a primary way of signifying relationships of power."[8] From this

3. Elizabeth Cady Stanton, ed., *The Woman's Bible* (New York: European, 1895; repr. Mineola, N.Y.: Dover, 2002). See Marie-Theres Wacker, "Historical, Hermeneutical, and Methodological Foundations," in Luise Schottroff, Silvia Schroer, and Wacker, *Feminist Interpretation: The Bible in Women's Perspective* (Minneapolis: Fortress, 1998), 3-35 (esp. 4-6); Carolyn De Swarte Gifford, "American Women and the Bible: The Nature of Woman as a Hermeneutical Issue," in *Feminist Perspectives on Biblical Scholarship*, ed. Adela Yarbro Collins. SBLBSNA 10 (Chico: Scholars, 1985), 11-33; "Politicizing the Sacred Texts: Elizabeth Cady Stanton and *The Woman's Bible*," in *Searching the Scriptures, 1: A Feminist Introduction*, ed. Elisabeth Schüssler Fiorenza (New York: Crossroad, 1993), 52-63.
4. Joan Wallach Scott, 18-21.
5. Joan Wallach Scott, 4.
6. Joan Wallach Scott, 4.
7. Joan Wallach Scott, 32.
8. Joan Wallach Scott, 42.

perspective, "the history of feminist thought is a history of the refusal of the hierarchical construction of the relationship between male and female . . . and an attempt to reverse or displace its operations."[9]

Needless to say, modern feminist thought is a good deal more complicated than this. Some theorists, for example, question the basic polarity of male and female, on the grounds that it is neither historically nor biologically universal.[10] Gender is viewed as "a *performative notion,* that is to say, as the activity of *acting as* men or women."[11] Or "Gender is a patriarchal plot that upholds the heterosexual norm."[12] In quite a different way, the discourse of feminism has been complicated by the emergence of "womanist"/African American, "mujerista"/Hispanic, and Asian theologians, who do not accept the experience and values of white American and European women as universal.[13] But our concern here is with the impact of feminism on biblical studies, primarily in Europe and North America, although there is a developing discourse on the subject also in Asia, Africa, and Latin America.[14] For our present purposes, this minimal sketch of developments in the general field of feminist studies will have to suffice.

Feminist Strategies in Biblical Studies

In the case of biblical studies, the task of feminist scholarship is further complicated by the fact that many of its practitioners still regard the Bible as an authoritative text. Mary Ann Tolbert, writing in 1983, admitted to "a

9. Joan Wallach Scott, 41.

10. Thomas Laqueur, *Making Sex: Body and Gender from the Greeks to Freud* (Cambridge, Mass.: Harvard University Press, 1990); Judith Butler, *Gender Trouble: Feminism and the Subversion of Identity* (London: Routledge, 1990).

11. Rosi Braidotti, "What's Wrong with Gender?" in *Reflections on Theology and Gender,* ed. Fokkelien van Dijk-Hemmes and Athalya Brenner (Kampen: Kok Pharos, 1994), 49-70 (64), characterizing the position of Judith Butler. See further, Nikki Sullivan, *A Critical Introduction to Queer Theory* (New York: New York University Press, 2003), 81-98.

12. Braidotti, 63.

13. E.g., Valentine M. Moghadam, ed., *Identity Politics and Women: Cultural Reassertions and Feminisms in International Perspective* (Boulder: Westview, 1994); Laura E. Donaldson and Kwok Pui-Lan, eds., *Postcolonialism, Feminism, and Religious Discourse* (London: Routledge, 2002). See also the comment of Butler, 1-6.

14. See, e.g., Phyllis A. Bird, ed., *Reading the Bible as Women: Perspectives from Africa, Asia, and Latin America.* Semeia 78 (Atlanta: Scholars, 1997).

bias in favor of the Bible. I frankly want to claim that text as a continuing resource for living in the modern age. I wish neither to relinquish its study to antiquarian motives nor to reject its concerns as unalterably oppressive."[15] Since there is much in the Bible that is undeniably patriarchal, scholars with such commitments find themselves faced with a dilemma. In the words of Letty Russell, "Are they to be faithful to the teachings of the Hebrew scriptures and the Christian scriptures, or are they to be faithful to their own integrity as whole human beings?"[16] It is not surprising, then, that some feminist biblical scholarship has a somewhat apologetic tone. In the terminology offered by *The Postmodern Bible,* this is the "hermeneutics of recuperation," which "is driven by a clear theological impulse — the redemption of traditions which seem to many to be utterly incompatible with feminist interests."[17] Various interpretative strategies are employed towards this end.[18]

Phyllis Trible, more than any other scholar, put feminist criticism on the agenda of biblical scholarship in the 1970s. Trible defined feminism not as a narrow focus on women but as "rather a critique of culture in light of misogyny."[19] In the context of biblical studies, this would mean a critique of misogynistic attitudes embedded in the text or in traditional interpreta-

15. Mary Ann Tolbert, "Defining the Problem: The Bible and Feminist Hermeneutics," in *The Bible and Feminist Hermeneutics.* Semeia 28 (Chico: Scholars, 1983), 113-26 (114). More recently, in her foreword to *Take Back the Word: A Queer Reading of the Bible,* ed. Robert E. Goss and Mona West (Cleveland: Pilgrim, 2000), ix, she writes that "the Bible will always be a book that I . . . love and value," but also "I do reject any theological position that claims the authority of the Bible as the primary guide for Christian life in the world today or in the world of the future."

16. Letty M. Russell, "Authority and the Challenge of Feminist Interpretation," in *Feminist Interpretation of the Bible* (Philadelphia: Westminster, 1985), 137-46 (137). See also the comments of Eryl W. Davies, *The Dissenting Reader: Feminist Approaches to the Hebrew Bible* (Aldershot: Ashgate, 2003), 10.

17. Pp. 245-46. Carolyn Osiek, "The Feminist and the Bible: Hermeneutical Alternatives," in Yarbro Collins, 93-105, distinguishes loyalist, revisionist, sublimationist, and liberationist approaches, all of which might be termed recuperative. See also Katherine Doob Sakenfeld, "Feminist Perspectives on Bible and Theology: An Introduction to Selected Issues and Literature," *Int* 42(1988): 5-18; and "Feminist Biblical Interpretation," *Theology Today* 46 (1989): 154-68.

18. Perdue, *Reconstructing Old Testament Theology,* 102-82, provides a wide-ranging review of recent work in feminist, womanist, and mujerista theology.

19. Phyllis Trible, *God and the Rhetoric of Sexuality.* OBT 2 (Philadelphia: Fortress, 1978), 7.

tion. This did not entail a rejection of the Bible or a critique of the view of God revealed therein. Rather, she claimed, "the nature of the God of Israel defies sexism,"[20] and "depatriarchalizing" is "a hermeneutic operating within Scripture itself."[21] Trible claimed that by proper use of rhetorical criticism she could arrive at the "intentionality" of the text: "the intentionality of biblical faith, as distinguished from a general description of biblical religion, is neither to create nor to perpetuate patriarchy but rather to function as salvation for both women and men. . . . The hermeneutical challenge is to translate biblical faith without sexism."[22] In some respects, this enterprise was a quintessentially Protestant one, of stripping away layers of traditional interpretation to recover the pristine intentionality of the text. It should be noted that Trible by no means glossed over patriarchal and misogynistic attitudes reflected in the text.[23] Her argument was rather that "the intentionality of Biblical faith" did not condone such attitudes, but rather invited the reader to critique them.

We shall return below to consider Trible's hermeneutic in action, in the interpretation of Genesis 1-3. For the present, we may note that postmodern literary criticism renders the idea of a single "intentionality of the text," or of intrinsic meaning, problematic.[24] Many scholars would now view with suspicion the attempt to salvage a pure grain of biblical faith from the husk of its cultural context. Trible's rhetorical criticism was heavily influenced by the literary criticism then in vogue, which concentrated "primarily on the text rather than on extrinsic factors such as historical background, archaeological data, compositional history" and claimed to interpret "the literature in terms of itself."[25] Again, we might question whether the text can be so easily detached from its context, or indeed whether "an intrinsic reading" that interprets a text only in terms of itself is even possible. This is not to deny for a moment that Trible has been extremely successful in demonstrating that many traditional interpretations

---

20. Phyllis Trible, "Depatriarchalizing in Biblical Interpretation," *JAAR* 41 (1973): 30-48 (34).

21. Trible, *JAAR* 41 (1973): 48.

22. Trible, *JAAR* 41 (1973): 31.

23. See esp. Phyllis Trible, *Texts of Terror: Literary-Feminist Readings of Biblical Narratives.* OBT 13 (Philadelphia: Fortress, 1984).

24. See esp. David Rutledge, *Reading Marginally: Feminism, Deconstruction and the Bible.* Biblical Interpretation 21 (Leiden: Brill, 1996), 41-42.

25. Trible, *God and the Rhetoric of Sexuality,* 8-9.

are unwarranted by the text, but only to question whether her critique was not unduly inhibited by her reverence for the Bible as Scripture.

Not all practitioners of recuperative feminist scholarship have relied on Trible's ahistorical brand of rhetorical criticism. There is also a kind of "culturally cued" literary criticism that gives greater weight to the cultural context of the ancient Near East.[26] Tikva Frymer-Kensky uses the mythology of the ancient Near East as the backdrop and foil for her discussion of women in the Bible. She concludes, counterintuitively, that the Bible has a "gender-free concept of humanity."[27] "Contrary to all assumptions — my own included," she writes, "the Hebrew Bible, unlike other ancient literature, does not present any ideas about women as the 'Other.' The role of woman is clearly subordinate, but the Hebrew Bible does not 'explain' or justify this subordination by portraying women as different or inferior."[28] Yet, amazingly, this "gender-free oncept of humanity contrasted sharply with Israelite reality. Life in ancient Israel was structured along gender lines. Women were overwhelmingly expected to concern themselves with domestic concerns; some men, at least, were to participate in public life."[29] Frymer-Kensky argues that

The gender-blindness of the biblical view of human nature . . . did not provide the language and tools for a biblical self-understanding of the gendered life of ancient Israel. As a result, this view of a unified humanity was eventually overlaid with new concepts that entered Israel at the end of the biblical period. The stories about women were reinterpreted, and these later reinterpretations, masquerading as the biblical message, were used to support sexist ideology and practice. The stories themselves remained to be rediscovered by an age that could understand and appreciate the biblical metaphysics of gender unity.[30]

26. The term of Sakenfeld, *Theology Today* 46 (1989): 161. Several good examples of culturally-informed approaches (among others) can be found in Alice Bach, ed., *Women in the Hebrew Bible: A Reader* (London: Routledge, 1999). See also Peggy L. Day, ed., *Gender and Difference in Ancient Israel* (Minneapolis: Fortress, 1989); and Phyllis A. Bird, *Missing Persons and Mistaken Identities: Women and Gender in Ancient Israel*. OBT (Minneapolis: Fortress, 1997). Not all culturally-cued interpretations are necessarily recuperative!

27. Tikva Frymer-Kensky, *In the Wake of the Goddesses: Women, Culture, and the Biblical Transformation of Pagan Myth* (New York: Free Press, 1992), 143.

28. Tikva Frymer-Kensky, *Reading the Women of the Bible* (New York: Schocken, 2002), xv.

29. Frymer-Kensky, *In the Wake of the Goddesses*, 143.

30. Frymer-Kensky, *In the Wake of the Goddesses*, 143.

All of this seems far too good to be true. We are left to wonder how we know about the gendered life of ancient Israel except for the fact that it is embedded, unquestioned, in the Bible. The lack of explicit statements on female inferiority cannot mask the pervasive patriarchy that suffuses biblical law as well as biblical narrative.[31] Moreover, the narratives, as well as the laws, have been taken traditionally as a prescriptive interpretation of culture, although, as Trible showed, the narratives can be read in other ways.[32] The idea of a gender-free Bible in tension with a patriarchal Israel does not do justice to the way that the biblical message is embedded in its narratives, laws, and other genres.

Yet another recuperative strategy can be illustrated by the work of Carol Meyers.[33] Meyers moves in the opposite direction from Frymer-Kensky. The biblical text is admittedly patriarchal, but the social reality was more complex. Even though ancient Israel was androcentric with respect to public roles, women may have had their own spheres of power and influence and enjoyed high status in their own roles.[34] The division of labor may have been functionally adaptive. Meyers is clear that such a society is still asymmetrical with regard to gender and insists that she does not intend to be apologetic. In part, her work may be credited with injecting an element of realism into a discussion that is often highly ideological. Nonetheless, this approach has its limitations. Our information about ancient Israelite society is limited, and this is especially true of women's roles. Meyers relies to a great degree on sociological and anthropological studies of peasant and "frontier" societies that are assumed to be comparable to ancient Israel. There is always some doubt as to whether the society in question is the appropriate background for a particular biblical text, as we shall see with reference to Genesis 2-3. Moreover, texts may have implica-

31. See Eryl Davies, 1-9.

32. See the critique of Esther Fuchs, *Sexual Politics in the Biblical Narrative: Reading the Bible as a Woman.* JSOTSup 310 (Sheffield: Sheffield Academic, 2000), 29: "the Bible's rhetorical art and its patriarchal ideology are inseparable and complementary." See also the studies of biblical narratives by J. Cheryl Exum, *Fragmented Women: Feminist (Sub)versions of Biblical Narratives* (Valley Forge: Trinity Press International, 1993); and *Plotted, Shot, and Painted: Cultural Representations of Biblical Women.* JSOTSup 215 (Sheffield: Sheffield Academic, 1996).

33. Carol Meyers, *Discovering Eve: Ancient Israelite Women in Context* (New York: Oxford University Press, 1988).

34. See now her short study, *Households and Holiness: The Religious Culture of Israelite Women.* Facets (Minneapolis: Fortress, 2005).

tions that transcend their original settings, and this is especially true in the case of a text like the Bible, which has enjoyed canonical authority for two thousand years.[35]

The editors of *The Postmodern Bible* contrast the "hermeneutic of re-cuperation" with the "hermeneutic of suspicion," which they associate especially with the work of Elisabeth Schüssler Fiorenza on the New Testament.[36] For Schüssler Fiorenza, "Not to defend biblical authority but to articulate the theological authority of women is the main task of a critical feminist hermeneutics."[37] She is willing, then, to reject the authority of texts she perceives as promoting oppression.[38] But she also engages in the retrieval of tradition. Her most influential book, *In Memory of Her,* is subtitled *A Feminist Theological Reconstruction of Christian Origins* and seeks to reconstruct the early Jesus movement as a resource for feminism.[39] In her presidential address to the Society of Biblical Literature, she affirmed the importance of historical-critical interpretation: "Such a historical reading seeks to give the text its due by asserting its original meanings over and against later dogmatic usurpations."[40] But she also called for "an *ethics of accountability* that stands responsible not only for the choice of theoretical interpretive models but also for the ethical consequences of the biblical text and its meanings."[41] Her interest is not in producing an "objective" history; she repeatedly polemicizes against the scientific positivism of what she calls "male-stream" scholarship.[42] Rather, her goal is to reconstruct the early Christian movement in a way that supports her feminist agenda: "My question," she writes, "was not 'did it actually happen?' but do we still have sufficient information and source texts to tell the story of the movement carrying Jesus' name *otherwise,* envisioning it as that of 'a disci-

---

35. See also the comments of Rutledge, 28-31.

36. Pp. 247-48.

37. Schüssler Fiorenza, *ABD* 2:785.

38. Cf. her comments contrasting her position with that of Renita Weems in Katie G. Cannon and Elisabeth Schüssler Fiorenza, eds., *Interpretation for Liberation.* Semeia 47 (Atlanta: Scholars, 1989), 4.

39. (New York: Crossroad, 1983).

40. Elisabeth Schüssler Fiorenza, "The Ethics of Biblical Interpretation: De-Centering Biblical Scholarship," *JBL* 107 (1988): 3-17 (14).

41. Schüssler Fiorenza, *JBL* 107 (1988): 15.

42. See, e.g., her essay, "Remembering the Past in Creating the Future: Historical-Critical Scholarship and Feminist Biblical Interpretation," in Yarbro Collins, *Feminist Perspectives on Biblical Scholarship,* 43-63.

pleship of equals'?"[43] Moreover, she argues: "If one cannot *prove* that wo/ men were not members of this group and did not participate in shaping the earliest Jesus traditions, one needs to give the benefit of the doubt to the textual traces suggesting that they did."[44] Schüssler Fiorenza is not a radical postmodernist. She insists that "the number of interpretations that can legitimately be given to a text are limited."[45] But her criteria of legitimacy are ethical (or, her critics would say, ideological) rather than calculations of plausibility.[46] Consequently, it is hardly surprising that her historical reconstructions have not been taken very seriously by more conventional historians.[47]

Schüssler Fiorenza, in fact, has been quite critical of postmodernism and poststructuralism for their political ambivalence,[48] although her work "finds many resonances with postmodernism," especially in her focus on rhetoric.[49] Among biblical feminists, her work is exceptional both in its overtly political character and in the vehemence of its rhetoric. It is not exceptional, however, in its "hermeneutic of suspicion." Perhaps the most thorough-going application of a hermeneutic of suspicion to the Hebrew Bible is that of Esther Fuchs.[50] Fuchs reads the Bible as a cultural-literary

43. Elisabeth Schüssler Fiorenza, *Jesus and the Politics of Interpretation* (New York: Continuum, 2000), 48-49,

44. Schüssler Fiorenza, *Jesus and the Politics of Interpretation*, 50.

45. Schüssler Fiorenza, *JBL* 107 (1988): 14.

46. Schüssler Fiorenza, *Jesus and the Politics of Interpretation*, 51, with reference to "the plausibility criterion" in historical Jesus research: "this criterion overlooks that what is regarded as 'common sense' or plausible in a culture depends on the hegemonic ideological understandings of 'how the world is.'"

47. Characteristically, she attributes the neglect of her work in "Historical-Jesus research" to "its positivist and empiricist discursive construction" and to "the continuing refusal of the discipline to critically reflect on and take responsibility for the public political implications of its research program"; *Jesus and the Politics of Interpretation*, 33.

48. Elisabeth Schüssler Fiorenza, *But She Said: Feminist Practices of Biblical Interpretation* (Boston: Beacon, 1992), 91.

49. See the response to Fiorenza's critique of postmodernism in *The Postmodern Bible*, 260-67 (266). See also her book, *Rhetoric and Ethic: The Politics of Biblical Studies* (Minneapolis: Fortress, 1999).

50. Fuchs, *Sexual Politics in the Biblical Narrative*. See already her essays, "The Literary Characterization of Mothers and Sexual Politics in the Hebrew Bible," and "Who Is Hiding the Truth? Deceptive Women and Biblical Androcentrism," both in Yarbro Collins, *Feminist Perspectives on Biblical Scholarship*, 117-36 and 137-44, respectively. Note also the "materialist" reading of the portrayal of women in the Bible by Gale A. Yee, *Poor Banished Children of Eve:*

text rather than as a religious or historical one.[51] Moreover, she construes the biblical narrative as "not merely a historical interpretation of past events, but a prescriptive interpretation of culture."[52] Her argument is that "the Hebrew Bible not only presents women as marginal, it also advocates their marginality. It is not merely a text authored by men — it also fosters a politics of male domination."[53] She is fiercely critical not only of scholars such as Trible who attempt to interpret the Bible without sexism, but also of those like Schüssler Fiorenza who try to combine a hermeneutic of suspicion with revisionist history.[54] She also objects to the labels "negative" or "rejectionist": "A critical reading of the Bible does not entail its rejection as an important cultural source, though it may very well reject its claim to divine or absolute truth."[55] While there is certainly much to learn from Fuchs's incisive analyses, she appears to reject not only claims of absolute truth, but any use of the Bible as a positive resource for gender relations.

Nonetheless, many scholars are reluctant to abandon the recuperative use of the Bible entirely. Schüssler Fiorenza, commenting on the hesitancy of African-American scholar Renita Weems to reject explicitly the authority of a biblical text that promotes violence and oppression, says that "those without power and authority cannot afford to relinquish lightly any authorizing resource and heritage in the struggle for survival, freedom and dignity."[56] For Weems, "the Bible is in many ways antagonistic to modern women's identity; yet, in other ways, it inspires and compels

---

Women as Evil in the Hebrew Bible (Minneapolis: Fortress, 2003). Yee's reading presupposes a setting in the context of the rise of the state, which is possible, but hardly necessary.

51. Fuchs, *Sexual Politics in the Biblical Narrative*, 11.

52. Fuchs, *Sexual Politics in the Biblical Narrative*, 29.

53. Fuchs, *Sexual Politics in the Biblical Narrative*, 11.

54. Fuchs, *Sexual Politics in the Biblical Narrative*, 22. A somewhat similar suspicion of theological ("confessional") feminism is articulated, but less vehemently, by Pamela Milne, "Toward Feminist Companionship: The Future of Feminist Biblical Studies and Feminism," in *A Feminist Companion to Reading the Bible: Approaches, Methods and Strategies*, ed. Athalya Brenner and Carole Fontaine (Sheffield: Sheffield Academic, 1997), 39-60 (esp. 57-60). See also Milne, "No Promised Land: Rejecting the Authority of the Bible," in *Feminist Approaches to the Bible: Symposium at the Smithsonian Institution*, ed. Hershel Shanks (Washington: Biblical Archaeology Society, 1995), 47-73.

55. Fuchs, *Sexual Politics in the Biblical Narrative*, 26

56. Elisabeth Schüssler Fiorenza, "Introduction," in Cannon and Schüssler Fiorenza, 4. Cf. Weems, "Gomer: Victim of Violence or Victim of Metaphor?" in Cannon and Schüssler Fiorenza, 87-104.

that identity."[57] *The Postmodern Bible* recognizes a third kind of feminist hermeneutics, a *hermeneutics of survival*, articulated especially among African American theologians and among interpreters from Latin America, Africa, and Asia.[58] (The label is borrowed from womanist theologian Delores Williams.) The Chinese theologian Kwok Pui Lan rejects both the sacrality of the text and appeals to the canon as guarantees of truth. Yet she insists that the Bible has not always been a tool of oppression and has often served as a paradigm of liberation. Accordingly, "the Bible offers us insights for our survival."[59] Ultimately, any feminist critique raises the question of biblical authority.[60] The problem that concerns feminists who remain attached to the biblical tradition is whether the insights for survival retain their power if they are stripped of the aura of canonicity and sacrality.

Not all feminist scholarship is as fiercely engaged in advocacy as Schüssler Fiorenza. Mieke Bal, dubbed "paradigmatic for postmodern biblical criticism" by *The Postmodern Bible*,[61] refuses to claim the Bible to be either a feminist resource or a sexist manifesto: "That kind of assumption can be an issue only for those who attribute moral, religious, or political authority to these texts, which is precisely the opposite of what I am interested in. It is the cultural function of one of the most influential mythical and literary documents of our culture that I discuss, as a strong representative instance of what language and literature can do to a culture, specifically to its articulation of gender."[62] In fact, whether one attributes moral or religious authority to these texts or not, the first task of feminist interpretation has to be to examine and expose the implications of the text for gender relations. In order to illustrate this process, I turn now to the biblical texts that have been most influential of all in the matter of gender, the opening chapters of Genesis.

---

57. Renita Weems, "Reading Her Way through the Struggle: African American Women and the Bible," in *Stony the Road We Trod: African American Biblical Interpretation*, ed. Cain Hope Felder (Minneapolis: Fortress, 1991), 57-77 (59).

58. P. 251.

59. Kwok Pui Lan, "Discovering the Bible in the Non-Biblical World," in Cannon and Schüssler Fiorenza, 25-42 (38).

60. Cf. David J. A. Clines, *What Does Eve Do to Help? and Other Readerly Questions to the Old Testament*. JSOTSup 94 (Sheffield: Sheffield Academic, 1990), 37.

61. P. 255.

62. Mieke Bal, *Lethal Love*, 1.

Adam and Eve

The well-founded consensus of scholarship distinguishes two creation stories, the Priestly (P) one in Gen 1:1–2:4a and the Yahwist (J) account in
2:4b–3:24. These stories can be read as complementary in the present text
of Genesis, and it may be that the Priestly account was composed to put
the story of human origins in a broader context, but the stories are quite
distinct nonetheless.[63] It is the second of these stories, which itself has two
distinct parts (roughly chs. 2 and 3), that has attracted most attention from
feminist scholars, because it is this story that has exerted the more fateful
influence on gender relations in the Western world.

Discussions of Genesis 2-3 often begin with a litany of unfounded assumptions that have dominated the interpretation of the story of Adam
and Eve.[64] Perhaps the most egregious example is the traditional Christian
doctrine of original sin, whereby a sinful state is inherited by all descendants of Adam. But the way in which Eve has been singled out for blame,
beginning with Ben Sira and the New Testament, also goes far beyond anything that we find in the text of Genesis.[65] Some other issues pertaining to
gender relations, however, remain controversial.

The most influential feminist analysis of this story is undoubtedly that of
Phyllis Trible.[66] Trible set out to strip away the layers of interpretation from
the story and "to contemplate it afresh as a work of art."[67] In the process, she
proposed a revised view of the original plan of creation and also a new interpretation of the consequences of disobedience of the primal couple.[68]

63. David M. Carr, *Reading the Fractures of Genesis: Historical and Literary Approaches*
(Louisville: Westminster John Knox, 1996), 15-22, 62-68; *The Erotic Word: Sexuality, Spirituality, and the Bible* (Oxford: Oxford University Press, 2003), 27-28.

64. See, e.g., Trible, *God and the Rhetoric of Sexuality*, 73; Meyers, *Discovering Eve*, 72-79;
Bal, *Lethal Love*, 109.

65. Sir 25:24: "From a woman sin had its beginning, and because of her we all die." 1 Tim
2:14: "Adam was not deceived, but the woman was deceived and became a transgressor." See
further Jean M. Higgins, "The Myth of Eve: The Temptress," *JAAR* 44 (1976): 639-47.

66. Trible, *God and the Rhetoric of Sexuality*, 72-143. Compare her earlier essays, *JAAR* 41
(1973): 30-48; "Eve and Adam: Genesis 2-3 Reread," *Andover Newton Quarterly* 13 (1973): 251-58.

67. Trible, *God and the Rhetoric of Sexuality*, 74.

68. Rutledge, 32-33, analyzes Trible's argument under five headings: a) the order of creation of the man and the woman; b) the disputed status of the woman as the man's "helper"; c)
the "naming" of the woman by the man; d) the dialogue between the woman and the serpent;
and e) the significance of the punishments meted out by Yahweh to the human couple.

The Original Plan of Creation

One of the oldest arguments for the subordination of women, found already in the Pastoral Epistles, is that "Adam was formed first, then Eve" (1 Tim 2:13). Against this, Trible argues that *hā'ādām* is not a proper name and is at first undifferentiated, neither male nor female. After the creation of the woman, *hā'ādām* "becomes a sexual reference so that it is used frequently, though not exclusively, for the male."[69] Trible continues: "But no ambiguity clouds the words *'iššâ* and *'îš*. One is female, the other male. Their creation is simultaneous, not sequential. One does not precede the other, even though the time line of this story introduces the woman first."[70] In this, she has been supported by Mieke Bal, who claims that "the biblical poetics of creation does not assign primacy to chronological priority" and further argues that there is no contradiction here between Genesis 1 and Genesis 2.[71] But the argument is undercut by the fact that *hā'ādām* is admittedly used for the male thereafter and is in fact the speaker in 2:23, when the man accepts the woman as flesh of his flesh and bone of his bone. In the words of Danna Nolan Fewell and David Gunn, while the argument that *hā'ādām* is initially ungendered "is logical, since maleness is meaningless before sexual differentiation, the text nevertheless asserts the illogical, namely 'the originality of maleness over femaleness.'"[72] Or, to put it differently, the male is presented as being continuous with the original *'ādām* in a way that the female is not. Consequently, as Susan Lanser has argued, "the masculine form of *hā'ādām* and its associated pronouns will, by inference, define *hā'ādām* as male."[73] Lanser does not argue that one cannot read *hā'ādām* as a sex-neutral figure, but that "readers *will* not ordinarily read Genesis 2 in this way."[74]

---

69. Trible, *God and the Rhetoric of Sexuality*, 98.

70. Trible, *God and the Rhetoric of Sexuality*, 98.

71. Bal, *Lethal Love*, 118.

72. Danna Nolan Fewell and David M. Gunn, *Gender, Power, and Promise: The Subject of the Bible's First Story* (Nashville: Abingdon, 1993), 32. Compare David Jobling, "Myth and Its Limits in Genesis 2.4b-3.24," in *The Sense of Biblical Narrative: Structural Analyses in the Hebrew Bible, II.* JSOTSup 39 (Sheffield: JSOT, 1986), 17-43.

73. Susan S. Lanser, "(Feminist) Criticism in the Garden: Inferring Genesis 2-3," in *Speech-Act Theory and Biblical Criticism*, ed. Hugh C. White. Semeia 41 (Decatur: Scholars, 1988), 67-84 (72),

74. Lanser, 72.

Given that the same word is used for a male later in the story, *hā'ādām* is assumed to be male unless there is clear indication to the contrary.[75] Related to the question of priority is the claim of the text that the woman was taken from the body of *hā'ādām*. This loses its significance on Trible's reading, but again the argument is undercut by the biblical terminology. When *hā'ādām* designates the woman as *'iššâ* in Gen 2:23, he says "for this one was taken *mē'îš*" — effectively designating the body from which she was taken as male. It is difficult to disagree with Carol Fontaine when she argues that this passage is a prime example of patriarchal propaganda by role-reversal.[76] In the words of Fewell and Gunn: "flying in the face of what every reader knows to be reality, he claims that woman comes out of man — claims for himself, that is, woman's biological function of child-bearing. A breathtaking claim, indeed!"[77] Trible is right that the statement that woman is taken from *hā'ādām* is primarily a matter of differentiation, and that, logically, "differentation . . . implies neither derivation nor subordination."[78] But the rhetorical effect remains. To say that the woman is built up from a rib taken from the man seems an odd basis for a relationship of mutuality and equality.

The fact that the woman is created in the course of a search for a "helper" for *hā'ādām* has also usually been taken as an indication of a subordinate role. Trible denies this implication, pointing out that God is sometimes cast as the helper of Israel, and dramatizes her point by translating the term as "companion."[79] This translation can hardly be justified. David Clines has argued persuasively that "though superiors may help inferiors, strong may help weak, gods may help humans, in the act of helping . . . they are subjecting themselves to a secondary, subordinate position. Their help may be necessary or crucial, but they are assisting some task that is already someone else's responsibility."[80] In the context of Genesis,

75. Cf. Carr, *The Erotic Word*, 29: "Soon it becomes evident that this first 'human' is, in fact, male."
76. Carole R. Fontaine, "The Abusive Bible: On the Use of Feminist Method in Pastoral Contexts," in Brenner and Fontaine, 84-113 (105). She continues: "Yes, we *can* read that first earth-creature as an androgynous, as do various Jewish traditions and many feminist biblical scholars; but this has seldom been the dominant reading in religious circles, and the reason for that is that the existing role reversal functions to privilege men over women."
77. Fewell and Gunn, 28.
78. Trible, *God and the Rhetoric of Sexuality*, 101. Cf. Bal, *Lethal Love*, 117.
79. Trible, *God and the Rhetoric of Sexuality*, 90.
80. Clines, *What Does Eve Do to Help?* 30-31.

The Impact of Feminist and Gender Studies

great weight has been placed on fact that the quest is for a helpmate
k^enegdô. Trible translates, "corresponding to it," and comments that this
word indicates identity, mutuality, and equality.[81] Meyers allows that a
helper can be either a superior or a subordinate, but argues that "the prep-
ositional phrase establishes a nonhierarchical relationship between the
two; it means 'opposite,' or 'corresponding to,' or 'parallel with,' or 'on a
par with.'"[82] It is certainly true that the phrase does not suggest subordination, but its precise connotation is still open to dispute. Fewell and Gunn
translate "counterpart" ("like-opposite") and argue that both difference
and similarity are required: "likeness is conjured by separation. Male and
female. Opposite and alike. Difference and sameness. Other and self."[83]
Clines asks astutely, "What does Eve do to help?" He concludes that the
only thing Adam needs Eve's help for, and the only task actually assigned to
her in Genesis 3, is procreation, in short to fulfill the command given in
Gen 1:28 ("Be fruitful and multiply, and fill the earth").[84] Clines's argument assumes that Genesis 1 is presupposed in Genesis 2-3, and this is
problematic. According to Gen 2:15, Adam was put in the garden "to till it
and keep it." In the context, we should expect that this is the task with
which she is to help Adam, even if she promptly gets distracted from her
task by the snake.

But why then is Adam provided with a woman rather than another
man? Frymer-Kensky notes the contrast with the Epic of Gilgamesh on
this point. When Gilgamesh needed a companion, the gods provided not a
woman but Enkidu, another male. For Frymer-Kensky, this contrast illus-
trates the Bible's "gender-free concept of humanity."[85] But the two situations are not entirely comparable. Adam is still the only human on earth.
Gilgamesh already had women galore. A clue may be provided here by the
parenthetical statement in Gen 2:24: "Therefore a man leaves his father
and his mother and clings to his wife." The story of Adam and Eve is,
among other things, an etiology. It is told to explain why things are the way
they are. Marriage and procreation are among the important facts of life
that have to be explained. Therefore the original human beings have to be
capable of procreation. They must also have the potential for heterosexual

81. Trible, *God and the Rhetoric of Sexuality*, 90.
82. Meyers, *Discovering Eve*, 85.
83. Fewell and Gunn, 27.
84. Clines, *What Does Eve Do to Help?* 34-37. See also Yee, 70.
85. Frymer-Kensky, *In the Wake of the Goddesses*, 143.

attraction, a potential highlighted here by their nakedness. Clines, then, is partially right, even if procreation is not the immediate purpose of the creation of Eve. The point of having a helpmate *kᵉnegdô* is sexual complementarity, and while there is certainly no implication of subordination, the term does not in itself address questions of relative status and does not necessarily imply identity, mutuality, or equality.

The climax, so to speak, of the creation of woman is found in Gen 2:23-25: "This at last is bone of my bones and flesh of my flesh. . . . Therefore a man leaves his father and his mother and clings to his wife, and they become one flesh. And the man and his wife were both naked, and were not ashamed." Many commentators have waxed lyrical at the idea of becoming one flesh with biblical approval. According to Trible: "The result of this convergence of opposites is a consummation of union: 'and they become one flesh.' No procreative purpose characterizes this sexual union; children are not mentioned. Hence, the man does not leave one family to start another; rather, he abandons (*ᶜzb*) familial identity for the flesh of sexuality."[86] But is there any other instance in the Hebrew Bible where marriage is not related to procreation? There is indeed a celebration of sexual love, without regard to procreation, in the Song of Songs, which Trible characterizes as "Love's Lyrics Redeemed,"[87] but the Song clearly envisions lovers who are not married at all.[88]

David Carr is even more rhapsodic in contemplating Gen 2:23. He finds here a "vision of non-reproductive, joyful sexuality," that "can be applied by extension to various forms of intimate, tender sexuality between partners who 'correspond' to each other: male-female, male-male, female-female."[89] By extension indeed! The text does not so much as acknowledge the possibility of same-sex relationships, let alone endorse them. As Fewell and Gunn put it, "the 'helper corresponding to [like-opposite]' the human/man is a sexual 'opposite.'"[90] They continue: "ac-

---

86. Trible, *God and the Rhetoric of Sexuality*, 104.

87. Trible, *God and the Rhetoric of Sexuality*, 144-65. On the Song as a celebration of sexual love, see Carey Ellen Walsh, *Exquisite Desire: Religion, the Erotic, and the Song of Songs* (Minneapolis: Fortress, 2000); Carr, *The Erotic Word*, 109-37.

88. Virginia Burrus and Stephen D. Moore, *BibInt* 11 (2003): 24-52, comment that while Trible explicitly represents the lovers as an unmarried couple, she implicitly represents them as exemplifying marriage as it was meant to be, by reading it against the foil of Genesis 2-3.

89. Carr, *The Erotic Word*, 32.

90. Fewell and Gunn, 29.

cording to this claim, human sexuality is clearly monogamous exogamous heterosexuality."[91] Whether it was necessarily monogamous might be disputed. Polygamy was accepted in ancient Israel and seems to have survived, if only in exceptional cases, down to the Roman period.[92] But there can be no doubt that, for better or worse, the story affirms normative heterosexuality.[93]

No procreative purpose is stated in Gen 2:23. It has often been assumed that the first couple were meant to be immortal. (Access to the tree of life was not prohibited.)[94] Procreation, then, would only have become necessary after the "Fall." Moreover, the fruit of the tree of the knowledge of good and evil has often been understood as a metaphor for sex. So it has been argued that "the divine command to abstain from the fruit of the tree of the knowledge of good and evil is thus designed to preclude the human discovery of procreativity."[95] (On this reading, incidentally, it would also diminish the joy of sex in the prelapsarian garden.) But the very next verse, 2:24, speaks of a man leaving his father and mother, and without procreation there would be no parents to leave (or rather the parents would have no son who could leave them). It is not Adam and Eve who are said here to become one flesh, but later couples who had fathers and mothers. In short, cleaving to each other and becoming one flesh is the postlapsarian condition, not the utopian, Edenic state. It is not apparent that Adam and Eve were supposed to have sex at all (or even permitted to do so, if we so interpret the prohibition of the fruit). Here again we must bear in mind the etiological character of the story. Sex and procreation are very much in view, whether they are supposed to have been initially on the agenda or not.

91. Fewell and Gunn, 29.

92. See John J. Collins, "Marriage, Divorce, and Family in Second Temple Judaism," in Leo G. Perdue et al., *Families in Ancient Israel* (Louisville: Westminster John Knox, 1997), 104-62 (121-12).

93. This is recognized also by Ken Stone, "The Garden of Eden and the Heterosexual Contract," in Goss and West, 57-70, although he seeks to destabilize the normativity of heterosexuality by noting tensions within the text. Yee, 71, regards the passage as an ideological subversion of patrilineal kinship in favor of the state.

94. It should be noted, however, that this understanding of Genesis is not found in the earliest interpreters, such as Ben Sira. See Sir 17:2; 41:4.

95. Sam Dragga, "Genesis 2-3: A Story of Liberation," *JSOT* 55 (1992): 3-13 (5).

The Post-Edenic Condition

In Trible's reading of the story, eros is contaminated by an act of disobedience.[96] Meyers has challenged the usual designation of this event as "the fall," on the grounds that there are no Hebrew words for "fall" or "sin" in the text.[97] In her view, this is a story of "emergence to reality," and it "must be seen primarily as helping highland settlers cope with life's demands."[98] Now it is certainly true that these chapters of Genesis are meant to explain how life came to be the way it is, not only for highland settlers but for all people. It is also quite possible to view the transition from a state where people were not conscious of being naked to life as we know it as a good thing. Think, for example, of Enkidu in the Epic of Gilgamesh, who is said to become human when he puts on clothes. From a modern perspective, one may admire Eve for her initiative in choosing the knowledge of good and evil over her naive Edenic state[99] or even suggest that God permits this course of events because it is for the best.[100] Yet it can not be denied that in Genesis this development has the character of a punishment. The speech of God begins in Gen 3:14 by cursing the serpent. He does not curse either the woman or the man, although the ground is cursed because of Adam. But he proclaims that henceforth their lives will be difficult, and he expels them from the garden. Insofar as the story offers an explanation of how life got to be the way it is, it places the blame on humanity (and the serpent) and, in the words of Gerhard von Rad, "is concerned to acquit God and his creation of all the suffering and misery that has come into the world."[101]

In the initial confrontation with the deity, the man tries to shift the blame to the woman, and the woman shifts it to the serpent. But feminist scholars, beginning with Trible, have been quite right to insist that the woman is not singled out for unique or primary blame by God. There is no

96. Trible, *God and the Rhetoric of Sexuality,* 105.

97. Meyers, *Discovering Eve,* 76-77, 87.

98. Meyers, *Discovering Eve,* 86, 93.

99. So Bal, *Lethal Love,* 125: "The woman promotes her own status in the narrative. Her disobedience is the first independent act, which makes her powerful as a character." Frymer-Kensky, *In the Wake of the Goddesses,* 108-10, views Eve as a culture-heroine, comparable to Prometheus.

100. Fewell and Gunn, 34-35.

101. Gerhard von Rad, *Genesis,* rev. ed. OTL (Philadelphia: Westminster, 1972), 101. See further Fewell and Gunn, 33.

warrant in Genesis for the statement in 1 Tim 2:14 that "Adam was not deceived, but the woman was deceived and became a transgressor." Nonetheless, she is to suffer consequences. The first is the painful labor associated with childbearing.[102] It is not clear that childbearing itself is a punishment. The point is rather that her primary role in the division of labor, childbearing, will be difficult, just as Adam's primary role of tilling the soil will be difficult for him.[103] Whether the man and woman were supposed to have gendered roles before they ate the fruit is not clear. Even before the woman was created, *hā'ādām* was put in the garden to till it and keep it. In the case of the man, then, the change in condition after Eden is not so much in his role as in the difficulty of discharging it. Whether this is also the case for the woman depends on whether procreation was part of the divine plan from the beginning.

A further consequence suffered by the woman is a clear change in status. The man "will rule over you" *(yimšol-bāk)*. Trible comments: "where once there was mutuality, now there is a hierarchy of division."[104] Bal, who denies that there is any sexist ideology in the text up to this point, allows that it may be identified here.[105] Trible is quite right that "the divine speeches to the serpent, the woman, and the man are not commands for structuring life."[106] "His supremacy is neither a divine right nor a male prerogative. Her subordination is neither a divine decree nor the female destiny. Both their positions result from shared disobedience. God describes this consequence but does not prescribe it as punishment."[107] It is not so easy, however, to distinguish between description of consequence and prescription of punishment. The consequence follows because God decrees it. It is not necessarily an eternal decree, and humanity is not prohibited from trying to diminish the laboriousness of life or from restructuring gender relations. But the state-

---

102. Meyers, *Discovering Eve*, 99-109, translates "I will greatly increase your toil and your pregnancies," and argues that the reference is to the amount of work the woman is expected to do, but the connection with childbirth seems clear in Gen 3:16b. Meyers's interpretation seems unduly dependent on her hypothesis that the story reflects life in the highland settlements.

103. Clines, *What Does Eve Do to Help?* 35

104. Trible, *God and the Rhetoric of Sexuality*, 128. It is not so clear that "the man will not reciprocate the woman's desire."

105. Bal, *Lethal Love*, 128.

106. Trible, *God and the Rhetoric of Sexuality*, 123.

107. Trible, *God and the Rhetoric of Sexuality*, 128.

ment "he shall rule over you" suggests an unambiguously patriarchal society and claims that it is brought into effect by a punitive divine decree. As Lanser has astutely observed, "this is the point where Bal's and Trible's readings reach their *aporia*. . . . For finally neither can explain why male dominance should be the particular consequence of a transgression for which both man and woman are equally, as they argue, responsible."[108]

A Patriarchal God?

The remark of Fewell and Gunn, that commentators on these chapters "have been remarkably reticent regarding the character of YHWH and, in particular, notably reluctant to put the deity under the same kind of critical scrutiny as the humans,"[109] is no less true of feminist commentators than of anyone else. Frymer-Kensky claims that radical monotheism promoted a "gender-free concept of humanity": "This view of the essential sameness of men and women is most appropriate to monotheism."[110] But is the God of Genesis gender-free? Most critics, I should think, would agree with David Rutledge that "Yahweh . . . is unmistakeably a male God, a father-figure to his creatures."[111] He may take unto himself powers and attributes that were once attributed to goddesses,[112] but in Genesis, his rule "exhibits all the characteristics of patriarchy."[113] The power relations in the story are thoroughly hierarchical, as reflected in Yahweh's demand for obedience, backed by the threat of death. The hierarchical, patriarchal character of God is increased by monotheism: "Within the Garden, creation is effected in solitary splendour by a male God who, in alone possessing the power to engender life, has no need of (or dependence upon) a fe-

---

108. Lanser, 75.

109. Fewell and Gunn, 22.

110. Frymer-Kensky, *In the Wake of the Goddesses*, 142.

111. Rutledge, 196.

112. See, e.g., Frymer-Kensky, *In the Wake of the Goddesses*, 97-99, on YHWH's role in procreation and childbirth.

113. Rutledge, 200. Cf. Erhard Gerstenberger, *Yahweh — The Patriarch* (Minneapolis: Fortress, 1996), esp. 81-98. The German original was entitled *Jahwe, ein patriarchaler Gott? Traditionelles Gottesbild und feministische Theologie* (Stuttgart: Kohlhammer, 1988). James M. Kennedy, "Peasants in Revolt: Political Allegory in Genesis 2-3," *JSOT* 47 (1990): 3-14, followed by Yee, 71, regards God, in this context, as a symbolic expression of the power of the state.

male consort."[114] Insofar as this creator God serves as a model for human imitation, he will hardly promote the importance of women.[115] In fact, as we have seen, the same expression, *hā'ādām*, is used both for the original creature and for the man after gender differentiation occurs. The woman, *'iššâ*, is defined as a split-off from the male *'îš* (Gen 2:23). While later tradition certainly exaggerated the misogyny of the story, a patriarchal structure was embedded in its core, not least in the depiction of the Creator.

Creation in the Image of God

Our focus in this discussion has been on Genesis 2-3. There is, of course, another account of creation, one that is usually considered less problematic from a feminist point of view. This is the Priestly account in Genesis 1, which famously includes the statement: "So God created *hā'ādām* in his image, in the image of God he created him, male and female he created them." This statement has often been taken as a remarkable statement of gender-neutrality and equality between the sexes.[116] Phyllis Bird, however, has cautioned rightly against taking this verse out of context.[117] It must be read not only in light of Genesis 1 as a whole, but also in light of the rest of the Priestly source, which is not conspicuously egalitarian in its view of women. Bird argues that the statement "male and female he created them" must be understood in connection with the command to be fruitful and multiply in Gen 1:28. The statement that *hā'ādām* is made in the image of God "offers no ground for assuming sexual distinction as a characteristic of *adam*, but appears rather to exclude it, for God *('ĕlōhîm)* is the defining term in the statement. The idea that God might possess any form of sexuality, or any differentiation analogous to it, would have been for P an ut-

---

114. Rutledge, 202.

115. On the positive potential of goddess worship for the status of women, see Carole R. Fontaine, "A Heifer from Thy Stable: On Goddesses and the Status of Women in the Ancient Near East," in Bach, 159-78.

116. E.g., Frymer-Kensky, *In the Wake of the Goddesses,* 142. But even Stanton held that Genesis 1 portrayed woman as "equal in power and glory with man" (20). See Clines, *What Does Eve Do to Help?* 41.

117. Phyllis A. Bird, "'Male and Female He Created Them': Gen 1:27b in the Context of the Priestly Account of Creation," in *Missing Persons and Mistaken Identities,* 123-54, originally published in *HTR* 74 (1981): 129-59.

terly foreign and repugnant notion. . . . *Unlike* God, but *like* the other creatures, *adam* is characterized by sexual differentiation."[118] It is not in virtue of being male and female that *hā'ādām* is in the image of God. (That attribute seems rather to refer to human domination of the animal world.) The verse "is not concerned with sexual roles, the status or relationship of the sexes to one another, or marriage,"[119] and it "contains no doctrine of the equality — or inequality — of the sexes, either explicit or implied."[120] It remains true, as Bird has also insisted, that women as well as men are created in the image of God, and this is essential to human identity. But "distinctions of roles, responsibilities, or social status on the basis of sex — or other characteristics — are not excluded by this statement."[121]

In the context of the Priestly source as a whole, gender equality is implausible. As Randall Garr has noted, "the Priestly tradition does not credit each parent with an equal role in producing descendants. . . . Like other ancient Near Eastern writers, the Priestly school downplays the female role in human reproduction. Women may not be completely absent from the process, yet the principal and active parent is male. . . . Males generally head the genealogical lineage as well as control the verbs of reproduction."[122] Males and females are valued differently in Leviticus.[123] Also, the Priestly worldview is thoroughly hierarchical. In Genesis 1, as in Genesis 2-3, God speaks with the voice of patriarchal authority. And need we add that the statement "male and female he created them" carries a strong implication of normative heterosexuality.[124]

Conclusion

Three decades of recuperative feminist scholarship have shown that the opening chapters of Genesis, and the Bible as a whole, are not as

118. Bird, "'Male and Female He Created Them,'" 142-43.

119. Bird, "'Male and Female He Created Them,'" 149.

120. Bird, "'Male and Female He Created Them,'" 151.

121. Bird, "'Male and Female He Created Them,'" 153.

122. W. Randall Garr, *In His Own Image and Likeness: Humanity, Divinity, and Monotheism.* CHANE 15 (Leiden: Brill, 2003), 130.

123. Clines, *What Does Eve Do to Help?* 45.

124. So also Stone, 62: "Genesis 1:27 lends itself to readings that buttress the heterosexual contract."

misogynistic as they have sometimes been made out to be. But in the end, in the words of Clines, "the text persists in its androcentric orientation, from which it cannot be redeemed."[125] Consequently, a feminist critique, no less than a "Canaanite" one, raises the question of biblical authority in an acute way. This is not to say that every text in the Bible is irredeemably patriarchal, although even texts that portray women in a sympathetic way, such as Ruth, often presuppose a patriarchal worldview. But the Bible furnishes rhetorical resources to support a patriarchal view of society far more readily than the reverse.

The most basic problem with the Bible from the perspective of postmodern gender theorists, however, does not lie in its reflection of an ancient patriarchal society. It lies in the assumption of a divinely ordained order of creation to which humanity must conform, as illustrated clearly in Genesis 1. In the egregious formulation of Karl Barth: "Men are simply male and female."[126] For contemporary theorists, gender is a human construct, which largely serves to indicate relationships of power. Humanity, it now appears, is not only male and female but admits of various permutations and combinations in between. From this perspective, the celebrated statement in Gen 1:27, "male and female he created them," is not only problematic, but oppressive. It has the effect of relegating whole categories of people (homosexual, transgender) to a status of abnormality.[127] There are, of course, real biological differences that cannot be denied, but the simple binary opposition does not do justice to the spectrum of human sexuality. One need not accept the constructionist view of gender theory in its most extreme forms to recognize that the biblical formulation is too simple.

As Esther Fuchs has rightly observed, the Bible is at least in part "a

---

125. Clines, *What Does Eve Do to Help?* 37.

126. Karl Barth, *Church Dogmatics,* III/4: *The Doctrine of Creation* (Edinburgh: T. & T. Clark, 1958), 186-87.

127. Ken Stone is one of the few biblical scholars, if not the only one, to address this problem directly. He offers no strategy for dealing with the normative heterosexuality of Genesis 1. In the case of Genesis 2-3, he dwells on the fact that at first Adam is created alone, and then, following the wildly speculative suggestion of Howard Ellberg-Schwartz, asks (67), "Is it possible that the representation of God's searching for an appropriate partner for Adam is a reflex of a felt need, on the part of the text's writer, to preclude the possibility of . . . (a) homoerotic relationship" between Yahweh and Adam? The question should probably be answered in the negative.

prescriptive interpretation of culture,"[128] and it has certainly been taken as such over the centuries. Insofar as the project of recuperative feminist biblical scholarship accepts that prescriptive interpretation, even in the basic binary distinction of male and female, it is inevitably problematic from the perspective of contemporary gender theory.

One may of course argue that the Bible is a safer guide to morality than postmodern gender theory and that society needs some ethical norms, even if those who do not conform to them feel discriminated against. But if one has any sympathy at all with the feminist enterprise, one will have to admit that the Bible is not an infallible guide, and that it is often very problematic. Biblical laws and narratives are all too clearly human constructs that reflect the culture of specific times and places and are not innocent in the matter of power relations. There is no reason to assume that the accounts of creation, Genesis 1 as well as the story of Adam and Eve, are any less culturally relative than the laws about slavery. Many other factors are relevant to discussions of sexuality and gender, but the fact that heterosexuality is depicted as normative in Genesis 1-2 cannot in itself be decisive for the modern discussion, any more than can the model of gender relations in these chapters.

The cultural value of the biblical stories is none the less for that. They provide ready grist for the mill of ideological criticism, and we have much to learn from them about the dynamics of gender relations. A "hermeneutic of resistance," such as that called for by Fuchs, is still a way of engaging the biblical text and acknowledging its importance.[129] But any approach that continues to treat the Bible as a prescriptive text for the modern world is rendered very problematic by feminist and gender criticism.

128. Fuchs, *Sexual Politics*, 29. On sexual prescriptions in the Bible, see Athalya Brenner, *The Intercourse of Knowledge: On Gendering Desire and "Sexuality" in the Hebrew Bible*. Biblical Interpretation 26 (Leiden: Brill, 1997), 90-152.

129. Fuchs, 29. Cf. also Eryl Davies, 109-12.

Israelite Religion:
The Return of the Goddess

The Hebrew Bible is in large part a purported history of the people Israel, with a primary focus on its religion. Consequently, scholars have often found it hard to distinguish between biblical theology and the history of Israelite religion.[1] The primary basis for a distinction lies in the weight given to nonbiblical sources in the latter enterprise. The so-called *Religionsgeschichtliche Schule* of a century ago was inspired in large part by the discovery of ancient texts from Mesopotamia and elsewhere, which offered the possibility of putting the biblical account in a broader cultural context.[2] For much of the 20th century, however, the history of religion was eclipsed by theology. The theological approach was concerned with the distinctiveness of Israel or, in the phrase of G. Ernest Wright, with setting "the Old Testament against its environment."[3] This approach was not confined to Christian theologians. Ironically, the most extreme disjunction of the Bible from ancient Near Eastern religion was

1. See James Barr, *The Concept of Biblical Theology: An Old Testament Perspective* (Minneapolis: Fortress, 1999), 100-39.

2. For a brief account, with further bibliography, see Hendrikus Boers, "Religionsgeschichtliche Schule," in *Dictionary of Biblical Interpretation,* ed. John H. Hayes (Nashville: Abingdon, 1999) 2:383-87. Key figures in relation to ancient Israel were Hermann Gunkel and Hugo Gressmann.

3. G. Ernest Wright, *The Old Testament against Its Environment.* SBT 2 (London: SCM, 1950). See Brevard S. Childs, *Biblical Theology in Crisis,* 47-50.

expressed in a book entitled *The Religion of Israel,* by the Israeli scholar
Yeḥezkel Kaufmann.[4]

The Antithesis of Israelite and Pagan

Kaufmann distinguished sharply between "pagan religion," based on "the
idea that there exists a realm of being prior to the gods and above them," and
"Israelite religion," whose basic idea is "that God is supreme over all."[5] Israelite religion was also characterized by a "remarkable absence of mythological
traits."[6] It was assumed that "only YHWH may be worshiped,"[7] and that
Moses staged a "monotheistic revolution."[8] Israelite religion "was absolutely
different from anything the pagan world ever knew; its monotheistic world
view had no antecedents in paganism."[9] In fact, Israelites could not even understand the nature of polytheism. As Ziony Zevit has remarked, "the monotheistic hypothesis" was not a conclusion of Kaufmann's work but an *a priori*
presupposition.[10] Kaufmann's view of Israelite religion has been especially
influential in Jewish scholarship.[11] Much, but not all, of it was shared by
Christian biblical theologians of the time. William F. Albright spoke for
many when he labelled Kaufmann's position extreme,[12] although he himself

4. Yeḥezkel Kaufmann, *The Religion of Israel: From Its Beginnings to the Babylonian Exile* (Chicago: University of Chicago Press, 1960). The Hebrew original ran to 8 volumes (Tel
Aviv: Bialik, 1937-1956). The title, תולדות האמונה הישראלית, might be translated more lit-
erally as "the history of Israelite faith."

5. Kaufmann, 21, 60.

6. Kaufmann, 61. Cf. the frequent antithesis of myth and history in works of biblical
theology of this period, and the critique of that antithesis by Bertil Albrektson, *History and
the Gods* (Lund: Gleerup, 1967).

7. Kaufmann, 61.

8. Kaufmann, 229.

9. Kaufmann, 2.

10. Ziony Zevit, *The Religions of Ancient Israel: A Synthesis of Parallactic Approaches*
(New York: Continuum, 2001), 48.

11. See the qualified defence of Kaufmann by Zevit, 43-48; also Baruch Halpern,
"'Brisker Pipes than Poetry': The Development of Israelite Monotheism," in *Judaic Perspectives on Ancient Israel,* ed. Jacob Neusner, Baruch A. Levine, and Ernest S. Frerichs (Philadelphia: Fortress, 1987), 77-115, who grants that Kaufmann's work had some "significant imper-
fections" (106).

12. William F. Albright, *Yahweh and the Gods of Canaan* (Garden City: Doubleday,
1968), 206.

used Canaanite religion primarily as a foil against which to highlight the religion of Israel.

In the last quarter of the 20th century, the pendulum of scholarly opinion swung decisively away from the kind of position represented by Kaufmann. Several factors have contributed to this shift.

The Impact of the Ugaritic Texts

The texts from Ugarit, first discovered in 1929, provided for the first time a substantial body of primary evidence about the language and religion of Canaan. The affinities with the Hebrew Bible were striking. Albright observed that "the Hebrew language and poetic style were quite certainly Canaanite in origin," although he found this paradoxical in view of the presumed Mesopotamian origin of the patriarchs.[13] Moreover, "the head of the Canaanite (Phoenician) pantheon was the god El (i.e., *the god*), just as among the Hebrews, where he was early called *El ʿElyôn*."[14] Albright went so far as to speculate that "early Hebrew popular religion was presumably similar [to that of other Semitic peoples], with a father, El, a mother whose specific name or names must remain obscure (perhaps Elat or Anath), and a son who appears as the storm-god, probably named Shaddai, 'the One of the Mountain(s).'"[15] By "early Hebrew" Albright meant pre-Mosaic. He still viewed Mosaic Israel as a new phenomenon and agreed with Kaufmann that "without monotheism, Israel, as we know it, could not have existed" and that "it was indeed Moses who was the principal architect of Israelite monotheism."[16] But he argued that "there was so much exchange of cultural influences between Israel and its neighbours on all sides of its tiny territory, and there were so many irruptions of paganism into Israel, that the ignorance presupposed by Kaufmann's view is simply incredible."[17] Albright's student, Frank Moore Cross, went further. He argued that the name Yahweh originated as a cultic name of El (*ʾēl yahweh ṣĕbāʾōt*, "El who creates the heavenly host").[18] Moreover, he showed that the

---

13. Albright, *Yahweh and the Gods of Canaan*, 153.

14. Albright, *From the Stone Age to Christianity*, 231.

15. Albright, *From the Stone Age to Christianity*, 247.

16. Albright, *Yahweh and the Gods of Canaan*, 206.

17. Albright, *Yahweh and the Gods of Canaan*, 207.

18. Frank Moore Cross, *Canaanite Myth and Hebrew Epic* (Cambridge, Mass.: Harvard University Press, 1973), 60-75.

descriptions of Yahweh's storm theophany are heavily indebted to Canaanite depictions of Baal.[19] Cross's theory that Yahweh split off from El is not without its problems,[20] but on any reckoning he showed that there was considerable continuity between Canaan and Israel in the depiction of deities. This continuity has been further elaborated by subsequent scholars such as Mark Smith and John Day.[21]

Morton Smith's Manifesto

Cross emphasized the continuities between Canaan and Israel, but he did not highlight the discrepancies between his reconstruction of Israelite religion and the biblical record. A much more controversial position was staked out by Morton Smith, in a book published two years before Cross's *Canaanite Myth and Hebrew Epic*.[22] Smith relied primarily on a critical reading of the biblical text. He argued that "although the cult of Yahweh is the principal concern of the Old Testament, it may not have been the principal religious concern of the Israelites."[23] In fact, there is abundant evidence in the biblical text that the people worshipped other deities. At the time of Josiah's reform,

> the priests throughout Judea had to be stopped from burning incense on the high places, not only to Baal, but also to the sun, the moon, the planets, and all the host of heaven; around Jerusalem the high places of "the satyrs" (?) and of the gods Astoreth, Kemosh, and Milkom had to be destroyed; and the temple of Yahweh itself had to be purged of the vessels of Baal, Asherah, and the host of heaven, the chariots of the sun,

19. Cross, 145-94.

20. See John Day, *Yahweh and the Gods and Goddesses of Canaan*. JSOTSup 265 (Sheffield: Sheffield Academic, 2000), 14.

21. Mark S. Smith, *The Origins of Biblical Monotheism: Israel's Polytheistic Background and the Ugaritic Texts* (New York: Oxford University Press, 2001); John Day, *God's Conflict with the Dragon and the Sea* (Cambridge: Cambridge University Press, 1985); *Yahweh and the Gods and Goddesses of Canaan*. See now also the recognition of "biblical myth" in Michael Fishbane, *Biblical Myth and Rabbinic Mythmaking* (Oxford: Oxford University Press, 2003), 31-92.

22. Morton Smith, *Palestinian Parties and Politics That Shaped the Old Testament* (New York: Columbia University Press, 1971; repr., London: SCM, 1987).

23. Morton Smith, 19.

and the houses of the sacred "prostitutes" where the women wove coverings for the pillar which symbolized the goddess Asherah.[24]

A few years later, Jeremiah and Ezekiel were still complaining about the worship of other deities. Smith rightly noted that these goings-on were not just at the high places in remote areas, but even in the temple of Yahweh in Jerusalem. He concluded that "syncretism was dominant in the cult of Yahweh at Jerusalem to the very last days of the first temple."[25] "All this indicates that to consider 'the religion of Israel' as a unique entity may be misleading. We shall better understand the state of affairs during the monarchies if we think of the religion of the Israelites as one form of the common religion of the ancient Near East."[26] There was, to be sure, a "Yahweh-alone party," represented by the Elijah stories and the prophet Hosea, but these were in the minority in the preexilic period, although their viewpoint eventually prevailed and came to dominate the biblical sources.

Smith's thesis, briefly stated and minimally argued, was taken up enthusiastically by the German scholar Bernhard Lang.[27] Lang claimed that during the period of the monarchy "the dominant religion is polytheistic and undifferentiated from that of its neighbours."[28] Yahweh's position as national god was undisputed, but no different from that of other national gods: "All the neighbouring peoples have *one single* national god each — the Moabites worship their Kemosh, the Ammonites Milcom, the Assyrians Ashur, and the Egyptians Amun-Re. Just as Israel is the people of Yahweh, so Moab is the 'people of Kemosh.'"[29] The enmity between Yahweh and Baal results from the fact that Yahweh is an interloper from Sinai, who has no kinship relations with the gods of Canaan.[30] Lang's theses sparked a lively controversy in Germany.[31] Some of the participants ob-

24. Morton Smith, 24.

25. Morton Smith, 25.

26. Morton Smith, 28.

27. Bernhard Lang, ed., *Der einzige Gott: Die Geburt des biblischen Monotheismus* (Munich: Kösel, 1981); *Monotheism and the Prophetic Minority: An Essay in Biblical History and Sociology* (Sheffield: Almond, 1983).

28. Lang, *Monotheism and the Prophetic Minority*, 20.

29. Lang, *Monotheism and the Prophetic Minority*, 21.

30. Lang, *Monotheism and the Prophetic Minority*, 35.

31. See esp. Ernst Haag, ed., *Gott, der Einzige: Zur Entstehung des Monotheismus in Israel.* Quaestiones disputatae 104 (Freiburg: Herder, 1985); Walter Dietrich and Martin A.

jected that the demand for exclusive worship of Yahweh was more deeply
rooted in Israelite tradition than Smith and Lang allowed, pointing especially to the pre-Priestly traditions in the book of Exodus.[32] Norbert
Lohfink called for a distinction between norm and practice, and argued
that "the empirical data" should not be taken for "the normative religion."[33] But there can be little doubt that Smith and Lang succeeded to a
great degree in undermining the common assumptions about the monotheistic nature of Israelite religion.[34]

Smith noted that the evidence of archaeology supports the view that
ancient Israel was polytheistic, noting especially the proliferation of figurines of naked women, presumably representing a goddess, but he devoted
only a single paragraph to the subject.[35] In fact, the reassessment of Israelite religion has been prompted above all by the discovery of a number of
inscriptions mentioning "Yahweh and his asherah."[36]

Klopfenstein, eds., *Ein Gott allein? JHWH-Verehrung und biblischer Monotheismus im
Kontext der israelitischen und altorientalischen Religionsgeschichte.* OBO 139 (Göttingen:
Vandenhoeck & Ruprecht, 1994); Werner H. Schmidt, "'Jahwe und. . .': Anmerkungen zur
sog. Monotheismus-Debatte," in *Die Hebräische Bibel und ihre zweifache Nachgeschichte:
Festschrift für Rolf Rendtorff zum 65. Geburtstag,* ed. Erhard Blum, Christian Macholz and
Ekkehard W. Stegemann (Neukirchen-Vluyn: Neukirchener, 1990) 435-48; Marie-Theres
Wacker and Erich Zenger, ed., *Der Eine Gott und die Göttin: Gottesvorstellungen des
biblischen Israel im Horizont feministischer Theologie.* Quaestiones disputatae 135 (Freiburg:
Herder, 1991). See also the volume by Dutch scholars Bob Becking, et al., *Only One God?
Monotheism in Ancient Israel and the Veneration of the Goddess Asherah.* Biblical Seminar 77
(London: Sheffield Academic, 2001).

32. E.g., Norbert Lohfink, "Zur Geschichte der Diskussion über den Monotheismus im
Alten Israel," in Haag, 9-25 (esp. 22-25); Erich Zenger, "Das jahwistische Werk: Ein
Wegbereiter des jahwistischen Monotheismus?" in Haag, 26-53; Schmidt, 442-46. See also
Halpern, "'Brisker Pipes than Poetry,'" 77-115, who notes the demand for exclusive devotion
in Exodus 20 and 34.

33. Lohfink, "Zur Geschichte der Diskussion," 22.

34. See, e.g., Robert Karl Gnuse, *No Other Gods: Emergent Monotheism in Israel.*
JSOTSup 241. (Sheffield: Sheffield Academic, 1997).

35. Morton Smith, 24-25.

36. William G. Dever, "Archaeology and the Ancient Israelite Cult: How the Kh. El-
Qôm and Kuntillet Ajrud 'Asherah' Texts Have Changed the Picture," *ErIsr* 26 (1999): 9*-15*.

The Inscriptions from Khirbet el-Qôm and Kuntillet ʿAjrud

The first of these was discovered in 1970, the year before Smith published his book, at Khirbet el-Qôm, 12 km. west of Hebron and approximately 10 km. southeast of Lachish.[37] The inscription, which dates to the late 8th century B.C.E.,[38] was chiselled out of a pillar in a burial cave. I cite the transcription and translation of Judith Hadley:

> ʾryhw.hˈšr.ktbh
> brk. ʾryhw.lyhwh
> wmṣryh lʾšrth hwšˈlh

> Uriyahu the rich wrote it.
> Blessed be Uriyahu by Yahweh
> for from his enemies by his asherah
> he has saved him.

Only single words can be read on the remaining lines. The fourth line reads a name Oniyahu, and the word asherah occurs again in the fifth line, and possibly also in the sixth.[39] There are various problems with the readings. The editor, and some other scholars, think the initial name should be preceded by a *lamed* ("belonging to Uriyahu"). Ziony Zevit reads a nominal form on line 1 ("his inscription") and a first person verb ("I blessed") on line 2,[40] but there is general consensus about the reference to "asherah," however it is construed.[41]

The reference to "asherah" in this inscription received indirect cor-

---

37. William G. Dever, "Iron Age Epigraphic Material from the Area of Khirbet el-Kôm," *HUCA* 40-41 (1969-1970): 139-204; *Did God Have a Wife? Archaeology and Folk Religion in Ancient Israel* (Grand Rapids: Wm. B. Eerdmans, 2005), 131-33.

38. André Lemaire, "Les inscriptions de Khirbet el-Qôm et l'Ashérah de YHWH," *RB* 84 (1977): 595-608 (603) proposed a date ca. 750 B.C.E., as did Dever, *HUCA* 40 [1970]: 165. Frank Moore Cross prefers a date ca. 700 B.C.E. (so Dever, *HUCA* 40 [1970]: 165, n. 53; Saul M. Olyan, *Asherah and the Cult of Yahweh in Israel.* SBLMS 34 [Atlanta: Scholars, 1988], 23).

39. Judith M. Hadley, *The Cult of Asherah in Ancient Israel and Judah: Evidence for a Hebrew Goddess.* University of Cambridge Oriental Publications 57 (Cambridge: Cambridge University Press, 2000), 86. So also G. I. Davies, *Ancient Hebrew Inscriptions* (Cambridge: Cambridge University Press, 1991), 106 (25.003).

40. Zevit, 361.

41. The reading is not beyond dispute. See Olyan, 24-25. On the problems of the inscription and the range of scholarly opinion see Hadley, *The Cult of Asherah*, 84-105.

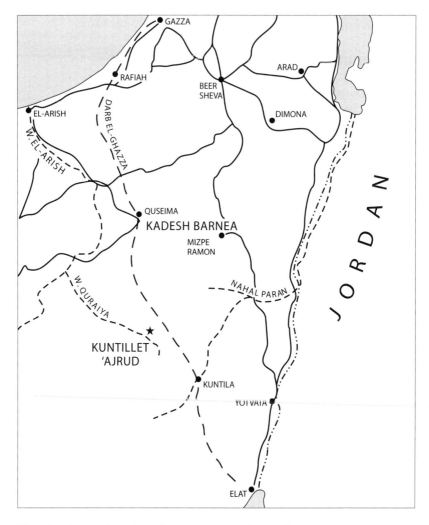

Map showing the location of Kuntillet ʿAjrud (P. Peck)

roboration from a number of inscriptions discovered in 1975-76 at Kuntillet ʿAjrud in the northeastern Sinai, ca. 70 km. southwest of Kadesh-barnea.[42] The site is located near the intersection of several ancient routes in the desert. The excavator, Zeʾev Meshel, regarded it as a religious center, mainly because of a number of inscriptions mentioning deities, including El and Baal as well as Yahweh.[43] This interpretation of the site has been disputed by Hadley, who regards it as a way station or caravanserai.[44] Many of the inscriptions are in Phoenician script. The Hebrew inscriptions refer to "Yahweh of Samaria" and "Yahweh of Teman," rather than to a resident deity of the site. There is no altar or unambiguous cultic installation. Hadley concludes that it was "a place which served a diversity of peoples from different linguistic groups, rather than a local shrine to one particular deity with its own resident priests."[45] Nonetheless, it must be acknowledged that the site also provided for the observance of religious ritual, as indicated by the inscriptions and by bowls and other artifacts dedicated to deities.[46]

The inscriptions are found on wall-plaster and on pithoi, or large storage vessels. They date to the beginning of the 8th century, and so are slightly earlier than the inscription from Khirbet el-Qôm.[47] Four of them mention Yahweh and asherah in conjunction. One of these is a plaster inscription and is poorly preserved. Hadley reads:

---

42. Zeʾev Meshel, *Kuntillet ʿAjrud: A Religious Centre from the Time of the Judaean Monarchy on the Border of Sinai* (Jerusalem: Israel Museum, 1978); "Did Yahweh Have a Consort?" *BAR* 5/2 (1979): 24-35.

43. He also noted the presence of vessels for votive offerings. So also Zevit, 374; William G. Dever, "Folk Religion in Early Israel: Did Yahweh Have a Consort?" in *Aspects of Monotheism: How God Is One,* ed. Hershel Shanks and Jack Meinhardt (Washington: Biblical Archeology Society, 1997), 27-56 (44). See now Dever, *Did God Have a Wife?* 160-67.

44. Hadley, *The Cult of Asherah,* 108-9.

45. Hadley, *The Cult of Asherah,* 109. So also Othmar Keel and Christoph Uehlinger, *Gods, Goddesses, and Images of God in Ancient Israel* (Minneapolis: Fortress, 1998), 247.

46. Brian B. Schmidt, "The Iron Age *Pithoi* Drawings from Horvat Teman or Kuntillet ʿAjrud: Some New Proposals," *JANER* 2 (2002): 91-125. I am grateful to Nicolas Wyatt for bringing this article to my attention.

47. P. Kyle McCarter, Jr., "Aspects of the Religion of the Israelite Monarchy: Biblical and Epigraphic Data," in *Ancient Israelite Religion: Essays in Honor of Frank Moore Cross,* ed. Patrick D. Miller, Paul D. Hanson, and S. Dean McBride (Philadelphia: Fortress, 1987), 137-55 (138). See also Zeʾev Meshel, "Kuntillet ʿAjrud," *ABD* 4:103-9 (109).

>... 'rk. ymm. wyšb'w ...
>... hyṯb. yhwh ... wy ...

and translates:

>May their day be long and may they be satisfied/swear ...
>Yahweh, prosper (them)/do good to (them).

Another fragment reads:

>... ytnw. l ... 'šrt

they will celebrate unto/give to ... asherah/Asherata[48]

Zevit combines these fragments:

>l]engthen their days and they will be filled, [and they] will give to
>[Y]HWH Teiman and to Asherat[[49]

The other inscriptions are found on fragments of pithoi, which were also covered with drawings. The first inscription appears above the heads of two figures, which are often taken as representations of the Egyptian dwarf deity or demon Bes, and overlaps with the headdress of one of them. There is also a seated figure playing a lyre in the immediate background. The inscription reads:

>'mr. ...'... h. ..k. 'mr. lyhl[l'l) wlyw'šh. w. .. brkt. 'tkm. lyhwh. šmrn.
>wl'šrth

X says: say to Yehal[lel'el] and to Yo'asah and ... I bless you by Yahweh of Samaria and by his asherah.[50]

The second inscription reads:

---

48. Hadley, *The Cult of Asherah*, 130. G. I. Davies, 80 (8.015), places this fragment after YHWH on the second line.

49. Zevit, 373. He restores a reference to Teiman after YHWH in the second line of the inscription. Cf. the readings of Shemuel Aḥituv and Meshel, cited by Hadley, *The Cult of Asherah*, 134.

50. Hadley, *The Cult of Asherah*, 121. G. I. Davies, 81 (8.017), reads *h[ml]k* (the king) before the second *'mr*.

'mr 'mryw 'mr l. 'dny hšlm. 't brktk. lyhwh tmn wl'šrth. ybrk. wyšmrk wyhy 'm. 'd[n]y . . . k

Amaryau says: say to my lord: Is it well with you? I bless you by Yahweh of Teman and by his asherah. May he bless you and keep you and be with my lord. . .[51]

The final inscription was not included in the original publication of the finds. It reads:

lyhwh htmn. wl'šrth[52]

for Yahweh of Teman and for his asherah

This appears above another inscription to which it may be related:

kl 'šr yš'l m'š ḥnn . . . wntn lh yhw klbbh

Whatever he asks from a man, may it be favoured . . . and let Yahw(eh) give unto him as he wishes (according to his heart)[53]

Ze'ev Meshel, the excavator of Kuntillet 'Ajrud, originally proposed that Yahweh Shom°ron ("Yahweh of Samaria") be read as "Yahweh, our guardian,"[54] but this possibility is excluded by the parallel usage of "Yahweh of Teman." Yahweh is linked with Teman, a region in Edom, in Hab 3:3: "God came from Teman, the Holy One from Mount Paran." Yahweh of Samaria and Yahweh of Teman are "local forms or manifestations of the national god."[55] Yahweh of Samaria is Yahweh as he was worshipped in Samaria, and the phrase strongly implies that there was a temple of Yahweh in the northern capital, besides the temple of Baal mentioned in 1 Kgs 16:32.[56] Hosea 8:5

51. Hadley, *The Cult of Asherah*, 125; G. I. Davies, 81 (8.021); Zevit, 394-95.

52. Hadley, *The Cult of Asherah*, 130.

53. Hadley, *The Cult of Asherah*, 129-30. This is taken as one inscription by Zevit, 398; Keel and Uehlinger, 227. G. I. Davies lists the first part as 8.016 and the second as 8.022.

54. Meshel, *Kuntillet 'Ajrud*. See Day, *Yahweh and the Gods and Goddesses of Canaan*, 49.

55. McCarter, 139. Cf. Keel and Uehlinger, 228.

56. Olyan, 35, against the older view of Albrecht Alt that the cult in Samaria was Canaanite, in contrast to the Yahwistic cult at Bethel and Dan. See Alt, "The Monarchy in the Kingdoms of Israel and Judah," in *Essays on Old Testament History and Religion* (Garden City: Doubleday, 1968), 311-35; Herbert Donner, "The Separate States of Israel and Judah," in

("he has spurned your calf, Samaria") suggests that the shrine there had a statue of a bull calf, like those at Bethel and Dan (1 Kgs 12:28-29). Whether there was a cult of Yahweh in Teman as late as the 9th or 8th century is debatable. John Emerton thought this unlikely and suggested that the reference merely meant that Yahweh had originally come from the region of Teman.[57] Saul Olyan counters that "Yahweh's close associations with the deep south in early texts suggests at least that his cult was present there, perhaps even prominent," although there is no direct evidence of it.[58] In any case, these references suggest a kind of "poly-Yahwism," in which Yahweh was worshipped in several different local manifestations. We might compare the different manifestations of El in Genesis (El Elyon, El Shaddai, etc.), the reference to multiple Baals in Hosea (Hos 2:13, 17), or the different manifestations of the Virgin Mary in Roman Catholicism (Our Lady of Lourdes, Fatima etc.). A related expression, "the God of Jerusalem," is found in an inscription from a burial cave at Khirbet Beit Lei, 8 km east of Lachish from approximately the same period.[59] This kind of poly-Yahwism was undermined by the centralizing reforms of kings Hezekiah and Josiah and seems to have died out in the dispersal of the Babylonian exile.[60]

Yahweh's Asherah

The main controversy initiated by these inscriptions, however, is not about local manifestations of Yahweh, but about the identity of "his asherah." Asherah is the Hebrew equivalent of Ugaritic atirat, wife of El and mother of his 70 sons. The question then arises, did Yahweh also have a wife, in the period of the monarchy?[61]

Israelite and Judaean History, ed. John H. Hayes and J. Maxwell Miller. OTL (Philadelphia: Westminster, 1977), 403. Hadley (123) adds further arguments against Alt's position.

57. J. A. Emerton, "New Light on Israelite Religion: The Implications of the Inscriptions from Kuntillet 'Ajrud," *ZAW* 94 (1982): 2-20.

58. Olyan, 28.

59. Zevit, 417-22; G. I. Davies, 89 (15.005); Frank Moore Cross, "The Cave Inscriptions from Khirbet Beit Lei," in *Near Eastern Archaeology in the Twentieth Century: Essays in Honor of Nelson Glueck,* ed. James A. Sanders (Garden City: Doubleday, 1970), 299-306.

60. McCarter, 142-43. McCarter does not claim that it was the purpose of the reforms to suppress the local Yahwehs, but that this was an effect of their emphasis on the unity of Yahweh. So he suggests that Deut 6:4 might be read "Yahweh, our god, is one Yahweh!"

61. Meshel, *BAR* 5/2 (1979): 24-35; William G. Dever, "Asherah, Consort of Yahweh?

The most energetic advocate of the view that Yahweh's asherah was a real live goddess has been William Dever, who writes dismissively about "the attempts of some Biblical scholars to get around this relatively clear reference to Asherah as a co-agent of blessing with Yahweh and undoubtedly conceived in popular circles as his consort."[62] The most persuasive of these attempts, one that even Dever has to acknowledge, appeals to Hebrew grammatical usage. In Hebrew idiom, pronominal suffixes are not attached to proper names, and this situation is not altered by the possibility that they are so attached in Ugaritic or other Semitic languages.[63] The point here is not that a pronominal suffix on a proper name would be a violation of Hebrew grammar, as understood by modern grammarians,[64] but that such usage is not attested. David Noel Freedman may possibly be right that this expression was an exception to the rule, intended to make the point that Asherah was consort of Yahweh, not Baal, and that one could speak of "Yahweh and his asherah" as Shakespeare spoke of "Juliet and her Romeo."[65] Nonetheless, an explanation in accordance with known Hebrew usage must be preferred. The same objection must be

---

New Evidence from Kuntillet ʿAjrûd," *BASOR* 255 (1984): 21-37. See now Dever, *Did God Have a Wife?* 196-236.

62. William G. Dever, "Ancient Israelite Religion: How to Reconcile the Differing Texts and Artifactual Portraits," in Dietrich and Klopfenstein, 105-25 (112). The immediate reference is to the Khirbet el-Qôm inscription. See also his comments in "Folk Religion in Early Israel." In support of Dever's interpretation, it should be noted that the word *lʾšrt* occurs in four inscriptions from Tel Miqne (Ekron), where it is most naturally taken as a divine name. See Seymour Gitin, "Seventh Century B.C.E. Cultic Elements at Ekron," in *Biblical Archaeology Today, 1990: Proceedings of the Second International Congress on Biblical Archaeology* (Jerusalem: Israel Exploration Society and Israel Academy of Sciences and Humanities, 1993), 248-58 (252); Zevit, 402.

63. See, among many, Emerton, 14; André Lemaire, "Who or What Was Yahweh's Asherah?" *BAR* 10 (1984): 42-51 (50); Olyan, 28; Judith M. Hadley, "Asherah: Archaeological and Textual Evidence," in Dietrich and Klopfenstein, 235-68 (245); Day, *Yahweh and the Gods and Goddesses,* 51. For possible instances of pronominal suffixes on proper names in Ugaritic, see Manfried Dietrich and Oswald Loretz, *"Jahwe und seine Aschera": Anthropomorphes Kultbild in Mesopotamien, Ugarit und Israel.* Ugaritisch-Biblische Literatur 9 (Münster: Ugarit Verlag, 1992), 98-101.

64. David Noel Freedman, "Yahweh of Samaria and His Asherah," *BA* 50 (1987): 241-49: "I believe the way to approach a strange grammatical construction is not by invoking a rule that somebody invented in the nineteenth century that says it is impossible but rather by investigating the possible reasons for such an unusual arrangement" (247).

65. Freedman, 249. Cf. Brian Schmidt, 107, who takes "his Asherah" as "the one whom Yahweh greatly endeared, 'his Asherah.'"

raised against several other ingenious proposals. Ziony Zevit proposes to read Asheratah, as a name with a double feminine ending, a form of the name that is otherwise unattested.[66] Other scholars have argued that the word means "his sanctuary," but this, again, is a meaning not attested in Hebrew.[67] The same problem defeats the proposal that the word asherah "represents a long-forgotten North-West Semitic noun . . . denoting 'wife, consort.'"[68] The simplest explanation in terms of Hebrew usage is to take the asherah to refer to a wooden cult object, either a carved object or a stylized tree. There are numerous references to asherahs in this sense in the Hebrew Bible, and this is how the word in the inscriptions is most often interpreted by modern scholars.[69]

The Symbolism of the Asherah

But what does this cult object symbolize? "Is it logical," asks Dever, "to suppose that an inanimate object, or even a sanctuary, could be mentioned on an equal footing with the principal deity as an *agent of blessing*, as the context demands both at 'Ajrûd and at el-Qôm?"[70] One might, of course, question whether "his asherah" is on an equal footing with the principal deity. More significantly, one might argue that "the cult symbol represents the goddess" so that it makes little difference whether "asherah" is taken as the name of the goddess or her symbol.[71] To quote Dever again, "whether 'a/Asherah' at 'Ajrud refers to the goddess herself or merely her symbol — an 'agent of blessing' that could be invoked alongside Yahweh — there was a widespread perception in ancient Israel of the goddess's reality, which

66. Zevit, 363-66.
67. So Edward Lipiński, "The Goddess Aṯirat in Ancient Arabia, in Babylon, and in Ugarit," *Orientalia Lovaniensia Periodica* 3 (1972): 101-19 (112). The interpretation in terms of a shrine appeals to usage in other Semitic languages. It is gainsaid by one of the Tel Miqne inscriptions, where the word *mqm (māqôm)* is used for the cult place and *'šrt* must mean something else (Zevit, 402).
68. Baruch Margalit, "The Meaning and Significance of Asherah," *VT* 40 (1990): 264-97 (284).
69. So among many others, Emerton, Hadley, Day, Olyan, McCarter.
70. Dever, *BASOR* 255 (1984): 21-37 (30).
71. So Olyan, 31, who compares the use of bull iconography to symbolize Yahweh and other storm gods, although strictly the bull was the pedestal on which the deity stood. Nicolas Wyatt, orally, suggests that the inscriptions may allude to the goddess without mentioning her directly.

gave the symbolism its efficacy."[72] Against this, it is observed that Asherah was no longer worshipped in Phoenicia in the 1st millennium[73] and that the possessive pronoun suggests that the symbol was attached to Yahweh rather than to a goddess.[74] In the words of Mark Smith: "'his asherah' should denote something that is 'his,' and not hers. In short, it appears preferable to take 'his asherah' as something that is 'his,' i.e., a symbol that once may have referred to the goddess by the same name, but functions in this context as part of Yahweh's symbolic repertoire, possibly with older connotations associated with the goddess."[75] In a somewhat similar vein, Kyle McCarter suggests that "we seem to have a case . . . of the personification of a cult object as a goddess."[76] More specifically, "in the cult Yahweh's *'ăšērâ*, his trace, sign, or effective presence, was marked with an upright wooden pole, called an asherah, which, along with an altar, a *maṣṣēbâ*, and other objects, constituted his sanctuary. At the same time, the *'ăšērâ* — the 'trace' of Yahweh in the cult — was attributed substance, personified, and worshiped as a hypostatic personality, following the widely attested Northwest Semitic pattern. . . . The asherah was thought of as feminine and thus as the consort of the deity."[77] Hadley speculates that "it may be that he [Yahweh] has absorbed the earlier indigenous fertility goddesses into his cult, and the statues which were formerly dedicated solely to the goddess Asherah have now become part of Yahweh's cultic paraphernalia. The asherah pole may have even become a hypostatization of Yahweh's fertility aspects."[78] She continues: "by the time of the deuteronomistic compilers, the distinction between Asherah the goddess and asherah the wooden cultic symbol had perhaps become totally obscured."[79]

Much of this discussion is obviously speculative. It is interesting to observe that already more than a hundred years ago, long before the discov-

---

72. Dever, "Folk Religion in Early Israel," 45.

73. This, however, would not hold if Asherah was identified with Tannit (so Olyan, private communication, following Frank Moore Cross).

74. It is possible, however, that the suffix should be translated as "its" and referred to Samaria or Teman.

75. Mark S. Smith, *The Early History of God,* 2nd ed. Biblical Resource Series (Grand Rapids: Wm. B. Eerdmans and Livonia: Dove, 2002), 121.

76. McCarter, 147.

77. McCarter, 149. See the criticism of Mark Smith, *The Early History of God,* 123-24.

78. Hadley, *The Cult of Asherah,* 80.

79. Hadley, *The Cult of Asherah,* 81.

ery of the Ugaritic texts, Robertson Smith had argued that "the opinion that there was a Canaanite goddess called Ashera, and that the trees or poles of the same name were her particular symbols, is not tenable; every altar had its ashera, even such altars as . . . were dedicated to Jehovah. This is not consistent with the idea that the sacred pole was a symbol of a distinct divinity."[80] After the discoveries at Ugarit, however, it is no longer possible to deny that there was a Canaanite goddess Asherah. The presence of asherah symbols at Yahwistic shrines does not necessarily show that they were not symbols of a distinct divinity, but rather raises the question of the relationship between the god and the goddess.

The discussion of the asherah in the inscriptions is further complicated by the drawings on the pithoi. On Pithos A, just below the inscription that mentions "Yahweh of Samaria," is a drawing of two standing figures with interlocking arms and a seated figure playing a lyre. (The inscription actually overlaps the headdress of the taller figure). These figures have been subjects of intense discussion.[81] Meshel already raised the question whether two of them may not represent Yahweh and his consort.[82] Several scholars think that the standing figures are bovine.[83] The smaller one appears to be standing behind the larger and also appears to have breasts, indicated by small circles. Objects hanging between the legs of both figures are likely to be tails rather than penises. If these figures are indeed meant to be bovine, they might be interpreted as "the 'bull of Jacob' and his lady," in the words of Michael Coogan.[84] (Compare also the bull images at Bethel and Dan and the reference to "the calf of Samaria" in Hos 8:6.) Against this interpretation, however, it is argued that bovine figures are "almost never portrayed frontally in ancient Near Eastern two-dimensional artistic works" and that the absence of horns tells against either of them being a bull.[85] Neither male genitals nor a cow's udder is portrayed (in contrast to another drawing, of a cow with a suckling calf, on the same pithos). The majority of commenta-

---

80. W. Robertson Smith, *Lectures on the Religion of the Semites* (London: Black, 1894; repr. New Brunswick: Transaction, 2002), 188-89. Cf. Margalit, 265.

81. Hadley, *The Cult of Asherah*, 136-37, provides a summary of the discussion.

82. Meshel, *BAR* 5/2 (1979): 31.

83. So Meshel, *BAR* 5/2 (1979): 31; Mordechai Gilula, "To Yahweh Shomron and His Asherah," *Shnaton* 3 (1978-79): 129-37 [Hebrew]; Margalit, 275; McCarter, 146-47.

84. Michael D. Coogan, "Canaanite Origins and Lineage: Reflections on the Religion of Ancient Israel," in Miller, Hanson, and McBride, 115-24 (119).

85. Keel and Uehlinger, 217-18, n. 47.

Hebrew inscription and drawing from Kuntillet ʿAjrud Pithos A depicting
"Yahweh of Samaria and his Asherah" (courtesy Zeʾev Meshel)

tors have preferred to identify the standing figures as depictions of the
Egyptian dwarf god Bes, who is usually represented frontal and squatting.[86]
Bes is usually depicted with leonine features and is occasionally depicted
with breasts or as a bisexual figure. Several Bes figures can stand side by
side.[87] Bes figures were very popular in Syria-Palestine and are attested at
several sites in Israel and Judah.[88] The woman playing the lyre is simply a

86. Pirhiya Beck, "The Drawings from Ḥorvat Teiman (Kuntillet ʿAjrud)," *Tel Aviv* 9 (1982): 3-68; Keel and Uehlinger, 217-23. For the iconography of Bes, see Veronica Wilson, "The Iconography of Bes with Particular Reference to the Cypriot Evidence," *Levant* 7 (1975): 77-103.

87. Hadley, *The Cult of Asherah*, 137-38.

88. See Zevit, 388.

human musician, playing for the deities.[89] The Bes figures are presumably drawn for apotropaic purposes. On this interpretation, the drawings are not related to the inscription. Indeed, as Othmar Keel and Christoph Uehlinger point out, there are several other drawings on the pithoi, and no one has argued that they should be related to any of the inscriptions.[90] Recently, however, precisely such an argument has been advanced by Brian Schmidt, who also argues that the overlap between the inscription and the figures is meant to indicate an association between them.[91] Hadley suggests that the goddess Asherah is depicted in another drawing on Pithos A (on the other side of the pithos), in the form of a sacred tree flanked by two ibexes.[92] But that drawing has no evident relationship to the inscription. It should be said that the interpretation of the standing figures as depictions of Bes is not without its problems.[93] Schmidt insists, reasonably, that "one cannot unequivocally assume that they must be the god Bes or that they cannot represent Yahweh and Asherah."[94] But nonetheless, it is very doubtful that the drawing can be used to shed any light on the inscription, while the discussion remains inconclusive.

To resolve the interpretation of the inscriptional references to "Yahweh and his asherah," then, we must look for context to the Hebrew Bible, where the word asherah occurs some 40 times.[95] Most of these occurrences can be understood to refer to a cult object — a pole or stylized tree planted by the altar. Olyan has argued persuasively that the asherah was a standard and legitimate part of the cult of Yahweh, in both the northern and the southern kingdoms.[96] Each of the reforming kings of Judah, Asa (1 Kgs 15:12-13), Hezekiah (2 Kgs 18:4), and Josiah (2 Kgs 23:4, 6, 7), is said to have removed the asherah from Jerusalem, and this suggests that

89. Dever, *BASOR* 255 (1984): 21-37 (22-25), argues that the seated figure is Asherah, but there is no clear evidence that ever shows a goddess playing a lyre, or with music at all. See Keel and Uehlinger, 223, 241.

90. Keel and Uehlinger, 241.

91. Brian Schmidt, 107-8.

92. Hadley, *The Cult of Asherah*, 153.

93. Hadley, *The Cult of Asherah*, 138-39.

94. Schmidt, 108.

95. Olyan, 1-22; Hadley, *The Cult of Asherah*, 54-83; Steve A. Wiggins, *A Reassessment of "Asherah": A Study According to the Textual Sources of the First Two Millennia B.C.E.* AOAT 235 (Neukirchen-Vluyn: Neukirchener, 1993), 91-131; Dever, *Did God Have a Wife?* 211-15.

96. Olyan, 9.

at other times it was not disputed.[97] Deuteronomy 16:21 commands: "You shall not plant for yourself an asherah, any tree, beside the altar of Yahweh your God." There would have been no need for the prohibition if the practice were not current. The practice of planting a tree beside the altar is attested already in Gen 21:33 ("Abraham planted a tamarisk tree in Beersheba, and called there on the name of Yahweh, El Olam"). It is anomalous that the asherah is sometimes linked with Baal (Judg 6:25, 28, 30). The anomaly can be explained as confusion of Asherah and Ashtart, whether accidental or willful.[98] Ashtart was a major consort of Baal in Canaanite religion and is also linked with him in several biblical passages.[99] It is noteworthy that while prophets such as Elijah and Hosea polemicize against the cult of Baal, they do not mention the asherah. Prophets of Asherah are mentioned in 1 Kgs 18:19, in the context of the Mount Carmel story, but unlike the prophets of Baal they are not said to be slaughtered. There is no clear mention of either the goddess or the cultic object in Hosea (although Wellhausen proposed one by emendation).[100] Opposition to the asherah is found primarily, even if not exclusively, in the so-called Deuteronomistic corpus and in a few other passages, notably Exod 34:13, where Deuteronomistic influence is highly probable.[101]

But was the asherah a symbol of the presence of Yahweh, in some way, or did it imply the continued worship of the goddess? (It should be noted

97. So also Susan Ackerman, "At Home with the Goddess," in *Symbiosis, Symbolism, and the Power of the Past: Canaan, Ancient Israel and Their Neighbors from the Late Bronze Age through Roman Palaestina*, ed. William G. Dever and Seymour Gitin (Winona Lake: Eisenbrauns, 2003), 455-68 (458).

98. Olyan (11) argues for willful confusion on the part of the Deuteronomistic historian.

99. Judg 2:13; 10:6; 1 Sam 7:3-4; 12:10; 1 Kgs 11:5, 33; 2 Kgs 23:13. Olyan, 10.

100. Julius Wellhausen, *Die kleinen Propheten*, 3rd ed. (Berlin: Reimer, 1898), 134, suggested that Hos 14:9 (Eng. 8), אני עניתי ואשורנו ("I have answered him and watched over him"), be emended to עני ענתו ואשרתו ("I am his Anath and his Asherah"). The emendation is generally rejected, but John Day argues, "That there is a word play on the names of these deities is plausible enough"; *Yahweh and the Gods and Goddesses of Canaan*, 58.

101. So esp. Olyan, 1-22. The case for Deuteronomistic additions to Exod 34:11-13 was made already by Martin Noth, *Exodus*. OTL (Philadelphia: Westminster, 1962), 262, although Wiggins (98) notes that it is not certain. Georg Braulik, "The Rejection of the Goddess Asherah in Israel," in *The Theology of Deuteronomy* (Berkeley: BIBAL, 1994), 165-82, insists that the Deuteronomists were not the originators of the opposition to Asherah. The evidence for a prophetic critique, however, lies primarily in Hos 4:17-19 and 14:9(8), and neither text is clear.

that the use of the article does not preclude reference to a goddess, as the article is used with Baal and Ashtart or Ashtoreth.)[102] A few texts, at least, seem to require an allusion to the goddess. Judges 3:7 says that the Israelites worshipped "the Baals and the Asherahs," but a reference to Ashtarts, as in Judg 2:13 and 10:6, would be more plausible in the context. This may also be the case in 1 Kgs 18:19, where Elijah challenges Ahab to assemble the 450 prophets of Baal and the 400 prophets of Asherah, who eat at Jezebel's table. The reference to Asherah here is problematic, as Asherah was no longer worshipped in Jezebel's home town of Sidon at this time, and besides, the prophets of Asherah do not appear again in the story. The reference, then, may well be secondary.[103] It is noteworthy, however, that whoever inserted the reference assumed that "the Asherah" was a deity with her own prophets. More significant is the notice in 1 Kgs 15:13 that King Asa removed his mother Maacah from being queen mother because she had made "an abominable image" for Asherah. Presumably, Maacah had not just planted a tree. In earlier times, Asherah had often been depicted as a naked woman.[104] In any case, it is clear that the object in question was made for a goddess. According to 2 Kgs 21:7, Manasseh made a carved image *(pesel)* of Asherah and set it in the temple of Yahweh. (The passage states earlier that he made "an asherah," that is, a pole or stylized tree, which was presumably a different object.[105]) 2 Kings 23:4 mentions "the vessels made for Baal, Asherah, and all the host of heaven," in the context of Josiah's purge of the temple. Since Baal and the host of heaven are deities, it is natural to assume that Asherah is a deity too. Mark Smith argues that this reading is not compelling: "All three are recipients of cultic paraphernalia, but there is no reason not to suppose that the asherah and not a goddess was the object of cultic items. This is precisely the way the asherah of the Jerusalem temple is presented in the same chapter."[106] 2 Kings 23:7 refers to women weaving for Asherah (or the asherah). But Smith here seems to miss the point of clothing a statue. In the words of A. Leo

102. Nicholas Wyatt, "Asherah," in *DDD*, 101.

103. So Olyan, 8. The reference is defended, however, by Wiggins, 111; Wyatt, 102. The passage is marked with an asterisk in Origen's Hexapla.

104. Ruth Hestrin, "Understanding Asherah: Exploring Semitic Iconography," *BAR* 17/5 (1991): 50-59.

105. Silvia Schroer, *In Israel gab es Bilder?* OBO 74 (Göttingen: Vandenhoeck & Ruprecht, 1987), 41, suggests that the image was in the form of a suckling cow.

106. Mark Smith, *The Early History of God*, 128.

Oppenheim apropos of ancient Mesopotamia: "The deity was considered present in its image if it showed certain specific features and paraphernalia and was cared for in the appropriate manner."[107] The statue represents the goddess, and offerings made to it are made to her. It is difficult to imagine why women would want to weave clothes for a stylized tree, or for an object that did not represent a deity.[108]

Jeremiah 2:27 also implies that there is a deity behind the sacred tree, so to speak, when he complains about those "who say to a tree, 'You are my father,' and to a stone, 'You gave me birth.'" This passage is evidently a parody of the usual accoutrements of the cult of Yahweh, the *maṣṣēbâ* and asherah, which reverses the paternal and maternal symbolism of the cult objects. But it implies that the worshippers did not look on these objects as "mere symbols," but as objects that represented and mediated the power of the deities.

In view of the fact that at various times there was an image of Asherah in the Jerusalem temple, it seems reasonable to assume that the cult of the goddess was alive and well before Josiah's reform and that Asherah had not simply been assimilated by Yahweh. Accordingly, the epigraphic references to "Yahweh and his asherah" should be assumed to imply recognition of the goddess too, even if the asherah is understood as the symbol of the goddess rather than the goddess herself. Olyan's conclusion that "naming the cult symbol of the deity is synonymous with naming the deity herself" may be somewhat overstated, but he is surely right that "the deity and his or her symbol are inseparable."[109]

To be sure, Asherah is subordinated to Yahweh, and her importance in the religion may have been no greater than that of the Virgin Mary in traditional Roman Catholicism. But she evidently had a prominent place both in northern Israel and in Judah and enjoyed official status more often than not. Her popularity in private devotion may well be indicated by the proliferation of terracotta female figurines, of which more than two thousand

107. A. Leo Oppenheim, *Ancient Mesopotamia: Portrait of a Dead Civilization* (Chicago: University of Chicago Press, 1964), 184.

108. Mark Smith finds a possible allusion to Asherah in Gen 49:25 and allows that she may have been consort of El, but not of Yahweh, in early Israelite religion.

109. Olyan, 32. Wiggins, 190, does not concur with Olyan, but nonetheless concludes that a relationship between Asherah and "the asherah" is most probable. See now also David Pinchansky, *Twilight of the Gods: Polytheism in the Hebrew Bible* (Louisville: Westminster John Knox, 2005), 75-89, who argues on the basis of the archaeological evidence that Asherah was consort of Yahweh.

have been found in all sorts of contexts.[110] These depict a female figure with large bare breasts, but the lower body is usually rendered as a pillar (hence the name, "pillar figurines"). They are not explicitly identified as Asherah, or even as a goddess, but they can hardly be dismissed as toys.[111]

Other Evidence of Polytheistic Worship

Asherah was not the only deity other than Yahweh who was venerated in ancient Israel, nor even the only goddess. It is clear from the biblical record that Baal was Yahweh's main rival, especially in northern Israel, although the worshippers may not have perceived the two gods as adversaries. At the time of Josiah's reform the Jerusalem temple was cluttered not only with the cultic paraphernalia of Baal and Asherah, but also that of "the whole host of heaven," especially the sun.[112] After the destruction of Jerusalem, Jer. 44:16-18 reports that Judeans who had fled to Egypt resolved to "do everything that we have vowed, make offerings to the queen of heaven and pour out libations to her, just as we and our ancestors, our kings and our officials, used to do in the towns of Judah and in the streets of Jerusalem. We used to have plenty of food, and prospered, and saw no misfortune. But from the time we stopped making offerings to the queen of heaven and pouring out libations to her, we have lacked everything and have perished by the sword and by famine." [113]

This cult was performed mainly by women, but as they say to Jeremiah, "do you think that we made cakes for her, marked with her image,

110. Dever, "Folk Religion in Early Israel," 51-52; *Did God Have a Wife?* 176-88; Raz Kletter, *The Judean Pillar Figurines and the Archaeology of Asherah* (Oxford: BAR, 1996). Cf. Zevit, 267-74; Hadley, *The Cult of Asherah,* 196-205; Hestrin, *BAR* 17/5 (1991): 57.

111. As was suggested by Dale W. Manor, "Cult Objects or Toys: A Re-evaluation of Figurines in the Levant," a paper read at the Annual Meeting of the Society of Biblical Literature (Boston, 5 December 1987). Tikva Frymer-Kensky, *In the Wake of the Goddesses,* 159, denies that these figurines represent personalized goddesses and characterizes them as "a visual metaphor . . . a kind of tangible prayer for fertility and nourishment."

112. See William G. Dever, "The Silence of the Text: An Archaeological Commentary on 2 Kings 23," in *Scripture and Other Artifacts: Essays on the Bible and Archaeology in Honor of Philip J. King,* ed. Michael D. Coogan, J. Cheryl Exum, and Lawrence E. Stager (Louisville: Westminster John Knox, 1994), 143-68.

113. See Susan Ackerman, *Under Every Green Tree: Popular Religion in Sixth-Century Judah.* HSM 46 (Atlanta: Scholars, 1992), 5-35.

and poured out libations to her without our husbands' being involved?" (Jer 44:19). The queen of heaven is most probably Ashtart, or perhaps a fusion of Ashtart and Ishtar,[114] but the passage provides resounding affirmation of goddess worship in ancient Judah in the Babylonian era.

There is also the evidence of polytheistic worship by the Jewish garrison at Elephantine in the south of Egypt in the 5th century B.C.E.[115] The deities acknowledged include Anathyahu and Anathbethel, presumably particular manifestations of the goddess Anath, who is well known from the Ugaritic texts.[116] One papyrus (AP 22) lists contributions not only for Yahu, as the God of Israel is called, but also for Eshembethel and Anathbethel. The suggestion of Bezalel Porten, that these funds may have been "a good-will gesture or may have been derived from Arameans whose names appeared on the lost columns,"[117] is a strained attempt to avoid the obvious implication of polytheism. A deity called Herembethel is also attested. The settlers had migrated to Egypt in the 6th century or earlier. Their religious observances may have been influenced by their Aramean neighbors at Elephantine. The name Bethel, and compounds thereof, do not necessarily refer to the Israelite town of that name. A god Bethel is known from the 7th century, mostly in an Aramaic context,[118] but also from Jer 48:13, which suggests that Bethel was to Israel as Chemosh was to Moab: "Then Moab shall be ashamed of Chemosh, as the house of Israel was ashamed of Bethel, their confidence." We do not know whether the ancestors of the Judeans in Elephantine had worshipped these deities before they migrated to Egypt.[119]

114. Ackerman, *Under Every Green Tree,* 34.

115. Karel van der Toorn, "Anat-Yahu, Some Other Deities and the Jews of Elephantine," *Numen* 39 (1992): 80-101.

116. Neal H. Walls, *The Goddess Anat in Ugaritic Myth.* SBLDS 135 (Atlanta: Scholars, 1992). William F. Albright, *Archaeology and the Religion of Israel* (Baltimore: Johns Hopkins University Press, 1942), 162-68, argued that the forms are not related to the Canaanite goddess, but that Anathyahu should be understood as "providence of Yahweh" (taking *anath* from the Aramaic noun for "time"). I do not find this proposal persuasive. See, however, Olyan, 56, n. 77.

117. Bezalel Porten, "The Jews in Egypt," in *The Cambridge History of Judaism,* 1: *Introduction; The Persian Period,* ed. W. D. Davies and Louis Finkelstein (Cambridge: Cambridge University Press, 1984), 372-400 (392). Porten grants that there is evidence for "individual Jewish contact with paganism" in letter-greetings and judicial oaths.

118. See Wolfgang Röllig, "Bethel," in *DDD,* 174.

119. Van der Toorn, *Numen* 39 (1992): 95, argues that "the concept of anat-Yahu came into existence on Israelite soil: yet . . . it was primarily at home in the Aramaean community there." Like many scholars, he assumes that the garrison had its origin in northern Israel.

There is no dispute that Yahweh was the national god of both Israel and Judah and that he was the deity most widely worshipped. The inscriptions from Khirbet el-Qôm and Kuntillet ʿAjrud confirm this. In a study published in 1986, Jeffrey Tigay calculated that 89 percent of Israelite theophoric names in the Hebrew Bible are Yahwistic, as against 11 percent that contain the names of pagan deities (excluding names with -el, which are ambiguous).[120] In the inscriptional evidence he surveyed, the ratio was 94.1 percent to 5.9 percent, and of the pagan deities mentioned in the Bible, only Baal is well represented, especially in the Samaria ostraca.[121] The numbers are misleading, since names that mention -el and names that mention no deity at all are excluded from the tally, and some names are excluded as non-Israelite. It has been estimated that a figure of ca. 46 percent would be more accurate for the percentage of names that are Yahwistic.[122] Moreover, as Tigay himself conceded, "even polytheists could give some or all of their children Yahwistic names if Yahweh was one of the gods they worshipped."[123] Ahab, husband of Jezebel, named sons Ahaziah and J(eh)oram, and Athaliah may have been his daughter. The Ammonite onomasticon is overwhelmingly dominated by El, and we do not know that the Ammonites were monotheists. Ashtart (Athtart), Athirat (Asherah), and Anath all received sacrifices at Ugarit, but Ashtart does not appear in any personal names, and Asherah only appears in one.[124] In short, names do not tell the whole story, and Tigay's findings about the onomasticon are not incompatible with the worship of other deities, and specifically goddesses, besides Yahweh.

Scholarly Reactions

Scholars have reacted to the evidence for goddess worship in various ways. Norbert Lohfink calls for a distinction between actual practice and what

120. Jeffrey H. Tigay, *You Shall Have No Other Gods: Israelite Religion in the Light of Hebrew Inscriptions.* HSS 31 (Atlanta: Scholars, 1986), 7. See also his essay, "Israelite Religion: The Onomastic and Epigraphic Evidence," in Miller, Hanson and McBride, 157-94.

121. Tigay, *You Shall Have No Other Gods,* 14.

122. Tilde Binger, *Asherah: Goddesses in Ugarit, Israel and the Old Testament.* JSOTSup 212 (Sheffield: Sheffield Academic, 1994), 30-35. I am grateful to Nicolas Wyatt for bringing this reference to my attention.

123. Tigay, *You Shall Have No Other Gods,* 17.

124. Tigay, *You Shall Have No Other Gods,* 19-20.

was normative.[125] But whose view was accounted normative? That of the prophets, or that of the kings? Patrick Miller distinguishes between "orthodox" and "heterodox" Yahwism. He grants, of course, that "orthodoxy is a somewhat slippery term, one practitioner's orthodoxy being another's heterodoxy and vice versa." But he continues: "There is some justification for suggesting that the tradition that became the end point of Israelite religion, or more accurately, the character it had as it moved into its two primary and immediately continuing streams, Judaism and Christianity, serves to define — in retrospect — what was orthodox and normative."[126] The first principle of orthodox Yahwism, we are told, was that "exclusive worship of the deity Yahweh was expected."[127] But expected by whom? By later Jews and Christians "in retrospect"? Exclusive worship of Yahweh was evidently demanded by the Deuteronomistic reformers and by other "Yahweh-alone" advocates (although it is striking that prophets like Amos and Hosea do not explicitly denounce Asherah). But to distinguish between orthodoxy and heterodoxy in this way is to impose a theological master-narrative on Israelite religion and to deny ancient history its own integrity.

More often, historians of the religion of Israel distinguish between "official" or "state" religion, on the one hand, and family or "popular" religion, on the other. Rainer Albertz has argued that "the kind of religion practised in the families in this time [i.e., before the monarchy] largely proves to be uninfluenced by the recent rise of Yahweh religion" and manifests "internal religious pluralism" that continued down to Josiah's reform.[128] But Albertz also affirms that "the popularity of the worship of a goddess alongside Yahweh throughout the whole pre-exilic period can hardly be overestimated. . . . Nor can this tradition simply be dismissed as 'popular piety.' The Ashera cult was demonstrably practised even in the royal family (I Kings 15.13) and in the Jerusalem state sanctuary (II Kings 23.4)."[129]

125. Lohfink, "Zur Geschichte der Diskussion," 22: "I regard it as methodologically incorrect to dismiss the idea that a group may have had a norm even if it was often not observed, and simply to regard the available data as reflecting the norm."

126. Patrick D. Miller, *The Religion of Ancient Israel* (Louisville: Westminster John Knox, 2000), 47.

127. Patrick D. Miller, 48.

128. Rainer Albertz, *A History of Israelite Religion in the Old Testament Period*. OTL (Louisville: Westminster John Knox, 1994), 1:95.

129. Albertz, *A History of Israelite Religion*, 1:86-87. On the problems associated with

A Tradition of Polytheism?

Neither can polytheism or goddess worship be attributed solely to "foreign influence" and the syncretism of the upper classes in the period of the monarchy. While Genesis is remarkably silent on the subject of goddess worship, we are told that Abraham planted a tamarisk tree in Beer-sheba and called there on the name of the Lord, El Olam (Gen 21:33). The tree beside a place of worship of El can reasonably be construed as an asherah, and the stone that Jacob erects in Bethel is explicitly called a *maṣṣēbâ* (Gen 28:18). The worship of Baal is well attested in Judges (2:11-13; 3:7; 6:25-32; 8:33; 9:4). In Judg 2:13 Baal is linked with the Ashtarts and in 3:7 with the Asherahs. The latter reference may be a mistake for Ashtarts, and some of these passages reflect a Deuteronomistic perspective and may be anachronistic,[130] but the temple of Baal-berith in Shechem, mentioned in Judg 9:4, is never mentioned again in the later books.[131] Kaufmann argued that Baal was an epithet of Yahweh in this period, and that loyal devotees of Yahweh such as David and Saul would not otherwise have given their sons names containing the element "baal" (such as Eshbaal or Meribbaal).[132] But this begs the question of whether the worship of Yahweh was exclusive in this period. Baal was certainly viewed as a different deity by the biblical editors, and the names Eshbaal and Meribbaal, which are preserved in 1 Chronicles 8-9, are altered to Ishbosheth ("man of shame") and Mephibosheth in 2 Samuel 2-4.

The admittedly meager evidence must be supplemented with the findings of archaeology. The so-called "Bull Site" in the territory of Manasseh from the 12th century is named for a bronze bull found at the site. The bull could symbolize Yahweh, as it does later, in the northern kingdom of Israel, but can more easily be associated with the Canaanite deity El.[133] It does not

---

"popular religion" in the Israelite context, see also Dever, "Ancient Israelite Religion," 114-15; *Did God Have a Wife?* 4-9.

130. The story of Gideon's destruction of the altar of Baal and the sacred pole (Judg 6:25, 28) looks suspiciously like Josiah's reform.

131. See Theodore J. Lewis, "Baal-berith," *ABD* 1:550-51; Martin J. Mulder, "Baal-berith," *DDD*, 141-44. There is also mention of a temple of El-berith in Judg 9:46.

132. Kaufmann, 138. Baal may in fact have been used as an epithet of Yahweh. Cf. Hos 2:18 (Eng. 2:16): "On that day, says the Lord, you will call me, 'My husband,' and no longer will you call me, 'My Baal.'"

133. So Dever, "Folk Religion in Early Israel," 29; *Did God Have a Wife?* 136.

10th-century cult stand from Taanach. The bottom tier depicts
a Canaanite goddess (courtesy Helga Weippert)

in itself demonstrate polytheism, but it does show the difficulty in distinguishing an Israelite cult site from a Canaanite one in the early period.

A cult stand from Taanach, near Megiddo, dated to the 10th century,
has four tiers of iconic representation. The top tier shows a quadruped carrying a winged sun-disk on its back. The next row contains a sacred tree
with two ibexes on their hind legs on either side. The third has a pair of
sphinxes or cherubim with female heads and lion bodies, with a vacant

space between them. Of greatest interest for this discussion is the bottom tier, which has two lions flanking a nude female figure, who holds them by the ears. This figure has been taken to represent either Asherah, Ashtart, or Anath. Dever insists, plausibly, that "she can be no other than Asherah, the Canaanite mother goddess. Asherah is known throughout the Levant in this period as the 'Lion Lady,' and she is often depicted nude, riding on the back of a lion."[134] Asherah is most probably also represented in the third tier (from the bottom) as the sacred tree. The vacant space on the second tier has been interpreted as the entrance to a shrine, guarded by cherubim.[135] Whether this object pertained to a Yahwistic cult depends on the interpretation of the top tier. The animal is variously interpreted as a young bull or as a horse. The solar disk is usually taken to represent a deity, whether Baal or Yahweh (if the animal is a bull) or simply as the sun-god, although Keel and Uehlinger argue that it represents "the heavens that crown the shrine" rather than any particular deity.[136] Solar metaphors are used for Yahweh in the Bible. For example, Ps 84:12 (Eng. 11) declares, "For a sun and a shield is Yahweh."[137] According to Judg 1:27-28, Taanach was one of the cities from which the tribe of Manasseh failed to drive out the Canaanites but later put them to forced labor.[138] In short, a Yahwistic interpretation of the cult stand is possible but uncertain. What this cult stand shows, again, is the pervasive Canaanite environment of early Israel and the difficulty of distinguishing with confidence between Israelite and Canaanite.

Nude female "plaque" figurines are well attested in Canaan in the Late Bronze Age. The "pillar figurines" that become common in the period of the monarchy are different in form, as they do not show the hips and pu-

134. Dever, "Folk Religion in Early Israel," 35; *Did God Have a Wife?* 219-21. See further Patrick D. Miller, 43-45; Keel and Uehlinger, 157-60; Zevit, 318-25, and esp. Hestrin, *BAR* 17/5 (1991): 50-59.

135. So Ruth Hestrin, "The Cult Stand from Ta'anach and Its Religious Background," in *Phoenicia and the East Mediterranean in the First Millennium B.C.*, ed. Edward Lipiński. Studia Phoenicia 5 (Louvain: Peeters, 1987), 61-77 (71).

136. Keel and Uehlinger, 160.

137. See further Mark Smith, *The Early History of God*, 148-59; Day, *Yahweh and the Gods and Goddesses*, 151-63; and the maximalist thesis of J. Glen Taylor, *Yahweh and the Sun: Biblical and Archaeological Evidence for Sun Worship in Ancient Israel*. JSOTSup 111 (Sheffield: JSOT, 1993). Taylor's interpretation of the cult stand can be found on pp. 24-36.

138. For the archeological evidence on Taanach, see Albert E. Glock, "Taanach," *ABD* 6:287-90.

denda, and it has been suggested that they reflect Phoenician influence rather than native development.[139] Nonetheless, as Hadley concludes, "although a 'direct descent' may not be proved, the possibility remains that there may be some sort of 'continuity of intent'; that is, the pillar figurines may be a typically Israelite way of portraying the goddess (albeit influenced by the Phoenician figurines), whereas the plaque figurines were the earlier Late Bronze Age method of representation."[140]

Sketchy and contested as all this evidence is, it renders unlikely the view that goddess worship in Israel and Judah was due to foreign influence in the period of the monarchy. In the words of Nicholas Wyatt:

> The Deuteronomistic historians have done their work so well that scholars are prone to talk of the asherah and other cultic elements as evidence of syncretism, or of (extraneous) 'Canaanite' elements in the Israelite and Judahite cults. In view of the epigraphic evidence . . . it is safer to begin from the supposition that the religion of both kingdoms only gradually moved towards monolatry and then monotheism . . . and was otherwise, at both popular and official levels, basically polytheistic in nature. Furthermore, there is no justification for ideas of 'foreignness' about the Canaanite elements in religion in Palestine. Israel and Judah are to be seen as wholly within that cultural tradition.[141]

The Significance of the Revisionist View

We should not conclude, of course, that there were no differences at all between Israel and Judah and their neighbors. The existence of a "Yahweh-alone" movement, even as a minority, would prove enormously important over time, and some such sentiment may have been quite old. On the evidence as yet available, Hebrew prophecy was significantly different from that of other Near Eastern peoples in the degree of its concern with moral and social issues.[142] The same might be said of biblical law. Moreover,

139. Miriam Tadmor, "Female Cult Figurines in Late Canaan and Early Israel: Archaeological Evidence," in *Studies in the Period of David and Solomon and Other Essays*, ed. Tomoo Ishida (Winona Lake: Eisenbrauns, 1982), 139-73.

140. Hadley, *The Cult of Asherah*, 196.

141. Wyatt, 102.

142. See Martti Nissinen, ed., *Prophecy in Its Ancient Near Eastern Context: Mesopo-*

there seems to have been an exclusivistic strain in Yahwistic religion from very early times, even if it did not always dominate.[143] The point here is not that any particular feature was entirely unique to Israel, but that differences in degree and emphasis give the religion a configuration that becomes quite distinctive over time.[144]

Furthermore, people with a taste for orthodoxy and normativity may well argue that all we have been discussing is the prehistory of the Bible. While the religion of Judaism in the Second Temple period was still not strictly monotheistic,[145] it was predominantly monolatrous,[146] and goddess worship seems to have died out[147] (despite occasional attempts to view the figure of Wisdom as a goddess).[148] It is still possible to argue, in the words of Raphael Patai, that "the introduction of monotheism into the consciousness of mankind is the greatest single achievement of the ancient Hebrews."[149]

The fact of the eventual triumph of monolatry can not be disputed. Nonetheless, it is salutary to remember that in the beginning it was not so.

---

tamian, Biblical, and Arabian Perspectives. SBLSymS 13 (Atlanta: Society of Biblical Literature, 2000).

143. So esp. Halpern, "'Brisker Pipes than Poetry.'"

144. See Peter Machinist, "The Question of Distinctiveness in Ancient Israel," in *Ah, Assyria — : Studies in Assyrian History and Ancient Near Eastern Historiography Presented to Hayim Tadmor,* ed. Mordechai Cogan and Israel Eph'al. Scripta Hierosolymitana 33 (Jerusalem: Magnes, 1991), 196-212; Theodore J. Lewis, "Divine Images and Aniconism in Ancient Israel," *JAOS* 118 (1998): 36-53 (esp. 53).

145. See my essay, "Jewish Monotheism and Christian Theology," in Shanks and Meinhardt, 81-105; Carey C. Newman, James R. Davila, and Gladys S. Lewis, eds., *The Jewish Roots of Christological Monotheism.* JSJSup 63 (Leiden: Brill, 1999).

146. See Larry W. Hurtado, *One God, One Lord* (Philadelphia: Fortress, 1988); *Lord Jesus Christ: Devotion to Jesus in Earliest Christianity* (Grand Rapids: Wm. B. Eerdmans, 2003), 29-48.

147. Wyatt suggests, orally, that the decline of Asherah worship may be related to the demise of the monarchy, as it was associated with the queen mother.

148. See Martin A. Klopfenstein, "Auferstehung der Göttin in der spätisraelitischen Weisheit von Prov 1-9?" in Dietrich and Klopfenstein, 531-42. Judith M. Hadley, "Chasing Shadows? The Quest for the Historical Goddess," in *Congress Volume Cambridge, 1995,* ed. John A. Emerton. VTSup 66 (Leiden: Brill, 1997), 169-84 (181), suggests that "the best interpretation of the apparent apotheosis of ḥokmâ in Israelite wisdom literature is that the gradual eradication (or assimilation into Yahweh) of legitimate goddesses such as Asherah and Astarte has prompted a counter reaction (perhaps even subconsciously) where the feminine needs to be expressed."

149. Raphael Patai, *The Jewish Mind* (New York: Scribner, 1977), 349.

And while some aspects of early Israelite religion, such as child-sacrifice,[150] are not to be lamented, the development of monotheism was not necessarily unqualified gain. The suppression of internal religious pluralism inevitably limited the acceptable forms of religious expression, and the centralization of the cult inevitably made it more difficult for some people to participate in rituals that were highly valued in the society. While goddess worship cannot be equated with women's religion, there is some reason to think that the traditional religious practices of women were especially disrupted by the reforms. As Phyllis Bird has remarked, "in general, women appear to be identified primarily with local rather than national or centralized forms of religious expression, and with 'folk' practice (often viewed as 'superstition') rather than the learned tradition."[151] The issue raised by any imposition of orthodoxy or normativity concerns the ability or right to define what is true religion or acceptable practice. There is always some tension between the demands of community cohesion and the freedom of individuals. The insistence on monolatry in the later biblical tradition served the cause of community solidarity well, but there was inevitably some cost in the suppression of practices deemed heterodox, which may have been harmless or even beneficial for the practitioners.

The revisionist scholarship on the religion of Israel has been driven primarily by historical criticism, especially by archaeological discoveries. It has postmodern overtones nonetheless, insofar as it involves resistance towards the biblical (especially Deuteronomistic) master-narrative and attempts to retrieve religious views that were relegated to the margins by the biblical editors. To a great degree, it has involved re-reading the biblical text against the grain of the editors' intentions, in effect deconstructing the canonical account of Israelite religion. The revisionist account is by no means final and will remain contested, because of both the limitation of the evidence and continuing archaeological discoveries. But it reminds us again that the biblical account is by no means a simple reflection of ancient reality. Rather, it is a highly ideological construction of a phenomenon that could be viewed very differently.

150. John Day, *Molech: A God of Human Sacrifice in the Old Testament* (Cambridge: Cambridge University Press, 1989); Jon D. Levenson, *The Death and Resurrection of the Beloved Son* (New Haven: Yale University Press, 1993), 3-17.

151. Phyllis A. Bird, "Israelite Religion and the Faith of Israel's Daughters," in *Missing Persons and Mistaken Identities*, 103-20 (111). Cf. the remarks of Dever, "Ancient Israelite Religion," 115.

Is a Postmodern Biblical
Theology Possible?

The changes in our views of the history and the religion of Israel and of the ethical import of the Old Testament for political and feminist liberation, which we have described in the last four chapters, do not, to any significant degree, result from postmodernist critical theory. They are, rather, the result of the ongoing pursuit of historical criticism and the widening of the circle of participants in biblical studies to include others besides white European and North American males.[1] They do, however, result from a postmodern situation, one that is characterised by pluralism and diversity, and by the collapse of paradigms that were once dominant and the absence of any consensus to replace them. To a great degree, the old paradigms in biblical studies were theological, tacitly if not explicitly. It is not surprising, then, that the impact of their collapse should be felt especially in the subfield of biblical theology.

---

1. Walter Brueggemann argues that precisely the expansion of the conversation constitutes the postmodern situation. Citing Richard Rorty to the effect that "objectivity is an agreement of everyone in the room," Brueggemann comments that "the problem is that in the great career of Western objectivity very few people were let into the room, which was peopled largely by white males of a certain class and perspective"; *Texts Under Negotiation: The Bible and Postmodern Imagination* (Minneapolis: Fortress, 1993), 8. For Rorty's view of objectivity as agreement, see his *Philosophy and the Mirror of Nature* (Princeton: Princeton University Press, 1979), 335.

The Nature of Biblical Theology

"The concept of biblical theology is a *contested* concept, and this is likely to remain so," writes James Barr.[2] Whether or not it is deemed a viable enterprise depends, naturally enough, on what one understands the nature of the enterprise to be. Historically, biblical theology was developed in German Protestantism of the late 18th century, in contrast to dogmatic theology, and carried overtones of Protestant commitment to *sola scriptura*.[3] Hence, there has been a persistent concern that biblical theology be based on "the text itself," although in practice it has often been shaped by the categories of systematic theology.[4] In the 20th century, the contrast was more often with the history of religion.[5] This has often led to an emphasis on the supposedly distinctive aspects of the religion of Israel. But biblical theology is distinguished primarily by its focus on the canonical text (as distinct from the ancient Near Eastern context) and its concern for the relevance of the material for the modern world and especially for the Christian churches. For some scholars, but by no means all, biblical theology presupposes a faith commitment or can only be done from a

2. James Barr, *The Concept of Biblical Theology*, 605.

3. See Ben C. Ollenburger, "From Timeless Ideas to the Essence of Religion: Method in Old Testament Theology before 1930," in *The Flowering of Old Testament Theology: A Reader in Twentieth-Century Old Testament Theology, 1930-1990*, ed. Ollenburger, E. A. Martens and Gerhard F. Hasel (Winona Lake: Eisenbrauns, 1992), 3-19, esp. 3-6; H.-J. Kraus, *Die Biblische Theologie* (Neukirchen-Vluyn: Neukirchener, 1970); Gerhard Hasel, *Old Testament Theology: Basic Issues in the Current Debate*, 4th ed. (Grand Rapids: Wm. B. Eerdmans, 1991), 10-18; John H. Hayes and Frederick C. Prussner, *Old Testament Theology: Its History and Development* (Atlanta: John Knox, 1985), 1-71.

4. See the remarks of Rolf Rendtorff, "Approaches to Old Testament Theology," in *Problems in Biblical Theology: Essays in Honor of Rolf Knierim*, ed. Henry T. C. Sun and Keith L. Eades (Grand Rapids: Wm. B. Eerdmans, 1997), 13-26, esp. 16-17, with reference to Walther Eichrodt, *Theology of the Old Testament*, 2 vols. OTL (Philadelphia: Westminster, 1961-67).

5. Barr, *The Concept of Biblical Theology*, 9-11. See esp. the classic debate between Otto Eissfeldt ("The History of Israelite-Jewish Religion and Old Testament Theology," in Ollenberger, Martens, and Hasel, 20-29) and Walther Eichrodt ("Does Old Testament Theology Still Have Independent Significance within Old Testament Scholarship?" 30-39). For a recent treatment of the subject, see Rainer Albertz, "Religionsgeschichte Israels statt Theologie des Alten Testaments! Plädoyer für eine forschungsgeschichtliche Umorientierung," *JBTh* 10 (1995): 3-24. This issue of the journal is entitled "Religionsgeschichte Israels oder Theologie des Alten Testaments?" See now also Leo G. Perdue, *Reconstructing Old Testament Theology*, 25-75.

specific confessional perspective.[6] For others, it is primarily a descriptive discipline, concerned first of all with "what it meant" and only secondarily with "what it means," in the famous distinction of Krister Stendahl.[7] Nonetheless, it is probably fair to say that it is the concern for "what it means" that is most distinctive about biblical theology. As Rudolf Bultmann put it with reference to the New Testament, in biblical theology historical reconstruction stands in the service of interpretation of the biblical writings, "under the presupposition that they have something to say to the present."[8] It is generally an attempt to sum up the abiding significance of the Bible for the modern world. Even a descriptive account of "what it meant" is usually assumed to have some authority or normative status for the present.[9]

My own comments on this topic proceed on the basis of two assumptions. First, the Bible, and specifically the Hebrew Bible or Old Testament, does indeed have abiding significance for the modern world. This much can be seen from the fact that it is regularly adduced in contemporary debates, for better or worse (and often, unfortunately, for worse) on matters of ethics and public policy. Its significance is not limited to inner-church matters, and is a matter of cultural heritage that has to be reckoned with, quite apart from one's faith perspective. Second, any responsible assessment of the Bible's enduring relevance must take account of developments

6. Such an assumption obviously underlies the "canonical approach" of Brevard S. Childs, *Old Testament Theology in a Canonical Context* (Philadelphia: Fortress, 1986); *Biblical Theology of the Old and New Testaments: Theological Reflection on the Christian Bible* (Minneapolis: Fortress, 1993); and the Christocentric approach of Francis Watson, *Text and Truth: Redefining Biblical Theology* (Grand Rapids: Wm. B. Eerdmans, 1997); but also, in quite different ways, the Roman Catholic approach of Roland de Vaux, "Is it Possible to Write a 'Theology of the Old Testament'?" in *The Bible and the Ancient Near East* (Garden City: Doubleday, 1971), 49-62; and the Jewish approach of Jon D. Levenson, *The Hebrew Bible, The Old Testament, and Historical Criticism*. In contrast, Wolfhart Pannenberg, "Problems in a Theology of (Only) the Old Testament," in Sun and Eades, 275-80, writes: "A theology of the Old Testament need not and should not be done on a confessional basis" (280).

7. Krister Stendahl, "Biblical Theology, Contemporary," *IDB* 1 (1962): 418-32.

8. Rudolf Bultmann, *Theology of the New Testament* 2 (New York: Scribner's, 1955): 251.

9. George Lindbeck, "Toward a Postliberal Theology," in *The Return to Scripture in Judaism and Christianity: Essays in Postcritical Scriptural Interpretation,* ed. Peter Ochs (New York: Paulist, 1993), 83-103 (84): "The descriptive task is also a normative one; theologians seek to describe speech and conduct that make sense in terms of a given religion's own standards (for example, its 'grammatical rules')."

in biblical scholarship, although it is under no obligation to accept these developments uncritically. It is, of course, possible to take an ostrichlike posture and persist in fundamentalism of whatever variety without regard for an outside world. My context, however, is an academic one, and my concern is for developing an approach to the Bible that takes account of current scholarship as fully as possible.[10] This concern, in my view, is also highly relevant to the churches, if they at all respect the intelligence and integrity of their members.

In some Christian circles, biblical theology is taken to require that the Old Testament be viewed through the lens of the New or that the two be construed as a unity.[11] Francis Watson goes so far as to say that the books of the Old Testament can be meaningful for Christians only in the full canonical context.[12] But this requires a peculiarly narrow and dogmatic view of Christianity. Many Christians find these books meaningful quite apart from any consideration of the New Testament. Even Brevard Childs, whose canonical approach is in many ways similar to that of Watson, protests that "the task of Old Testament theology is . . . not to Christianize the Old Testament by identifying it with the New Testament witness, but to hear its own theological testimony to the God of Israel."[13] And the theological interpretation of these books, construed as the discussion of what they have to say to the modern world, is of interest to others besides Christians. My interest lies in examining the problems raised by any theological interpretation of biblical texts rather than in conforming the Old Testament or Hebrew Bible to Christian dogma.

---

10. On the different contexts of theological discussion, see David Tracy, *The Analogical Imagination* (New York: Crossroad, 1981), 3-46.

11. So, in different ways, Hartmut Gese, *Vom Sinai zum Zion: Alttestamentliche Beiträge zur biblischen Theologie.* BEvT 64 (Munich: Kaiser, 1974); *Zur biblischen Theologie.* BEvT 78 Munich: Kaiser, 1977); *Essays on Biblical Theology* (Minneapolis: Augsburg, 1981), who favors a traditio-historical approach; and Watson, esp. 177-329 ("The Old Testament in Christological Perspective"). Watson's approach is canonical, but more Christological in focus than that of Childs.

12. Watson, 181. Cf. the notorious remark of Eichrodt, *Theology of the Old Testament,* 1:26, that Judaism has only "a torso-like appearance . . . in separation from Christianity." Watson does not intend to disparage Judaism, but implies that for Christians the Old Testament has a torso-like appearance without the New.

13. Childs, *Old Testament Theology in a Canonical Context,* 9.

The Problem of Diversity

Perhaps the most obvious problem confronting anyone who attempts to sum up what the Old Testament means is the obvious diversity within it. This is, after all, a collection of books, written over several hundred years on any account and shaped to a great degree by the historical crises of ancient Israel and Judah. Johann P. Gabler, whose inaugural address at the University of Altdorf in 1787 is generally accepted as foundational for subsequent biblical theology, already recognized that not everything found in Scripture is normative for modernity.[14] "Who," he asked, "would apply to our times the Mosaic rites which have been invalidated by Christ, or Paul's advice about women veiling themselves in church?"[15] Accordingly, Gabler called for a separation of "those things which in the sacred books refer most immediately to their own times and to the men of those times from those pure notions which divine providence wished to be characteristic of all times and places."[16] In positing such "universal ideas," Gabler was very much a child of his time, the heyday of the Enlightenment.[17]

Later biblical theology tried to address this problem by looking for a "center" of biblical theology — one concept, such as "the covenant" or "election," which was taken as the key to the unity underlying the diversity of the biblical books.[18] It was the great merit of Gerhard von Rad that he quite decisively rejected this quest:[19] "What's it all about with this almost *unisono* asked question about the 'unity', the 'center' of the Old Testament? Is it something so self-evident its proof belongs, so to speak, as a *conditio sine qua non* to an orderly Old Testament theology? . . . Or is this postulate less a matter of historical or theological recognition than a speculative-philosophical principle that becomes effective as an unconscious prem-

---

14. Johann P. Gabler, "An Oration on the Proper Distinction between Biblical and Dogmatic Theology and the Specific Objectives of Each," in Ollenberger, Martens, and Hasel, 489-502.

15. Gabler, 500.

16. Gabler, 496.

17. See the comments of John Sandys-Wunsch and Laurence Eldredge, "J. P. Gabler and the Distinction between Biblical and Dogmatic Theology: Translation, Commentary, and Discussion of His Originality," *SJT* 33 (1980): 133-58, esp. 147.

18. Hasel, 139-71; Rendtorff, 14-15.

19. Gerhard von Rad, *Old Testament Theology,* 2:362: "On the basis of the Old Testament itself, it is truly difficult to answer the question of the unity of that Testament, for it has no focal-point such as is found in the New."

ise?"[20] Not all biblical theologians have taken the point. The *Old Testament Theology* of Horst Dietrich Preuss opts for "election" as the center.[21] But most recent proposals have given up the quest for a center of the Old Testament and celebrate rather the pluralism of different viewpoints.[22]

While von Rad rejected the idea that any one concept or motif could be identified as the center, he also posited an underlying unity in the Old Testament. While acknowledging "the tremendous differences evinced in the specific literary units," he affirmed that "none the less we must anticipate, and mention briefly, what unites them all. . . . The Old Testament writings confine themselves to representing Jahweh's relationship to Israel and the world in one aspect only, namely as a continuing divine activity in history. This implies that in principle Israel's faith is grounded in a theology of history . . . and was shaped and re-shaped by factors in which it saw the hand of Jahweh at work."[23] Von Rad was typical of his generation in construing the Old Testament as history. This was also true of the so-called Biblical Theology movement associated with G. Ernest Wright.[24] But already by the time von Rad wrote, the "salvation history" approach to biblical theology was seen to be problematic.[25] On the one hand, there is much

20. Gerhard von Rad, "Offene Fragen im Umkreis einer Theologie des Alten Testaments," *ThLZ* 88 (1963): 401-16, repr. in his *Gesammelte Studien zum Alten Testament* 2. ThB 48 (Munich: Kaiser, 1973), 289-312, quoted in English by Rendtorff, 14-15.

21. Horst Dietrich Preuss, *Old Testament Theology*, 2 vols. OTL (Louisville: Westminster, 1995-96; German original, Stuttgart: Kohlhammer, 1991), 1:24. Preuss lists and criticizes more than a dozen other proposals.

22. See, e.g., Paul D. Hanson, *The Diversity of Scripture: A Theological Interpretation.* OBT 11 (Philadelphia: Fortress, 1982); Walter Brueggemann, *Theology of the Old Testament: Testimony, Dispute, Advocacy* (Minneapolis: Fortress, 1997); Erhard S. Gerstenberger, *Theologies in the Old Testament* (Minneapolis: Fortress, 2002). Rolf Knierim, "The Task of Old Testament Theology," *HBT* 6 (1984): 25-57 (repr. in Ollenburger, Martens, and Hasel, 467-86) begins: "The Old Testament contains a plurality of theologies. This fact is well established exegetically." See also the comments from a Jewish perspective by Benjamin D. Sommer, "Unity and Plurality in Jewish Canons: The Case of the Oral and Written Torahs," in *One Scripture or Many? Canon from Biblical, Theological, and Philosophical Perspectives,* ed. Christine Helmer and Christoph Landmesser (Oxford: Oxford University Press, 2004), 108-50, esp. 144-46.

23. Von Rad, *Old Testament Theology,* 1:106.

24. G. Ernest Wright, *God Who Acts.* See the comments of Brevard S. Childs, *Biblical Theology in Crisis,* 39-44, and, from a postmodern perspective, David Penchansky, *The Politics of Biblical Theology: A Postmodern Reading* (Macon: Macon University Press, 1995).

25. See esp. Langdon B. Gilkey, "Cosmology, Ontology, and the Travail of Biblical Language," *JR* 41 (1961): 194-205.

material in the Old Testament that does not fit the paradigm. On the other hand, much of the "historylike" material is shown by archaeology and critical analysis to be unhistorical. So, writes von Rad, "These two pictures of Israel's history lie before us — that of modern critical scholarship and that which the faith of Israel constructed — and for the present, we must reconcile ourselves to both of them."[26] The problem is not greatly alleviated by claiming that "the kerygmatic picture too (and this even at the points where it diverges so widely from our historical picture) is founded in the actual history and has not been invented."[27] Von Rad had, in effect, deconstructed his whole approach to biblical theology by honestly pointing to the problem that undermined it. Many scholars agreed with James Barr that "story" rather than "history" was the proper category for the biblical narratives.[28] But this suggestion did not actually advance matters very far. Stories are of different kinds, and since the basic biblical stories were admittedly "historylike," their relation to history as critically reconstructed could not be finessed.[29]

The Collapse of the Foundations

The shift from "history" to "story" is, however, indicative of a broader shift in theological and philosophical discourse away from the quest for secure foundations. For the "Biblical Theology movement" of the mid-20th century, history provided "the foundations of our faith," in the phrase of Roland de Vaux.[30] But, as the discussion of the history of Israel in the last quarter century has shown, these foundations are subject to erosion.[31] Neither have Gabler's "universal ideas," valid in all times and places, stood the

26. Von Rad, *Old Testament Theology,* 1:107.

27. Von Rad, *Old Testament Theology,* 1:108.

28. James Barr, "Story and History in Biblical Theology," *JR* 56 (1976): 1-17. See also Barr, *The Concept of Biblical Theology,* 345-61; and the updated discussion by Ernest Nicholson, "Story and History in the Old Testament," in *Language, Theology and the Bible: Essays in Honour of James Barr,* ed. Samuel E. Balentine and John Barton (Oxford: Clarendon, 1994), 135-50.

29. See further John J. Collins, "The 'Historical Character' of the Old Testament in Recent Biblical Theology," *CBQ* 41 (1979): 185-204, esp. 199.

30. De Vaux, 56-57.

31. See esp. Leo G. Perdue, *The Collapse of History.*

test of time. Even the moral teaching of the Bible is undercut by commandments that are repugnant to modern (and even to ancient) sensibilities.[32] The great story of liberation from Egypt loses its luster when it is viewed from a Canaanite perspective, and biblical concern for the rights of man is too often oblivious to the rights of women. Are there left then any grounds for biblical authority that might claim our allegiance in the modern world?

There is in fact a whole movement in contemporary philosophy and theology that makes a virtue out of necessity and argues that any quest for foundations, in the sense of unassailably certain beliefs, is not only futile but misguided. "Foundationalism" is often associated with the quest of René Descartes for a secure starting point for philosophical reflection and characterized somewhat dismissively as "the Cartesian Anxiety."[33] "Nonfoundationalism" in philosophy is a movement that has its roots in the pragmatism of William James and Charles Sanders Peirce and in Wittgenstein's theory of "language games."[34] Truth is not the correlation of mind and reality, but a matter of coherence within a set of shared beliefs. The most vocal contemporary advocate of nonfoundationalism is probably Richard Rorty.[35] Rorty holds that "it is pictures rather than propositions, metaphors rather than statements, which determine most of our philosophical convictions"[36] and that even "reason is no longer an agency that directs other traditions; it is a tradition in its own right with as much (or as little) claim to the center of the stage as any other tradition."[37] For

32. Gerd Lüdemann, *The Unholy in Scripture;* Jonneke Bekkenkamp and Yvonne Sherwood, eds., *Sanctified Aggression: Legacies of Biblical and Post Biblical Vocabularies of Violence.* JSOTSup 400 (London: T. & T. Clark, 2003).

33. Richard J. Bernstein, *Beyond Objectivism and Relativism* (Philadelphia: University of Pennsylvania Press, 1983), 16-20.

34. John E. Thiel, *Nonfoundationalism.* Guides to Theological Inquiry (Minneapolis: Fortress, 1994), 1-12.

35. Rorty, *Philosophy and the Mirror of Nature; Consequences of Pragmatism; Contingency, Irony, and Solidarity* (Cambridge: Cambridge University Press, 1989). In moral philosophy the major nonfoundationalist voice has been that of Alasdair MacIntyre, *After Virtue: A Study in Moral Theory* (Notre Dame: University of Notre Dame Press, 1981); *Whose Justice? Which Rationality?* See further William M. Sullivan, "After Foundationalism: The Return to Practical Philosophy," in *Anti-Foundationalism and Practical Reasoning,* ed. Evan Simpson (Edmonton: Academic, 1987), 21-44.

36. Rorty, *Philosophy and the Mirror of Nature,* 12.

37. So Paul Feyerabend, *Science in a Free Society* (London: NLB, 1978), 8-9. See the discussion of Rorty by Bernstein, 197-207.

Rorty, there are no transcendent, metaphysical standards. The heart of pragmatism is "willingness to talk, to listen to other people, to weigh the consequences of our actions upon other people," without any guarantee of success.[38] There is no neutral ground from which to evaluate competing claims: "There is no chance that someone can take up a vantage point for comparing conceptual schemes by temporarily shedding his own."[39] Rorty denies that he is a relativist. He does not hold that every belief on a certain topic is as good as any other. But he denies that it is possible to give objective, definitive grounds for one's preference for one view over another.[40]

The idea that there are no self-evident foundations on which our beliefs might be based is somewhat unsettling to most people when they first encounter it, but it has been welcomed by some, primarily Protestant, theologians. "It is time," writes William Stacy Johnson, "that we recognized this foundationalist way of thinking for what it is. In its Christian guise, it represents not the strength of faith but the result of a faith that has lost its nerve. The Christian Scriptures set themselves up not so much as truth claims to be defended by philosophical foundations but as witnesses to the transforming power that no truth claim itself can contain. The gospel is not a 'foundation' to render our traditional notions of rationality secure but a remaking of everything, including rationality itself."[41] Theological nonfoundationalism may draw on its philosophical counterpart to varying degrees. George Lindbeck bases his "postliberal theology" on a cultural-linguistic model that is in principle applicable to any religion.[42] Stanley Hauerwas is more explicitly confessional: "The Church's One Foundation Is Jesus Christ Her Lord."[43] But in any case, nonfoundational

38. Richard Rorty, "Pragmatism, Relativism, and Irrationalism," *Proceedings and Addresses of the American Philosophical Association* 53 (1980): 719-38 (734).

39. So Donald Davidson, "On the Very Idea of a Conceptual Scheme," *Proceedings and Addresses of the American Philosophical Association* 47 (1974): 5-20; repr. in *Inquiries into Truth and Interpretation* (Oxford: Clarendon, 1983), 183-98 (185).

40. Rorty, *Proceedings and Addresses of the American Philosophical Association* 53 (1980): 727-28.

41. William Stacy Johnson, "Reading the Scriptures Faithfully in a Postmodern Age," in *The Art of Reading Scripture*, ed. Ellen F. Davis and Richard B. Hays (Grand Rapids: Wm. B. Eerdmans, 2003), 109-24 (112).

42. Lindbeck, "Toward a Postliberal Theology," 83-84; *The Nature of Doctrine: Religion and Theology in a Postliberal Age* (Philadelphia: Westminster, 1984), 32-42.

43. Hauerwas, "The Church's One Foundation Is Jesus Christ Her Lord; Or in a World without Foundations All We Have Is the Church," in *Theology Without Foundations: Reli-*

THE BIBLE AFTER BABEL

or antifoundational theology is indebted far more to Karl Barth than to Rorty or Ludwig Wittgenstein. Barth held that there could be no "foundation, support, or justification" for theology in any philosophy, theory, or epistemology[44] and famously and emphatically rejected any form of natural theology.[45] The debt to Barth is especially obvious in the predilection of postliberal theologians for the category "story."[46] Lindbeck argues that the diverse materials in the Bible are held together in "an overarching story. . . . It is as if the Bible were a 'vast, loosely-structured, non-fictional novel' (to use a phrase David Kelsey applies to Karl Barth's view of scripture)."[47] Whether or not there is such a thing as "a non-fictional novel," the affinity between Barthian theology and philosophical nonfoundationalism is superficial. To affirm that the church has one foundation, whether Christ or the Scriptures, is quite incompatible with philosophical nonfoundationalism, which rejects any foundation at all.[48]

In the field of Old Testament theology, the most influential nonfoundational approach (in the theological sense) is undoubtedly that of Brevard Childs. Childs distances himself from Lindbeck's cultural-linguistic model as insufficiently explicit in its theological claims: "The role of the Bible is not . . . simply as a cultural expression of ancient peoples, but as a testimony pointing beyond itself to a divine reality to which it bears witness."[49] Nonetheless, there are significant similarities. Both approaches are intratextual. Both vest the authority of Scripture in the ca-

gious Practice and the Future of Theological Truth, ed. Hauerwas, Nancey Murphy, and Mark Nation (Nashville: Abingdon, 1994), 143-62.

44. Karl Barth, *Church Dogmatics*, I/1: *The Doctrine of the Word of God*, 2nd ed. (Edinburgh: Clark, 1986), xiii; Thiel, 50. Thiel notes that Barth shows no familiarity with (or interest in) philosophical nonfoundationalism.

45. See his debate with Emil Brunner in Brunner and Barth, *Natural Theology* (London: Bles, 1946), and the critique of James Barr, *Biblical Faith and Natural Theology*, 102-37.

46. The use of the category "story" by James Barr, noted above, is decidedly *not* Barthian in its implications.

47. Lindbeck, "Toward a Postliberal Theology," 95. Cf. David Kelsey, *The Uses of Scripture in Recent Theology* (Philadelphia: Fortress, 1975), 48. See also Hans Frei, *The Eclipse of Biblical Narrative* (New Haven: Yale University Press, 1974); Stanley Hauerwas, *A Community of Character: Toward a Constructive Christian Social Ethic* (Notre Dame: University of Notre Dame Press, 1981). On Barth's use of story, see further David Ford, *Barth and God's Story* (Frankfurt: Lang, 1981).

48. So also Thiel, 87.

49. Childs, *Biblical Theology of the Old and New Testaments*, 9. This remark is made approvingly apropos of the work of Gerhard Ebeling.

nonical text. Neither is concerned to reconstruct the history behind the text or to support the claims of the text by appeal to any other kind of foundation.[50] In view of the problems encountered by the Biblical Theology movement, and even by von Rad, a biblical theology that does not rely on history is attractive. It is also a strength of the approach that it embraces the whole canon and does not attempt to identify a "center." Nonetheless, problems remain.[51] Here I shall mention only two, which are among the most persistent problems in biblical theology.

First, the historical status of biblical narratives remains problematic. According to Childs, "the divine imperatives are no longer moored in the past, but continue to confront the hearer in the present as truth."[52] But Childs does not insist on the historical truth of the biblical narratives. He acknowledges with some sympathy that "von Rad was unable to overcome the radical tension between the picture of critically reconstructed history and the portrayal of history confessed in Israel's sacred tradition."[53] But neither has he any solution to offer: "Biblical Theology offers neither a new philosophy of history nor a fresh theory of language, but rather it suggests that the church's path of theological reflection lies in its understanding of its scripture, its canon, and its christological confession which encompass the mystery of God's ways in the world with his people."[54] In short, history is a mystery. This conclusion is not much help to one seeking understanding, whether in the name of faith or of anything else. Childs's treatment of the problem of history is a good illustration of the formalism of the canonical approach. In this case, it amounts to little more than an insistence on a reverential attitude towards the text and a refusal to accept modes of interpretation, such as sociology, which take seriously the human historicity of the biblical "witness."

The import of the canonical approach is more clearly in evidence in the second problem. Another Yale colleague, Roland Bainton, had raised

---

50. See the remarks of Mark G. Brett, *Biblical Criticism in Crisis? The Impact of the Canonical Approach on Old Testament Studies* (Cambridge: Cambridge University Press, 1991), 9-10, 156-67.

51. See the extensive critiques of Childs's work by Barr, *The Concept of Biblical Theology*, 378-438; Brueggemann, *Theology of the Old Testament*, 89-93; John Barton, *Reading the Old Testament: Method in Biblical Study*, rev. ed. (Louisville: Westminster John Knox, 1996), 89-103.

52. Childs, *Biblical Theology of the Old and New Testaments*, 86.

53. Childs, *Biblical Theology of the Old and New Testaments*, 200.

54. Childs, *Biblical Theology of the Old and New Testaments*, 206.

the question of how the Old Testament could be regarded as authoritative in the light of the gross immoralities of the patriarchs.[55] Childs responds that, "if one looks at how these stories were heard in the rest of the Old Testament . . . a very clear pattern emerges. Everything that happened to the patriarchs has been encompassed within the rubric of God's wonderful works and his mighty deeds of redemption."[56] Here there is a clear attempt to solve a problem by innerbiblical intertextuality. But is the problem solved? Is the morality of the patriarchs any less problematic for being subsumed into God's wonderful works? And while one might well argue that the Bible does not approve the deceitful practices of the patriarchs, what are we to make of cases where divine commands are repugnant (the command to sacrifice Isaac or to slaughter the Canaanites)? It is significant that Childs does not acknowledge an ethical problem with the conquest at all in the theological reflections on Joshua in his *Introduction*.[57] A reverential posture towards the text as a witness to divine reality makes it difficult to practice ideological criticism, an enterprise that Childs would in any case rule out as inappropriate. This refusal to acknowledge the problematic nature of the text seems to me to be a major shortcoming, not only in Childs's canonical approach, but also in other postliberal theologies that speak of the text shaping the imagination and perceptions of the reader or of the reader being conformed to the text.[58] It is possible, of course, to acknowledge some problems within the biblical tradition while still being shaped by the whole, but criticism is inhibited, nonetheless, by the submissive posture towards the text.

A Postmodern Biblical Theology?

Childs may be termed antifoundationalist in the theological sense, insofar as he refuses to appeal to any philosophical or other universal criteria to

55. Roland H. Bainton, "The Immoralities of the Patriarchs according to the Exegesis of the Late Middle Ages and of the Reformation," *HTR* 23 (1930): 39-49.

56. Childs, *Biblical Theology of the Old and New Testaments*, 679-80.

57. Brevard S. Childs, *Introduction to the Old Testament as Scripture* (Philadelphia: Fortress, 1979), 239-53.

58. The language is that of Lindbeck, "Toward a Postliberal Theology," 90, 95. At least in the latter case, Lindbeck has the Gospels in mind, and it is difficult to know how he would apply what he says to a book like Joshua.

support his biblical faith, but he is certainly no postmodernist.[59] His approach arises from the precritical Protestant principle of *sola scriptura* rather than from philosophical nonfoundationalism. To my knowledge, the only scholar who has attempted to formulate a theology of the Old Testament that is explicitly postmodern is Walter Brueggemann.[60] Brueggemann argues quite rightly that "in every period of the discipline, the questions, methods, and possibilities in which study is cast arise from the sociointellectual climate in which the work must be done."[61] He uses the term "postmodern" to characterize the contemporary situation. This is characterized above all by pluralism: "The great new fact of interpretation is that we live in a pluralistic context, in which many different interpreters in many different specific contexts representing many different interests are at work on textual (theological) interpretation. . . . The great interpretive reality is that there is no court of appeal behind these many different readings. There is no court of appeal beyond the text itself. . . . The postmodern situation is signified precisely by the disappearance of any common, universal assumption at the outset of reading."[62] Furthermore, "we now recognize that there is no interest-free interpretation, no interpretation that is not in the service of some interest and in some sense advocacy."[63]

Brueggemann's own theology might be described as postmodern in two respects. First is the role of rhetoric. Since there is no foundation outside the text, "speech constitutes reality, and who God turns out to be in Israel depends on the utterance of the Israelites or, derivatively, the utterance of the text."[64] Second, while the primary characterization of the biblical material is "testimony," Brueggemann recognizes deconstructive moments of "counter-testimony" and even "unsolicited testimony" that do not fit his dominant paradigm.

One can only admire the scope and courage of Brueggemann's undertaking and the irenic spirit in which it is carried out. There are, however,

---

59. This is also true of Jon Levenson.

60. Brueggemann, *Theology of the Old Testament.* See also his earlier book, *Texts under Negotiation,* and his article, "Biblical Theology Appropriately Postmodern," *BTB* 27 (1997): 4-9.

61. Brueggemann, *Theology of the Old Testament,* 11.

62. Brueggemann, *Theology of the Old Testament,* 61-62.

63. Brueggemann, *Theology of the Old Testament,* 63.

64. Brueggemann, *Theology of the Old Testament,* 65.

some problems with the project, both in regard to its relationship to postmodernism and in regard to its own coherence. One cannot fail to be struck by the frequency with which he appeals to "the text itself" as if this were unproblematic. Study in the tradition of Enlightenment historicism was "a study that in principle had to distort or deny the most defining characteristics of the text itself."[65] Historical criticism has "made the text unavailable on its own terms."[66] As Barr observes: "Brueggemann sometimes writes as if the text was a living person, who can decide how it is to be treated, 'presenting itself' for this and 'refusing' that, 'closing itself' to something else. All these, surely, are really Brueggemann's own decisions, not those of the text."[67] There is no recognition here that any reading of a text involves a construal, whether one construes the text as history or as testimony, and Brueggemann seems to have forgotten his own declaration that no construal or interpretation is innocent or interest-free. It is noteworthy in this context that he never declares his own interest.[68]

Further tension with postmodern sensibilities is evident in Brueggemann's discussion of "metanarratives." He cites Jean-François Lyotard's well-known characterization of the postmodern situation as one in which there is no confidence in metanarratives.[69] But Brueggemann argues that we should not too readily accept this view: "I prefer to think that our situation is one of conflict and competition between deeply held metanarratives, which are seldom enunciated and only evidenced in bits and pieces."[70] This view then allows him to set up "Israel's Yahwistic construal of reality" as an alternative to "the dominant metanarrative of Western society," military consumerism.[71] Lyotard, I suspect, might well agree that the world is full of competing metanarratives, but his point is that a postmodern intellectual should view all of them with suspicion, the alternatives as well as the domi-

---

65. Brueggemann, *Theology of the Old Testament*, 15.

66. Brueggemann, *Theology of the Old Testament*, 85.

67. Barr, *The Concept of Biblical Theology*, 550.

68. One significant clue may be found in a footnote where Brueggemann notes that "the appeal to testimony as a ground of certitude has particular and peculiar importance for the thought of Karl Barth"; *Theology of the Old Testament*, 119, n. 6). He also notes others for whom this category is important, ranging from the Gospel of John to Elie Wiesel. Brueggemann's appropriation of Barth is very different from that of Childs.

69. Jean-François Lyotard, *The Postmodern Condition*.

70. Brueggemann, *Theology of the Old Testament*, 712.

71. Brueggemann, *Theology of the Old Testament*, 718.

nant ones. Like most nonfoundationalist theologians, Brueggemann wants to exempt the sacred text from the suspicion to which all other meta-narratives are subjected. His appropriation of postmodernism, then, is partial, and has a familiar Protestant, Barthian, look. And, in view of the pluralism that is admittedly characteristic of "the text itself," is it so simple to speak of "Israel's Yahwistic construal of reality"?

Brueggemann does devote considerable time to the countertestimony of the text, those elements that question and deconstruct the dominant characterization of God.[72] He concludes that both the testimony and the countertestimony must be held in tension. "Lived faith in this tradition consists in the capacity to move back and forth between these two postures of faith, one concerned to submit to Yahweh, culminating in *self-abandoning praise,* the other concerned to assert self in the face of God, culminating in *self-regarding complaint.*"[73] In different contexts, one testimony or the other may be appropriate. This is probably a fair enough description of the way the Bible has traditionally been used.[74] But noting the tensions within the tradition stops well short of ideological criticism in the manner of Michel Foucault or David Clines.[75] Despite his recognition that all interpretation is influenced by its context, Brueggemann pays no attention to the historical contexts of the biblical texts, an omission all the more surprising since he has paid attention to these contexts in the past.[76] And, in good antifoundationalist fashion, he insists that "what 'happened'

72. Brueggemann, *Theology of the Old Testament,* 337-406.

73. Brueggemann, *Theology of the Old Testament,* 400-1. For an illuminating discussion of the ways in which different views can be held in tension, see the dialogic approach to biblical theology advocated by Carol A. Newsom, "Bakhtin, the Bible, and Dialogic Truth," *JR* 76 (1996): 290-306, and exemplified in her treatment of the book of Job, *The Book of Job: A Contest of Moral Imaginations* (New York: Oxford University Press, 2003).

74. Cf., from a quite different theological perspective, James A. Sanders, "Adaptable for Life: The Nature and Function of Canon," in *Magnalia Dei: The Mighty Acts of God: Essays on the Bible and Archaeology in Memory of George Ernest Wright,* ed. Frank Moore Cross, Werner E. Lemke, and Patrick D. Miller (New York: Doubleday, 1976), 531-60.

75. The inadequacy of Brueggemann's treatment of "the dark side of the Bible" is noted by Brian Rice McCarthy, "Response: Brueggemann and Hanson on God in the Hebrew Scriptures," *JAAR* 68 (2000): 615-20.

76. See, e.g., his essay, "Trajectories in Old Testament Literature and the Sociology of Ancient Israel," *JBL* 98 (1979): 161-85, where he outlines different, even contradictory, trajectories in the biblical text and aligns them with trajectories in modern scholarship. Brueggemann's neglect of historical context is incisively criticized by Paul D. Hanson in his review, "A New Challenge to Biblical Theology," *JAAR* 67 (1999): 447-59, esp. 450-51.

(whatever it may mean) depends on testimony and tradition that will not submit to any other warrant."[77] But here his basic metaphor of testimony becomes problematic. As he himself notes, "the proper setting of testimony is a court of law, in which various and diverse witnesses are called to 'tell what happened,' to give their version of what is true. . . . The court must then detemine, with no other data except testimony, which version is reality."[78] Of course, this is not just a matter of accepting whatever testimony is presented. "In any serious courtroom trial, testimony is challenged by other, competing testimony. In any serious trial, no unchallenged testimony can expect to carry the day easily."[79] But in this case Brueggemann allows no other testimony than what is found in the Bible itself: this testimony will not submit to any other warrant. But what kind of trial is this, where one may cross-examine the witness only for "countertestimony" in his or her own evidence and not adduce other witnesses? Is not the testimony of archaeology relevant to any discussion of "what happened"? Should not the full tradition of moral discussion in the Western world (at least) be brought to bear on a discussion of biblical ethics? Here Brueggemann's position is illustrative of the basic problem with all nonfoundational theology that tries to exempt the Scripture from external warrants. No one in modern pluralist society can live in a world that is shaped only by biblical narrative. We are all heirs to other traditions as well, including the Enlightenment and sundry other intellectual movements.[80] We may agree that none of these provides secure foundations from which to judge the others, but neither does the Bible, or rather the particular mode of interpretation to which we subscribe, whether critical or confessional. For, *pace* Brueggemann, the Bible does not speak for itself any more than any other book but can only be viewed through whatever interpretive lens and filter of human interests that we bring to it.

The most radical part of Brueggemann's proposal is undoubtedly his insistence that "speech is constitutive of reality." "Yahweh lives in, with, and under this speech, and in the end depends on Israel's testimony for an access point in the world."[81] At first blush, this position might seem com-

77. Brueggemann, *Theology of the Old Testament*, 714.

78. Brueggemann, *Theology of the Old Testament*, 120.

79. Brueggemann, *Theology of the Old Testament*, 715,

80. See Charles Taylor, *Sources of the Self: The Making of the Modern Identity* (Cambridge, Mass.: Harvard University Press, 1989).

81. Brueggemann, *Theology of the Old Testament*, 713-14.

parable to Derridean deconstruction, which "seeks . . . to pull the bottom from under all metaphysics."[82] "Old Testament theology," writes Brueggemann, "is endlessly seduced by the ancient Hellenistic lust for Being, for establishing ontological reference behind the text."[83] Yet in a footnote he pulls back: "It is not my intention to be anti-ontological. It is rather to insist that whatever might be claimed for ontology in the purview of Israel's speech can be claimed only in and through testimonial utterance. That is, once the testimony of Israel is accepted as true — once one believes what it claims — one has ontology, one has the reality of Yahweh. But to have the reality of God apart from the testimony of Israel is sure to yield some God other than the Yahweh of Israel."[84] In short, there is a reality of God behind or beyond the text, but it is known *sola fide, sola scriptura.* This is not as radical a departure from traditional Protestant theology as it may have seemed. But if the God of Israel is supposed to be the God of all creation, it seems to me problematic to say that this God can be known only through the Bible, and indeed there is considerable material in the biblical corpus that can be marshalled against Brueggemann's position on this point.[85]

It seems to me that if one wishes to be nonfoundationalist, and treat the text as if it were a novel or a drama,[86] then one has to forgo any claim of ontological reality. In Ludwig Wittgenstein's famous phrase, whereof we cannot speak, thereof we must be silent, however important it may be. Brueggemann is right that the biblical text can seldom if ever be construed as an ontological argument.[87] What we have, indeed, are writings in vari-

---

82. Edward L. Greenstein, "Deconstruction and Biblical Narrative," *Prooftexts* 9 (1989): 43-71 (53).

83 Brueggemann, *Theology of the Old Testament,* 714.

84. Brueggemann, *Theology of the Old Testament,* 714, n. 21.

85. See Barr, *Biblical Faith and Natural Theology.* The main, but not the only, resources for natural theology or creation theology in the Old Testament are found in the Wisdom literature. See John J. Collins, "The Biblical Precedent for Natural Theology," *JAAR* 45 (1977) Sup B: 35-67; Leo G. Perdue, *Wisdom and Creation: The Theology of Wisdom Literature* (Nashville: Abingdon, 1994).

86. So Brueggemann, *Theology of the Old Testament,* 69.

87. Hanson, *JAAR* 67 (1999): 449, asks, "Why should biblical theology shy away from questions of ontology when Israelite religion assumes an historical ontology that sets it apart from the mythopoeic worldviews of surrounding cultures? It is an ontology predicated on the perception of divine initiatives in profane history." But the problems involved in predicating ontology on divine acts in profane history were exposed a long time ago. See esp. Gilkey.

ous genres that make claims about God that defy any process of verification, by philosophy, history, or any other means. A consistently postmodernist biblical theology, or for that matter a consistently historical-critical one, can describe these claims, deconstruct them by noting problems and countertestimonies, and clarify and explain them to some extent, but any positive claims it makes must be "under erasure," in Derrida's phrase.[88] In short, a postmodernist theology would have to be considerably more modest, and less convinced in its claims, than any proposed hitherto, even those proposed in the name of antifoundationalism.

Postmodernism and Ethics

The relevance of the Bible to the modern world has never depended only on its metaphysical affirmations. It has always lain largely in its ethical teachings. Moreover, it is an axiom of pragmatic, nonfoundationalist philosophy that systems of thought must be judged by the practices they support. Does postmodernist thought have any light to shed on the question of biblical ethics?

At first blush, it would seem unlikely that it does. Derridean deconstruction has been accused, with some justification, of "the endless deferral of sense,"[89] of covering the clarity of decisions with "a film of undecidability,"[90] and consequently of tending towards "the indeterminacy of guilt and the conceit of evasiveness."[91] This tendency was painfully in evidence in the reaction of deconstructionist critics to the revelation that Paul de Man had published anti-Semitic writings during World War II,[92] although in that case the reluctance to condemn de Man may

88. Cf. Greenstein, 53. Cf. Derrida's own reflections on what it means to call on God in Yvonne Sherwood and Kevin Hart, *Derrida and Religion*, 37-38.

89. Somer Brodribb, *Nothing Mat(t)ers*, 8.

90. John D. Caputo, *Against Ethics: Contributions to a Poetics of Obligation with Constant Reference to Deconstruction* (Bloomington: Indiana University Press, 1993), 4.

91. Caputo, *Against Ethics*, 3-4. Cf. Derrida's own statement: "I try where I can to act politically while recognizing that such action remains incommensurate with my intellectual project of deconstruction"; in Richard Kearney, *Dialogues with Contemporary Continental Thinkers*, (Manchester: University of Manchester Press, 1984), 120.

92. Werner Hamacher, Neil Hertz, and Thomas Keenan, eds., *Wartime Journalism, 1939-1943* by Paul de Man (Lincoln: University of Nebraska Press, 1988); *Responses: On Paul de Man's Wartime Journalism* (Lincoln: University of Nebraska Press, 1989), esp. the ago-

have been due in some part to a concern for the reputation of the deconstructionist enterprise.[93] In a related vein, some critics speak of a "tendency to political inertia"[94] and of providing "a sophisticated rationale for its own political paralysis."[95] But in fact, postmodernist critics have not been exceptionally reticent about addressing political issues. Foucault, for example, supported the Iranian revolution of the Ayatollah Khomeini because it represented "the collective will of a people."[96] (One wonders what he would have said had he visited Berlin in the late 1930s.) What is characteristic of postmodern ethics is not a refusal to take positions but a refusal to ground those positions in principles or absolute values.[97]

Both the strength and the weakness of one strand of postmodern ethics can be illustrated from a brief op-ed piece by Stanley Fish, published in the *New York Times* scarcely a month after the terrorist attack on the World Trade Center in New York.[98] Fish was responding to the question whether the events of September 11 meant the end of postmodernist relativism. "The problem, according to the critics, is that since postmodernists deny the pos-

---

nized reflections of Jacques Derrida, "Like the Sound of the Sea Deep Within a Shell: Paul de Man's War," 127-64. Hamacher, "Journals, Politics: Notes on Paul de Man's Wartime Journalism," 438-67, argues that de Man's collaboration "was *not* founded on pro-Nazi sympathies . . . but rather on a realism to which force appears as an authority that produces facts and justice" (454). See the comments of Brodribb, 34-35.

93. Derrida, "Like the Sound of the Sea," 156, speaks of "those who would like to exploit the recent 'revelations' against deconstruction." J. Hillis Miller attributes the "attacks" on de Man to "unreasoning hostility," in response to "the genuine threat posed by de Man's work and by that of the so-called deconstructionists generally to a powerful tradition of ideological assumptions"; "An Open Letter to Professor Jon Wiener," in Hamacher, Hertz, and Keenan, 334-42 (342).

94. Paul Lakeland, *Postmodernity: Christian Identity in a Fragmented Age.* Guides to Theological Inquiry (Minneapolis: Fortress, 1997), 33.

95. Terry Eagleton, *The Illusions of Postmodernism*, 69, with reference to one side of the work of Foucault. See also Eagleton's critique of deconstructionist ethics in his essay, "Deconstruction and Human Rights," in *Freedom and Interpretation: The Oxford Amnesty Lectures, 1992*, ed. Barbara Johnson (New York: Basic Books, 1993), 121-45.

96. Michel Foucault, *Politics, Philosophy, Culture: Interviews and Other Writings, 1972-1977* (New York: Routledge, 1988), 215: "personally, I thought that the collective will was like God, like the soul, something one would never encounter. I don't know whether you agree with me, but we met, in Tehran and throughout Iran, the collective will of a people. Well, you have to salute it, it doesn't happen every day."

97. See esp. Stanley Fish, *The Trouble with Principle.*

98. Stanley Fish, "Condemnation without Absolutes," *New York Times*, 15 October 2001, A 19.

sibility of describing matters of fact objectively, they leave us with no firm basis for either condemning the terrorist attacks or fighting back." Not so, writes Fish. "Postmodernism maintains only that there can be no independent standard for determining which of many rival interpretations of an event is the true one. The only thing postmodern thought argues against is the hope of justifying our response to the attacks in universal terms that would be persuasive to everyone, including our enemies." Fish goes on to give several examples of "false universals,"[99] which describe the conflict as a war between good and evil or as a war against international terrorism. He quite rightly argues that it is unhelpful to think of the terrorists as irrational or simply as evil. They, no less than we, have a history that supplies them with reasons and motives for their actions, and we would do well to try to understand it. So far so good. Fish is also right that the basic reason for any response to the attacks of September 11 is self-defense. But what is most striking in his piece is the further grounding he proposes: "We have grounds enough for action and condemnation in the democratic ideals we embrace, without grasping for the empty rhetoric of universal absolutes." But these democratic ideals are not preferred because they are superior by any universal standard. Rather, "our convictions are by definition preferred, that is what makes them *our* convictions." And, of course for the members of al-Qaida, their convictions are by definition preferred, because they are *their* convictions. As we have noted above, Richard Rorty also denies that it is possible to give objective grounds for preferring one point of view over another, but for Rorty the solution to this predicament is "willingness to talk, to listen to other people, to weigh the consequences of our actions upon other people,"[100] in short, to enter into the give and take of dialogue. Fish seems to regard dialogue as pointless, especially in matters involving religious convictions, since he holds that "it is the nature of religious dogma to resist and even condemn challenges from perspectives other than its own."[101] Dogma, he tells us, "is a word that once had a positive meaning: it meant the unqualified assertion of a priori truths and was indistinguishable from a truly strong religiosity."[102] Fish likes his religiosity, and other convic-

99. Fish, *New York Times*, 15 October 2001, A 19. He attributes this phrase to Edward Said.

100. Rorty, *Proceedings and Addresses of the American Philosophical Association* 53 (1980): 734.

101. Fish, *The Trouble with Principle*, 37.

102. Fish, *The Trouble with Principle*, 261.

tions, strong and has nothing but contempt for liberal religion.[103] Such convictions admit of negotiation with people of other persuasion, as a matter of practical necessity, but they do not lend themselves to dialogue where one might be persuaded to modify one's own views.

Not all postmodernists are necessarily as agonistic as Fish, although he is not unique in this regard.[104] One would think that deconstruction, with its systematic attention to the trace of contradictory views in any assertion, would undermine the certainty of any dogmatism.[105] But also the polemic against universals is misdirected. Fish declares that "Invoking the abstract notions of justice and truth to support our cause wouldn't be effective anyway because our adversaries lay claim to the same language. (No one declares himself to be an apostle of injustice.)"[106] Indeed. That is why conversation is possible as to what justice and truth entail. As Terry Eagleton has remarked, it is no disproval of human universals to point out that they are differently constructed by different cultures.[107] Moreover, the understandings of what justice and truth entail — at least in the great monotheistic traditions of Christianity, Judaism and Islam — are not as incommensurable as Fish would claim.[108] But of course, if the understanding of justice were the subject of genuine dialogue, then it would no longer be adequate to say that "our convictions are by definition preferred."[109]

---

103. See his critique of the works of Franklin Gamwell and Ronald Thiemann in *The Trouble with Principle*, 189-91. He complains that "a fanatic in Thiemann's vocabulary is someone who holds to his position with an inappropriate 'degree of certainty'"; 190, with reference to Thiemann, *Religion in Public Life: A Dilemma for Democracy* (Washington: Georgetown University Press, 1996), 137.

104. See the comments of Terry Eagleton, *After Theory*, 192.

105. Cf. David J. A. Clines, "Ethics as Deconstruction, And, Deconstruction as Ethics," in *The Bible in Ethics: The Second Sheffield Colloquium*, ed. John W. Rogerson, Margaret Davies, and M. Daniel Carroll R. JSOTSup 207 (Sheffield: Sheffield Academic, 1995), 77-106 (105): "What I find deconstruction does in the realm of ethics is to problematize traditional categories and distinctions."

106. Fish, *New York Times*, 15 October 2001, A 19, col. 1.

107. Eagleton, *The Illusions of Postmodernism*, 48-49.

108. See Hans Küng and Karl-Josef Kuschel, eds., *A Global Ethic: The Declaration of the Parliament of the World's Religions* (New York: Continuum, 1993).

109. Cf. the critique of Rorty and Fish as fideists, who refuse to justify their basic convictions, in Eagleton, *After Theory*, 54-55.

Concern for the Other

There is however another strand in postmodernist thought that is more promising for an approach to biblical ethics. Deconstruction is famously concerned with difference, or as Derrida would say, "differance."[110] Accordingly, at least some critics speak of "a responsibility to otherness."[111] In his reflections on the de Man affair, Derrida declared that the "first rule" is "respect for the other, that is, for his right to difference, in his relation to others but also in his relation to himself."[112] It is certainly true that postmodernist scholarship is especially sensitive to voices from the margins, and it takes a negative view of any claims that might be considered hegemonic or totalizing. Even a critic of postmodernism such as Eagleton acknowledges that its politics "have been at once enrichment and evasion," the enrichment lying in its attempt to give a voice to the humiliated and the reviled.[113]

The philosopher who has developed the concern for otherness most eloquently as a moral issue is Emmanuel Lévinas, an older contemporary and friend of Derrida who was also trained in the philosophy of phenomenology.[114] Lévinas shared with Derrida and other postmodernists a distrust of totality, born in no small part of the experience of totalitarianism,

110. Jacques Derrida, "Differance," in *Speech and Phenomena, and Other Essays on Husserl's Theory of Signs* (Evanston: Northwestern University Press, 1973), 129-60; *Writing and Difference* (Chicago: University of Chicago Press, 1978).

111. Gary A. Phillips, "The Ethics of Reading Deconstructively, or Speaking Face to Face: The Samaritan Woman Meets Derrida at the Well," in *The New Literary Criticism and the New Testament*, ed. Edgar V. McKnight and Elizabeth S. Malbon. JSNTSup 109 (Sheffield: Sheffield Academic, 1994), 283-325 (315).

112. Derrida, "Like the Sound of the Sea," 154. See also his essay "Deconstruction and the Other," in Kearney, *Dialogues with Contemporary Continental Thinkers*, 107-26.

113. Eagleton, *The Illusions of Postmodernism*, 24.

114. Lévinas was born in Lithuania in 1905 and died in Paris in 1995. His final academic position was at the Sorbonne. See the brief sketch by Tamara Cohn Eskenazi, "Introduction: Facing the Text as Other: Some Implications of Lévinas's Work for Biblical Studies," in *Lévinas and Biblical Studies*, ed. Eskenazi, Gary A. Phillips and David Jobling. Semeia Studies 43 (Atlanta: SBL, 2003), 1-16 (2). See also the reflections of Derrida on the legacy of Lévinas, *Adieu to Emmanuel Lévinas* (Stanford: Stanford University Press, 1999). On the philosophical exchanges between Lévinas and Derrida, see Susan E. Shapiro, "'And God Created Woman': Reading the Bible Otherwise," in Eskenazi, Phillips, and Jobling, 159-95, n. 3 (160-61). On the influence of Lévinas on Derrida, see Brian M. Britt, "Erasing Amalek: Remembering to Forget with Derrida and Biblical Tradition," in Sherwood and Hart, 61-77 (72-73).

and also the attention to otherness as a primary category for reflection.[115] But while he recognized that European institutions had been highly compromised by the events of the 20th century, he continued to admire universal principles.[116] Unlike Derrida, moreover, Lévinas gave the other a human face. In the words of Robert Gibbs: "Lévinas' phenomenology climaxes in the moment I am face to face with another person. The face is the experience that lies at the root of ethics for Lévinas. . . . The separation between the other and myself is an inassimilable difference proclaimed in the other's face. I cannot make him mine, nor reduce him to my cognition of him."[117] Or in Lévinas' own words: "The facing position, opposition par excellence, can be only as a moral summons. This movement proceeds from the other. The idea of infinity, infinitely more contained in the less, is concretely produced in the form of a relation with the face."[118] "The infinite . . . gleams in the face of the Other, in the total nudity of his defenceless eyes, in the nudity of the absolute openness of the Transcendent."[119]

Lévinas's appreciation of the face of the other is not derived only from philosophical analysis.[120] He relates it explicitly to Jewish tradition, grounded ultimately in the Hebrew Bible, as read in the Talmud and Midrash.[121] So the phenomenon of greeting and blessing in the name of the Lord, illustrated in Ruth 2:4 and Judg 6:12, leads him to say that "the epiphany of God is invoked in the human face. The face of the other, irreducible difference, bursting into all that gives itself to me, all that is understood by

115. William Stacy Johnson (122) describes Lévinas's philosophy as "a relentless critique of all totalizing forms of reason that make no place for the Other."

116. Emmanuel Lévinas, "Zionisms: Assimilation and New Culture," in *The Lévinas Reader,* ed. Seán Hand (Oxford: Blackwell, 1989), 284: "We continue to admire universal principles and whatever can be deduced by sound logic from them."

117. Robert Gibbs, *Correlations in Rosenzweig and Lévinas* (Princeton: Princeton University Press, 1992), 165.

118. Emmanuel Lévinas, *Totality and Infinity: An Essay on Exteriority.* Duquesne Studies: Philosophical Series 24 (Pittsburgh: Duquesne University Press, 1969), 196.

119. Lévinas, *Totality and Infinity,* 199.

120. Claire Elise Katz, *Lévinas, Judaism, and the Feminine: The Silent Footsteps of Rebecca* (Bloomington: Indiana University Press, 2003), 10-11, argues that Lévinas subordinates philosophy to religion. Cf. Lévinas, "On Jewish Philosophy," in *In the Time of the Nations* (Bloomington: Indiana University Press, 1994), 167-83. He writes, however, as a philosopher in the tradition of phenomenology. See Eskenazi, 4-5.

121. Edith Wyschogrod, *Emmanuel Lévinas: The Problem of Ethical Metaphysics,* 2nd ed. (New York: Fordham University Press, 2000), 176-221; Eskenazi, 1-16.

me and belongs to my world; an appearance in the world which un-makes and dis-orders the world, worries me and keeps me awake."[122] And the obligation to the Other is ultimately an obligation to God: to follow the Most High "is also to know that nothing is greater than to approach one's neighbor, than the concern for the lot of the 'widow and orphan, the stranger and poor' and that to approach them with empty hands is not to approach them at all."[123] The actual motif of the "face" appears in an ancient Jewish text that Lévinas is unlikely to have known, as it is not part of the rabbinic corpus. The apocalypse of 2 Enoch, which is preserved in Slavonic but was probably composed by a Hellenistic Jew around the end of the 1st century C.E., says: "The Lord with his own two hands created mankind; and in a facsimile of his own face. Small and great the Lord created. Whoever insults a person's face insults the face of the Lord."[124]

The attractiveness of Lévinas's approach for biblical ethics lies in its obvious affinity with themes that are prominent in the biblical text. Lévinas does not argue from biblical authority, but his philosophy is influenced by biblical tradition. As Tamara Cohn Eskenazi writes, "It is exhilarating to see this biblical 'vocabulary' (i.e., frames of reference) and basic ideas applied to an interpretation of reality that extends beyond the confines of specifically biblical or even religious discourse." [125] Lévinas, in fact, stands in a long tradition, attested both in ancient Judaism and in the New Testament, that holds that the whole biblical law can be summed up under the headings of obligation to God and duty to one's neighbor.[126] "The Bible," he writes, "teaches us that man is he who loves his neighbor, and that the fact of loving his neighbor is a modality of meaningful life, of a thinking as funda-

122. Emmanuel Lévinas, "On the Jewish Reading of Scriptures," in Eskenazi, Phillips, and Jobling, 17-31 (28-29).

123. Emmanuel Lévinas, "Revelation in the Jewish Tradition," in *Beyond the Verse: Talmudic Readings and Lectures* (Bloomington: Indiana University Press, 1994), 129-50 (142). See Wyschogrod, 176-85, on Lévinas's view of Judaism as an ethical community.

124. 2 En 44:1-2; cf. 52:6; 60:1. For the text, see Francis I. Andersen, "2(Slavonic Apocalypse of) Enoch," in *The Old Testament Pseudepigrapha* 1, ed. James H. Charlesworth (Garden City: Doubleday, 1983), 91-213. See the discussion by Katell Berthelot, L'"Humanité de l'autre Homme" dans la Pensée Juive Ancienne. JSJSup 87 (Leiden: Brill, 2004), 183-89.

125. Eskenazi, 4.

126. See, e.g., Philo, *Spec* 2.62-63 (282); Mark 12:28-31; Matt 22:34-40; Luke 10:25-28. See Klaus Berger, *Die Gesetzesauslegung Jesu.* WMANT 40 (Neukirchen-Vluyn: Neukirchener, 1972), 17-76; Andreas Nissen, *Gott und der nächste im antiken Judentum.* WUNT 15 (Tübingen: Mohr Siebeck, 1974).

mental — I would say more fundamental — than the knowledge of an object, than truth as knowledge of objects."[127] The Bible demands "a reversal of ontology into ethics": "The Torah demands, in opposition to the natural perseverance of each being in his or her own being (a fundamental ontological law), care for the stranger, the widow and the orphan, a preoccupation with the other person. A reversal of the order of things!"[128] Or again, "The original perseverance of realities in their being . . . is inverted in the man announced to humanity in Israel."[129] This view of the Bible is appealing to Christians as much as to Jews. "The Jewish Bible I quote," Lévinas says, "is not the originality of an ethnic particularism no more so than is the Hellenic rationality of knowledge. The Bible signifies for all authentically human thought, for civilization *tout court,* whose authenticity can be recognized in peace, in *shalom,* and in the responsibility of one man for another."[130] His attention to "the face of the other" also acquires poignant force from the recollection of the Holocaust, which surely had an impact on his thinking, even if it does not figure very prominently in his writings.[131]

Attractive as this view of the Bible is, however, it suffers from some of the same problems that beset any attempt to identify a center of biblical theology. There is much in the Bible that does not illustrate the responsibility of one man for another, let alone the responsibility of man for woman.[132] Statements about "the man announced to humanity in Israel" are altogether too simple. That "man" will surely look different depending on whether one is an Israelite or a Canaanite. In fairness to Lévinas, he did not set out to construct a biblical theology as such, but drew from the Bible what suited his philosophy.

127. Emmanuel Lévinas, *Is It Righteous to Be? Interviews with Emmanuel Lévinas,* ed. Jill Robbins (Stanford: Stanford University Press, 2001), 64.

128. Lévinas, *In the Time of the Nations,* 61-62.

129. Lévinas, *In the Time of the Nations,* 133.

130. Lévinas, "On Jewish Philosophy," 171-72.

131. During the Second World War, Lévinas was imprisoned in a labor camp for Jewish prisoners outside Hanover. His family in Lithuania was killed. His wife and daughter were hidden in a convent. See Scott Hennessy, "Creation, Chaos, and the Shoah," in Eskenazi, Phillips, and Jobling, 49-63.

132. While feminist scholars have appreciated the potential of Lévinas's focus on the Other, many are critical of his own views on woman and the feminine. See L. Irigaray, "Questions to Levinas: On the Divinity of Love," in *Re-Reading Lévinas,* ed. Robert Bernasconi and Simon Critchley (Bloomington: Indiana University Press, 1991), 109-18; Tamara Cohn Eskenazi, "Love Your Neighbor as an Other: Reflections on Lévinas's Ethics and the Hebrew Bible," in Eskenazi, Phillips, and Jobling, 145-57; Shapiro.

Nonetheless, he tended to speak of the Bible in idealistic terms and also enter-tained a rather romantic view of the vocation of the state of Israel: "Is it just 'a State like any other', plus a lot of eloquence?" he asks. "Really! . . . Beyond the concern to provide a shelter for those without a country, and beyond the sometimes astonishing, sometimes doubtful, accomplishments of the State of Israel, has it not been a matter above all of creating on its own land the con-crete conditions for political innovation? That is Zionism's ultimate end, and probably one of the great events of human history."[133] One might have hoped for a little more attention to the face of the Palestinian "Other."

But while Lévinas's concern for "the face of the other" is problematic if it is taken *tout court* as a summary of biblical ethics, it has much to com-mend it if it is taken as a criterion by which biblical ethics may be judged. It is by no means a foreign criterion, imported into the Bible from philoso-phy. It has strong support in both Jewish and Christian traditions, but it also has a strong claim to validity as a universal principle[134] — not that it is universally recognized, of course. If it were, we would have a world free from oppression. But what civilized person would deny that genocide is an outrage or indeed that there are actions that can properly be categorized as crimes against humanity? The force of such a principle does not derive from scriptural revelation, or from the fact that it is enshrined in the tradi-tions of Western democracies, but from a sensibility of what it means to be human, granted that this sensibility is constantly being refined. Equally, the validity of such a principle is not limited to any segment of humanity, but is applicable to humanity as such. There is much in the Bible that would have to be judged deficient by such a criterion, even some material that is cast as divine commandment, but it is nonetheless a criterion that is well supported in the biblical record.[135]

133. Emmanuel Lévinas, "Zionisms," in Hand, 283.

134. Küng and Kuschel, 34. Cf. Eagleton, *The Illusions of Postmodernism*, 124: "The par-ticular and the universal are not necessarily at odds. Cultures can be criticized by universalist criteria not only from the standpoint of some other culture, but from within themselves."

135. Knierim, 473, argues for a criterion to determine "which theology or theological as-pect or notion governs others, and which is relative to, or dependent on, or governed by oth-ers." He identifies this principle as "the universal dominion of Yahweh in justice and righ-teousness" (480). This kind of criterion differs from what I am proposing in two respects. Knierim believes that this criterion is given by the text itself, and it is not clear to me that he is willing to apply it so as judge some theologies found in the text as invalid or deficient. In contrast, Perdue, *Reconstructing Old Testament Theology*, 343, states frankly: "There are ideol-ogies present in scripture that are demonic."

There are, of course, other ways in which concern for the other might be formulated besides that of Lévinas, and these ways may carry a different, and arguably superior, nuance. The traditional Christian command to "love your neighbor as yourself" may lack the emotional power of "the face of the Other, in the total nudity of his defenceless eyes," but it allows that "care of self" is an integral part of ethical behavior, as Western philosophy from the Greeks to Foucault has maintained,[136] without compromising its biblical roots. It is not my present purpose, however, to argue the fine points of ethical priorities. The contribution of Lévinas, as I see it, is to show that there is still a place for a universal principle in ethical discussion, and that the imperative to care for others is a compelling one, not necessarily the only one.

I am not suggesting, of course, that the identification of such a principle resolves all problems of biblical ethics or removes the need for deconstructive reading. As Fish remarked, no one declares himself an apostle of injustice. Lévinas's own blind spots on feminist issues and on the Israeli-Palestinian issue remind us that the claims of the Other are not self-evident, and in any case we may often be confronted (as in the case of Palestine) with competing claims from multiple others. But at least such a principle offers some guidance and provides a context within which competing claims may be discussed if not resolved.

In the context of biblical theology, it is axiomatic that this discussion brings us back to the biblical text. The Bible, even just the Hebrew Bible, contains more than one ethical vision and frames it with more than one worldview: contrast, for example, the empirical wisdom of Qoheleth with the apocalypticism of Daniel. The postmodern view that "words like 'justice' (recalling MacIntyre's *Whose Justice?*) and other uplifting words such as 'peace,' 'freedom,' and 'human dignity' have very little meaning outside the context of communal narratives and practices that inform and contextualize these terms"[137] seems to me somewhat exaggerated. It re-

136. Michel Foucault, "The Ethics of a Concern for the Self as a Practice of Freedom," in *The Essential Foucault: Selections from Essential Works of Foucault, 1954-1984,* ed. Paul Rabinow and Nikolas Rose (New York: New Press, 2003), 25-42; Alison Leigh Brown, *On Foucault* (Belmont: Wadsworth, 2000), 76-88. See also John Milbank, "The Midwinter Sacrifice," in *The Blackwell Companion to Postmodern Theology,* ed. Graham Ward (Oxford: Blackwell, 2001), 107-30.

137. Gavin D'Costa, "Postmodernity and Religious Plurality: Is a Common Global Ethic Possible or Desirable?" in Ward, 131-43 (137).

mains true, however, that biblical ethics are embedded in very specific contexts and derive their force in large part from their specificity. No principle or criterion can ever dispense with the reading of specific biblical texts.

Amos Revisited

By way of an illustration, I would like to return to the article of David Clines, "Metacommentating Amos," which I mentioned in the opening chapter.[138] Clines quite rightly observes that, despite Amos's proclamation of impending judgment on Israel because of its social abuses, "the truth about political and economic disaster and well-being is probably far too complex to be explained by the behaviour of individuals."[139] For the present, however, I wish to focus on the prophet's characterization of the social classes. The critique of the wealthy of Samaria is based not only on their perceived excess but also on the fact that they "are not grieved over the ruin of Joseph!" (Amos 6:6). Amos, we might say, is looking at the face of the poor, naked, and defenseless. But, says Clines, how does the prophet know what the rich feel and don't feel? "Would it perhaps be just as true to say, Amos hates the rich because he is not one of them? . . . It's easy to condemn other people's lifestyle and to blame the ills of society on them."[140]

Now, I grant readily enough that commentators on Amos have often been carried away by their zeal in seconding the denunciations of the prophet. And I also grant that we have limited knowledge of conditions in Israel beyond what the prophet tells us[141] and that it would be very interesting to have an account of social conditions from the perspective of the upper class. But nonetheless, my guess is that the prophet's description of the situation was not too far wide of the mark. The situation, after all, is not unfamiliar. It would not take a great act of imagination to conjure up a prophet from the third world fulminating against the luxury of the decadent West, even against what we might regard as the very modest luxury enjoyed by mild-mannered academics who are peacefully unaware of the distress of their fellow human beings. And we would be hard put to say

138. David J. A. Clines, "Metacommentating Amos," in *Interested Parties,* 76-93
139. Clines, "Metacommentating Amos," 80.
140. Clines, "Metacommentating Amos," 80.
141. See, however, Philip J. King, *Amos, Hosea, Micah: An Archaeological Commentary* (Philadelphia: Westminster, 1988).

that the fulminations were without basis, unless, of course, we took the position that our own situation was by definition preferred. So in this case, I am inclined to think that Clines is playing the deconstructionist game by imposing a fog of undecidability on a moral issue. But, interestingly enough, the issue could be clarified only by a thicker description of the social reality. Old-fashioned historical criticism still has its uses in the context of postmodern ethical discussion.[142]

Clines also questions the assumption in the text that sin should be punished by destruction by the deity, with the assistance of human agents.[143] The mentality reflected in the text is by no means outdated, even if most moderns prefer a less theological idiom. In Lars von Trier's film, "Dogville," the long-suffering heroine, Grace (played by Nicole Kidman), has a late and unexpected opportunity to turn the tables on the townspeople who have made her life miserable. At first, she is inclined to be merciful and forgiving. She thinks, we might say, of the faces of these people with whom she has lived and is inclined to overlook their faults. But then the moonlight grows clearer, and she sees that these faces do not inspire so much compassion after all. She also thinks of the possibility that other unfortunate people may wander into this town in the future and be subjected to abuse as she was. So she decides that it is her moral responsibility to improve the state of humanity, if only by a little, and has everyone in the town wiped out. Incubated as I have been in biblical imagery, I felt an impulse to cheer, but it occurred to me that such a reaction might be perceived as politically incorrect. But if there was division of opinion about the fate of Dogville, it should be noted that there was some division of opinion about divine judgment in the Hebrew Bible too. The God of Amos was resolved to wipe a sinful people off the face of the earth (Amos 9:8), but the God of Jonah was concerned about the great city Nineveh, whose inhabitants were surely no saints, and even about their animals.[144]

In short, acceptance of a principle such as "concern for others" is not likely to leave us with any lack of ethical issues to debate. But it does provide a context for our debates, one that is not dependent on assertions about our views because they are ours or the traditions to which we happen to belong.

---

142. Cf. the remarks of F. W. Dobbs-Allsopp, *BibInt* 7 (1999): 251.
143. Clines, "Metacommenting Amos," 90-92.
144. In van Trier's film the dog survives.

Conclusion

" What I find deconstruction does in the realm of ethics," says Clines, "is to problematize traditional categories and distinctions. And what such problematization does is to weaken the authority of traditional ethics. And what such weakening does is to turn more ethical issues over to the decision of individuals. And what the taking charge of one's own ethical decisions does is to make one more of an ethical person."[145] The first three sentences of that statement are surely right, although Clines's insistence on individual responsibility goes against the grain of postmodernist attempts to deconstruct the notion of the self. The last sentence of the quotation requires some qualification. Hitler presumably took charge of his own ethical decisions. He was not for that reason more of an ethical person. The issue is not whether one is autonomous, but what kind of decisions one makes, and on what grounds one makes them.

Much of what Clines says about deconstruction is also true of historical criticism, which has also eroded certitude and weakened the authority of traditional ethics, even if not to quite the same degree. As Fish recognizes, one of the surest ways to deconstruct premature universals is to examine the particular historical circumstances that gave rise to them.[146] But, unlike the postmodernism of Fish, historical criticism does not deny the possibility of universal principles, which is to say, of principles on which people from different cultures can agree. In this respect, the approach of Lévinas is much more congenial to historical criticism, although Lévinas himself seems to have had a limited appreciation of the historicity of human knowledge.[147]

It should be clear, however, that ethical principles, or theological truth, are not simply given by the Bible, regardless of whether one operates within a historical-critical or a postmodernist paradigm. The internal pluralism of the Bible, both theological and ethical, has been established be-

---

145. Clines, "Ethics as Deconstruction," 105.

146. Fish, *The Trouble with Principle*, 4-7.

147. Emmanuel Lévinas, *Nine Talmudic Readings* (Bloomington: Indiana University Press, 1990), cited in Wyschogrod, 186: "No one can refuse the insights of history. But we do not think they are sufficient for everything." According to Wyschogrod, Lévinas "rejects what he considers to be the chief obstacle in a strictly historical approach, namely the presupposition that thought unfolds historically, that before certain historical epochs certain thoughts were unthinkable."

yond dispute. Even within a single book, Deuteronomy, we find both a moving concern for one set of others, the widow, the orphan, and the alien, and a complete disregard for another, the Canaanites. Biblical theology, and biblical ethics, are never just a matter of telling the biblical story, whether one regards it as historical or not, but require a criterion by which different elements in the text may be evaluated. Such a criterion may be found within the text, but it is never the only one on offer. Biblical theology and biblical ethics, in short, can never be determined *sola scriptura*, by appeal to "the text itself," but always have the nature of a dialogue between the Bible as we understand it and whatever knowledge we may have from other sources. Biblical theology, then, must be a critical enterprise, which does not simply affirm the values of the text but weighs them in comparison and contrast with other sources.[148]

The main gain of postmodernist criticism, in my view, is that it has expanded the horizons of biblical studies, by going out to the highways and by-ways to bring new "voices from the margin" to the conversation. The persistent attention to the Other, or to the other way of reading, is a salutary exercise. These horizons will inevitably continue to expand in the 21st century. Conversely, the main danger of postmodernism is the disintegration of the conversation into a cacophony of voices, each asserting that their convictions are by definition preferred, because they are *their* convictions, or what Yvonne Sherwood and Kevin Hart call "cultures of mutual indifference,"[149] or worse. This danger is considerable, but not unavoidable. Biblical theology and biblical ethics will have to be more skeptical and self-critical in the wake of postmodernism, but they remain viable enterprises for people who are willing to enter a conversation in good faith and to pursue consensus, but not assume it.

---

148. Cf. Perdue, *Reconstructing Old Testament Theology,* 349.
149. Sherwood and Hart, 8.

Bibliography

Ackerman, Susan. "At Home with the Goddess." In *Symbiosis, Symbolism, and the Power of the Past: Canaan, Ancient Israel, and Their Neighbors from the Late Bronze Age through Roman Palaestina*, ed. William G. Dever and Seymour Gitin, 455-68. Winona Lake: Eisenbrauns, 2003.

————. *Under Every Green Tree: Popular Religion in Sixth-Century Judah*. HSM 46. Atlanta: Scholars, 1992.

Adam, A. K. M. "Post-modern Biblical Interpretation." In *Dictionary of Biblical Interpretation*, ed. John H. Hayes, 2:305-9. Nashville: Abingdon, 1999.

————. *What Is Postmodern Biblical Criticism?* GBS. Minneapolis: Fortress, 1995.

————, ed. *Handbook of Postmodern Biblical Interpretation*. St. Louis: Chalice, 2000.

————. *Postmodern Interpretations of the Bible: A Reader*. St. Louis: Chalice, 2001.

Ahlström, Gösta W. *The History of Ancient Palestine from the Palaeolithic Period to Alexander's Conquest*. JSOTSup 146. Sheffield: Sheffield Academic, 1993.

Aichele, George. *Sign, Text, Scripture: Semiotics and the Bible*. Sheffield: Sheffield Academic, 1997.

————, et al. (The Bible and Culture Collective). *The Postmodern Bible*. New Haven: Yale University Press, 1995.

Albertz, Rainer. "An End to the Confusion? Why the Old Testament Cannot Be a Hellenistic Book!" In *Did Moses Speak Attic?* ed. Lester L. Grabbe, 30-46. Sheffield: Sheffield Academic, 2001.

————. "Die Exilszeit als Ernstfall für eine historische Rekonstruktion ohne biblische Texte: Die neubabylonischen Königsinschriften als 'Primärquelle.'" In *Leading Captivity Captive,* ed. Lester L. Grabbe, 22-39. Sheffield: Sheffield Academic, 1998.

————. *A History of Israelite Religion in the Old Testament Period.* 2 vols. OTL. Louisville: Westminster John Knox, 1994.

————. *Israel in Exile: The History and Literature of the Sixth Century B.C.E.* Atlanta: SBL, 2003.

————. "Religionsgeschichte Israels statt Theologie des Alten Testaments! Plädoyer für eine forschungsgeschichtliche Umorientierung," *JBTh* 10 (1995): 3-24.

Albrektson, Bertil. *History and the Gods.* ConBOT 1. Lund: Gleerup, 1967.

Albright, William F. *Archaeology and the Religion of Israel.* Baltimore: Johns Hopkins University Press, 1942.

————. *From the Stone Age to Christianity: Monotheism and the Historical Process.* 2nd ed. New York: Doubleday, 1957.

————. *Yahweh and the Gods of Canaan.* Garden City: Doubleday, 1968.

Alt, Albrecht. "The Monarchy in the Kingdoms of Israel and Judah." In *Essays on Old Testament History and Religion,* 313-35. Garden City: Doubleday, 1968.

Alter, Robert. *The Pleasures of Reading in an Ideological Age.* New York: Simon and Schuster, 1989.

Appleby, Joyce, Lynn Hunt, and Margaret Jacob. *Telling the Truth about History.* New York: Norton, 1994.

Ashcroft, Bill, Gareth Griffiths, and Helen Tiffin. *The Empire Writes Back: Theory and Practice in Post-colonial Literatures.* London: Routledge, 1989.

————. *Key Concepts in Post-Colonial Studies.* London: Routledge, 1998.

————. *The Post-Colonial Studies Reader.* London: Routledge, 1995.

Assman, Jan. *Moses the Egyptian: The Memory of Egypt in Western Monotheism.* Cambridge, Mass.: Harvard University Press, 1997.

Ateek, Naim Stifan. *Justice, and Only Justice. A Palestinian Theology of Liberation.* Maryknoll: Orbis, 1989.

Auld, A. Graeme. *Joshua Retold: Synoptic Perspectives.* Edinburgh: T. & T. Clark, 1998.

Bach, Alice, ed. *Women in the Hebrew Bible: A Reader.* London: Routledge, 1999.

Bainton, Roland H. "The Immoralities of the Patriarchs according to the Exegesis of the Late Middle Ages and of the Reformation." *HTR* 23 (1930): 39-49.

Bal, Mieke. *Death and Dissymmetry: The Politics of Coherence in the Book of Judges.* Chicago: University of Chicago Press, 1988.

————. *Lethal Love: Feminist Literary Readings of Biblical Love Stories.* Bloomington: Indiana University Press, 1987.

163

Barr, James. *Biblical Faith and Natural Theology*. Oxford: Clarendon, 1993.

———. *The Concept of Biblical Theology: An Old Testament Perspective*. Minneapolis: Fortress, 1999.

———. *History and Ideology in the Old Testament*. Oxford: Oxford University Press, 2000.

———. "Story and History in Biblical Theology." *JR* 56 (1976): 1-17.

Barstad, Hans. "History and the Hebrew Bible." In *Can a "History of Israel" Be Written?* ed. Lester L. Grabbe, 37-64. Sheffield: Sheffield Academic, 1997.

———. "The Strange Fear of the Bible: Some Reflections on the 'Bibliophobia' in Recent Ancient Israelite Historiography." In *Leading Captivity Captive*, ed. Lester L. Grabbe, 120-27.

Barth, Fredrik, ed. *Ethnic Groups and Boundaries: The Social Organization of Cultural Difference*. Boston: Little, Brown, 1969.

Barth, Karl. *Church Dogmatics*, I/1: *The Doctrine of the Word of God*. 2nd ed. Edinburgh: T. & T. Clark, 1986.

———. *Church Dogmatics*, III/4: *The Doctrine of Creation*. Edinburgh: T. & T. Clark, 1958.

Barton, John. "Historical-critical Approaches." In *The Cambridge Companion to Biblical Interpretation*, 9-20.

———. *Reading the Old Testament: Method in Biblical Study*. Rev. ed. Louisville: Westminster John Knox, 1996.

———, ed. *The Cambridge Companion to Biblical Interpretation*. Cambridge: Cambridge University Press, 1998.

Bauman, Zygmunt. *Postmodern Ethics*. Oxford: Blackwell, 1993.

Becking, Bob; M. Dykstra; M. C. A. Korpel; and K. J. H. Vriezen. *Only One God? Monotheism in Ancient Israel and the Veneration of the Goddess Asherah*. New York: Sheffield: Sheffield Academic, 2001.

Beck, Pirhiya. "The Drawings from Ḥorvat Teiman (Kuntillet ʿAjrud)." *Tel Aviv* 9 (1982): 3-68.

Bekkenkamp, Jonneke, and Yvonne Sherwood, eds. *Sanctified Aggression: Legacies of Biblical and Post Biblical Vocabularies of Violence*. JSOTSup 400. London: T. & T. Clark, 2003.

Bellis, Alice Ogden, and Joel S. Kaminsky, eds. *Jews, Christians, and the Theology of the Hebrew Scriptures*. SBLSymS 8. Atlanta: Society of Biblical Literature, 2000.

Benjamin, Walter. *One Way Street, and Other Writings*. London: New Left, 1979.

Bentley, Michael. *Modern Historiography: An Introduction*. London: Routledge, 1999.

Berger, Klaus. *Die Gesetzesauslegung Jesu*. WMANT 40. Neukirchen-Vluyn: Neukirchener, 1972.

Berkhofer, Robert F. *Beyond the Great Story.* Cambridge, Mass.: Harvard University Press, 1995.

Bernstein, Richard J. *Beyond Objectivism and Relativism.* Philadelphia: University of Pennsylvania Press, 1983.

Berthelot, Katell. *L'"Humanité de l'autre Homme" dans la Pensée Juive Ancienne.* JSJSup 87. Leiden: Brill, 2004.

Betz, Hans Dieter. *The Sermon on the Mount.* Hermeneia. Minneapolis: Fortress, 1995.

Biran, Avraham, and Joseph Naveh. "The Tel Dan Inscription: A New Fragment." *IEJ* 45 (1995): 1-18.

Bird, Phyllis A. "Israelite Religion and the Faith of Israel's Daughters." In *Missing Persons and Mistaken Identities,* 103-20.

———. "'Male and Female He Created Them': Gen 1:27b in the Context of the Priestly Account of Creation." In *Missing Persons and Mistaken Identities,* 123-54.

———. *Missing Persons and Mistaken Identities: Women and Gender in Ancient Israel.* OBT. Minneapolis: Fortress, 1997.

———, ed. *Reading the Bible as Women: Perspectives from Africa, Asia, and Latin America.* Semeia 78. Atlanta: Scholars, 1997.

Bloch, Marc. *The Historian's Craft.* New York: Knopf, 1953.

Bloch-Smith, Elizabeth. "Israelite Ethnicity in Iron I: Archaeology Preserves What Is Remembered and What Is Forgotten in Israel's History." *JBL* 122 (2003): 401-25.

———, and Beth Alpert Nakhai. "A Landscape Comes to Life." *NEA* 62 (1999): 62-92, 101-27.

Boer, Roland. "Night Sprinkle(s): Pornography and the Song of Songs." In *Knockin' on Heaven's Door: The Bible and Popular Culture,* 53-70. New York: Routledge, 1999.

———. "The Second Coming: Repetition and Insatiable Desire in the Song of Songs." *BibInt* 8 (2000): 276-301.

Boers, Hendrikus. "Religionsgeschichtliche Schule." In *Dictionary of Biblical Interpretation,* ed. John H. Hayes, 2:383-87. Nashville: Abingdon, 1999.

Boff, Leonardo, and Clodovis Boff. *Liberation Theology: From Confrontation to Dialogue.* San Francisco: Harper & Row, 1986.

———. *Salvation and Liberation: In Search of a Balance between Faith and Politics.* Maryknoll: Orbis, 1984.

Boyarin, Daniel. *A Radical Jew: Paul and the Politics of Identity.* Berkeley: University of California Press, 1994.

Boyarin, Jonathan. "Reading Exodus into History." *New Literary History* 23 (1992): 523-54.

Braidotti, Rosi. "What's Wrong with Gender?" In *Reflections on Theology and Gender,* ed. Fokkelien van Dijk-Hemmes and Athalya Brenner, 49-70. Kampen: Kok Pharos, 1994.

Braude, William G., and Israel J. Kapstein, trans. *Pesikta de-Ra̲b̲ Kahana.* 2nd ed. Philadelphia: Jewish Publication Society of America, 2002.

Braulik, Georg. "The Rejection of the Goddess Asherah in Israel." In *The Theology of Deuteronomy,* 165-82. Berkeley: BIBAL, 1994.

Brenner, Athalya. *The Intercourse of Knowledge: On Gendering Desire and "Sexuality" in the Hebrew Bible.* Biblical Interpretation 26. Leiden: Brill, 1997.

————, and Carol R. Fontaine, eds. *A Feminist Companion to Reading the Bible: Approaches, Methods and Strategies.* Sheffield: Sheffield Academic, 1997.

Brett, Mark G. *Biblical Criticism in Crisis? The Impact of the Canonical Approach on Old Testament Studies.* Cambridge: Cambridge University Press, 1991.

————. "The Ethics of Postcolonial Criticism." *Semeia* 75 (1996): 219-28.

————. "Israel's Indigenous Origins: Cultural Hybridity and the Formation of Israelite Ethnicity." *BibInt* 11 (2003): 400-12.

Brettler, Marc Zvi. *The Creation of History in Ancient Israel.* London: Routledge, 1995.

Bright, John. *A History of Israel.* 4th ed. Louisville: Westminster John Knox, 2000. (1st ed., Philadelphia: Westminster, 1959).

Britt, Brian M. "Erasing Amalek: Remembering to Forget with Derrida and Biblical Tradition." In *Derrida and Religion,* ed. Yvonne Sherwood and Kevin Hart, 61 pp. New York: Routledge, 2005

Brodribb, Somer. *Nothing Mat(t)ers: A Feminist Critique of Postmodernism.* North Melbourne: Spinifex, 1992.

Brown, Alison Leigh. *On Foucault.* Belmont: Wadsworth, 2000.

Brueggemann, Walter. "Biblical Theology Appropriately Postmodern." *BTB* 27 (1997): 4-9.

————. *The Land: Place as Gift, Promise, and Challenge in Biblical Faith.* OBT. Philadelphia: Fortress, 1977. 2nd ed., Minneapolis: Fortress, 2002.

————. "Pharaoh as Vassal: A Study of a Political Metaphor." *CBQ* 57 (1995): 27-51.

————. *Texts Under Negotiation: The Bible and Postmodern Imagination.* Minneapolis: Fortress, 1993.

————. *Theology of the Old Testament: Testimony, Dispute, Advocacy.* Minneapolis: Fortress, 1997.

————. "Trajectories in Old Testament Literature and the Sociology of Ancient Israel." *JBL* 98 (1979): 161-85.

Brunner, Emil, and Karl Barth. *Natural Theology.* London: Bles, 1946.

Bultmann, Rudolf. *Theology of the New Testament*. 2 vols. New York: Scribner's, 1951-55.

Burnett, Fred W. "Postmodern Biblical Exegesis: The Eve of Historical Criticism." *Semeia* 51 (1990): 51-80.

Burrus, Virginia, and Stephen D. Moore. "Unsafe Sex: Feminism, Pornography, and the Song of Songs." *BibInt* 11 (2003): 24-52.

Butler, Judith. *Gender Trouble: Feminism and the Subversion of Identity*. London: Routledge, 1990.

Buttrick, George A., et al., eds. *Interpreter's Dictionary of the Bible*. 4 vols. New York: Abingdon, 1962.

Cannon, Katie G., and Elisabeth Schüssler Fiorenza, eds. *Interpretation for Liberation*. Semeia 47. Atlanta: Scholars, 1989.

Caputo, John D. *Against Ethics: Contributions to a Poetics of Obligation with Constant Reference to Deconstruction*. Bloomington: Indiana University Press, 1993.

———. *The Prayers and Tears of Jacques Derrida*. Bloomington: Indiana University Press, 1997.

Carr, David M. *The Erotic Word: Sexuality, Spirituality, and the Bible*. Oxford: Oxford University Press, 2003.

———. *Reading the Fractures of Genesis: Historical and Literary Approaches*. Louisville: Westminster John Knox, 1996.

Carroll, Robert P. "Poststructuralist Approaches: New Historicism and Postmodernism." In *The Cambridge Companion to Biblical Interpretation*, ed. John Barton, 50-66. Cambridge: Cambridge University Press, 1998.

Charlesworth, James H., ed. *The Old Testament Pseudepigrapha*. 2 vols. Garden City: Doubleday, 1983-84.

Childs, Brevard S. *Biblical Theology in Crisis*. Philadelphia: Westminster, 1970.

———. *Biblical Theology of the Old and New Testaments: Theological Reflection on the Christian Bible*. Minneapolis: Fortress, 1993.

———. *Introduction to the Old Testament as Scripture*. Philadelphia: Fortress, 1979.

———. *Old Testament Theology in a Canonical Context*. Philadelphia: Fortress, 1986.

Clines, David J. A. "Ethics as Deconstruction, And, Deconstruction as Ethics." In *The Bible in Ethics: The Second Sheffield Colloquium*, ed. John W. Rogerson, Margaret Davies, and M. Daniel Carroll R., 77-106. JSOTSup 207. Sheffield: Sheffield Academic, 1995.

———. *Interested Parties: The Ideology of Writers and Readers of the Hebrew Bible*. JSOTSup 205. Sheffield: Sheffield Academic, 1995.

———. "Metacommentating Amos." In *Interested Parties*, 76-93.

————. "The Postmodern Adventure in Biblical Studies." In *Auguries: The Jubilee Volume of the Sheffield Department of Biblical Studies,* ed. Clines and Stephen D. Moore, 276-91. JSOTSup 269. Sheffield: Sheffield Academic, 1998.

————. *What Does Eve Do to Help? and Other Readerly Questions to the Old Testament.* JSOTSup 94. Sheffield: Sheffield Academic, 1990.

Collingwood, R. G. *The Idea of History.* Oxford: Oxford University Press, 1946.

Collins, John J. "The Biblical Precedent for Natural Theology." *JAAR* 45 (1977) Sup B: 35-67.

————. "The Development of the Exodus Tradition." In *Religious Identity and the Invention of Tradition,* ed. Jan Willem van Henten and Anton Houtepen, 144-55. Assen: van Gorcum, 2001.

————. "The Exodus and Biblical Theology." *BTB* 25 (1995): 152-60. Repr. in *Jews, Christians, and the Theology of the Hebrew Scriptures,* ed. Alice Ogden Bellis and Joel S. Kaminsky, 247-261. Atlanta: SBL, 2000.

————. "Faith Without Works: Biblical Ethics and the Sacrifice of Isaac." In *Recht und Ethos im Alten Testament: Gestalt und Wirkung.* Festschrift für Horst Seebass zum 65. Geburtstag, ed. Stefan Beyerle, Günther Mayer, and Hans Strauss, 115-31. Neukirchen-Vluyn: Neukirchener, 1999.

————. "The 'Historical Character' of the Old Testament in Recent Biblical Theology." *CBQ* 41 (1979): 185-204.

————. "Jewish Monotheism and Christian Theology." In *Aspects of Monotheism,* ed. Hershel Shanks and Jack Meinhardt, 81-105. Washington: Biblical Archeology Society, 1987.

————. "Marriage, Divorce, and Family in Second Temple Judaism." In *Families in Ancient Israel,* ed. Leo G. Perdue et al., 104-62. Louisville: Westminster John Knox, 1997.

————. "The Politics of Biblical Interpretation." In *Biblical and Near Eastern Essays: Studies in Honour of Kevin J. Cathcart,* ed. Carmel McCarthy and John F. Healey, 195-211. JSOTSup 375. London: T. & T. Clark, 2004.

————. "Temporality and Politics in Jewish Apocalyptic Literature." In *Apocalyptic in History and Tradition,* ed. Christopher Rowland and John Barton, 26-43. JSPSup 43. Sheffield: Sheffield Academic, 2002.

————. "The Zeal of Phinehas: The Bible and the Legitimation of Violence." *JBL* 122 (2003): 3-21. Repr. as *Does the Bible Justify Violence?* Minneapolis: Fortress, 2004.

Coogan, Michael D. "Canaanite Origins and Lineage: Reflections on the Religion of Ancient Israel." In *Ancient Israelite Religion,* ed. Patrick D. Miller, Paul D. Hanson, and S. Dean McBride, 115-24. Philadelphia: Fortress, 1987.

Cook, Albert. *History/Writing.* Cambridge: Cambridge University Press, 1988.

Cooper, Alan. "Biblical Studies and Jewish Studies." In *The Oxford Handbook of*

Jewish Studies, ed. Martin Goodman, 14-35. Oxford: Oxford University Press, 2002.

Cott, Jeremy. "The Biblical Problem of Election." *Journal of Ecumenical Studies* 21 (1984): 199-228.

Cox, Jeffrey N., and Larry J. Reynolds. "The Historicist Enterprise." In *New Historical Literary Study: Essays on Reproducing Texts, Representing History,* 3-38. Princeton: Princeton University Press, 1993.

Croatto, J. Severino. *Biblical Hermeneutics: Toward a Theory of Reading as the Production of Meaning.* Maryknoll: Orbis, 1987.

————. *Exodus: A Hermeneutics of Freedom.* Maryknoll: Orbis, 1978.

Cross, Frank Moore. *Canaanite Myth and Hebrew Epic.* Cambridge, Mass.: Harvard University Press, 1973.

————. "The Cave Inscriptions from Khirbet Beit Lei." In *Near Eastern Archaeology in the Twentieth Century: Essays in Honor of Nelson Glueck,* ed. James A. Sanders, 299-306. Garden City: Doubleday, 1970.

Culler, Jonathan D. *On Deconstruction: Theory and Criticism after Structuralism.* Ithaca: Cornell University Press, 1982.

Davidson, Donald. "On the Very Idea of a Conceptual Scheme." *Proceedings and Addresses of the American Philosophical Association* 47 (1974): 5-20. Repr. in *Inquiries into Truth and Interpretation,* 183-98. Oxford: Clarendon, 1983.

Davies, Eryl W. *The Dissenting Reader: Feminist Approaches to the Hebrew Bible.* Aldershot: Ashgate, 2003.

Davies, G. I. *Ancient Hebrew Inscriptions.* Cambridge: Cambridge University Press, 1991.

Davies, Philip R. "'House of David' Built on Sand: The Sins of the Biblical Maximizers," *BAR* 20/4 (1994): 54-55.

————. *In Search of "Ancient Israel."* JSOTSup 148. Sheffield: Sheffield Academic, 1992.

————. "Method and Madness: Some Remarks on Doing History with the Bible." *JBL* 114 (1995): 699-705.

————. *Whose Bible Is it Anyway?* JSOTSup 204. Sheffield: Sheffield Academic, 1995.

————. "Whose History? Whose Israel? Whose Bible? Biblical Histories, Ancient and Modern." In *Can a "History of Israel" Be Written?* ed. Lester L. Grabbe, 104-22. Sheffield: Sheffield Academic, 1997.

Davies, W. D. *The Territorial Dimension of Judaism, with a Symposium and Further Reflections.* Minneapolis: Fortress, 1991.

Day, John. *God's Conflict with the Dragon and the Sea.* Cambridge: Cambridge University Press, 1985.

————. *Molech: A God of Human Sacrifice in the Old Testament.* Cambridge: Cambridge University Press, 1989.

————. *Yahweh and the Gods and Goddesses of Canaan.* JSOTSup 265. Sheffield: Sheffield Academic, 2000.

Day, Peggy L, ed. *Gender and Difference in Ancient Israel.* Minneapolis: Fortress, 1989.

D'Costa, Gavin. "Postmodernity and Religious Plurality: Is a Common Global Ethic Possible or Desirable?" In *The Blackwell Companion to Postmodern Theology,* ed. Graham Ward, 131-43. Oxford: Blackwell, 2001.

Derrida, Jacques. *Adieu to Emmanuel Lévinas.* Stanford: Stanford University Press, 1999.

————. "Circumfession: Fifty-nine Periods and Periphrases." In *Jacques Derrida,* ed. Geoffrey Bennington and Derrida, 155-56. Chicago: University of Chicago Press, 1993.

————. "Deconstruction and the Other." In *Dialogues with Contemporary Continental Thinkers,* ed. Richard Kearney, 107-26. Manchester: University of Manchester Press, 1984.

————. "Differance." In *Speech and Phenomena, and Other Essays on Husserl's Theory of Signs,* 129-60. Evanston: Northwestern University Press, 1973.

————. "Faith and Knowledge: The Two Sources of 'Religion' at the Limits of Reason Alone." In *Religion,* ed. Derrida and Gianni Vattimo, 1-78. Cambridge: Polity, 1998.

————. *The Gift of Death.* Chicago: University of Chicago Press, 1995.

————. "Like the Sound of the Sea Deep Within a Shell: Paul de Man's War." In *Responses,* ed. Werner Hamacher, Neil Hertz, and Thomas Keenan, 127-64.

————. *Of Grammatology.* Baltimore: Johns Hopkins University Press, 1976.

————. "Des Tours de Babel." In *Poststructuralism and Exegesis,* ed. David Jobling and Stephen D. Moore, 3-34. Semeia 54 (Atlanta: Scholars, 1991).

————. *Writing and Difference.* Chicago: University of Chicago Press, 1978.

Dever, William G. "Ancient Israelite Religion: How to Reconcile the Differing Texts and Artifactual Portraits." In *Ein Gott allein,* ed. Walter Dietrich and Martin A. Klopfenstein, 105-25. Göttingen: Vandenhoeck & Ruprecht, 1994.

————. "Archaeology and the Ancient Israelite Cult: How the Kh. el Qôm and Kuntillet Ajrud 'Asherah' Texts Have Changed the Picture." *ErIsr* 26 (1999): 9*-15*.

————. "Asherah, Consort of Yahweh? New Evidence from Kuntillet ʿAjrûd." *BASOR* 255 (1984): 21-37.

————. *Did God Have a Wife? Archaeology and Folk Religion in Ancient Israel.* Grand Rapids: Wm. B. Eerdmans, 2005.

————. "Folk Religion in Early Israel: Did Yahweh Have a Consort?" In *Aspects of Monotheism,* ed. Hershel Shanks and Jack Meinhardt, 27-56. Washington: Biblical Archeology Society, 1997.

———. "Iron Age Epigraphic Material from the Area of Khirbet el-Kôm." *HUCA* 40-41 (1969-1970): 139-204.

———. "Revisionist Israel Revisited: A Rejoinder to Niels Peter Lemche." *CurBS* 4 (1996): 35-50.

———. "The Silence of the Text: An Archaeological Commentary on 2 Kings 23." In *Scripture and Other Artifacts: Essays on the Bible and Archaeology in Honor of Philip J. King,* ed. Michael D. Coogan, J. Cheryl Exum, and Lawrence E. Stager, 143-68. Louisville: Westminster John Knox, 1994.

———. "What Did the Biblical Writers Know, and When Did They Know It?" In *Hesed ve-Emet: Festschrift for Ernest Frerichs,* ed. Jodi Magness and Seymour Gitin, 241-53. BJS 320. Atlanta: Scholars, 1998.

———. *What Did the Biblical Writers Know and When Did They Know It?* Grand Rapids: Wm. B. Eerdmans, 2001.

———. *Who Were the Early Israelites and Where Did They Come From?* Grand Rapids: Wm. B. Eerdmans, 2003.

Dietrich, Manfried, and Oswald Loretz. *"Jahwe und seine Aschera": Anthropomorphes Kultbild in Mesopotamien, Ugarit und Israel.* Ugaritisch-Biblische Literatur 9. Münster: Ugarit, 1992.

Dietrich, Walter, and Martin A. Klopfenstein, eds. *Ein Gott allein? JHWH-Verehrung und biblischer Monotheismus im Kontext der israelitischen und altorientalischen Religionsgeschichte.* OBO 139. Göttingen: Vandenhoeck & Ruprecht, 1994.

Dobbs-Allsopp, F. W. "Rethinking Historical Criticism." *BibInt* 7 (1999): 235-71.

Donaldson, Laura E. "Postcolonialism and Biblical Reading: An Introduction." In *Postcolonialism and Scriptural Reading,* 1-14. Semeia 75. Atlanta: Scholars, 1996.

———, and Kwok Pui Lan, eds. *Postcolonialism, Feminism, and Religious Discourse.* London: Routledge, 2002.

Donner, Herbert. "The Separate States of Israel and Judah." In *Israelite and Judaean History,* ed. John H. Hayes and J. Maxwell Miller, 381-434. OTL. Philadelphia: Westminster, 1977.

Dragga, Sam. "Genesis 2–3: A Story of Liberation." *JSOT* 55 (1992): 3-13.

Dussel, Enrique. "Exodus as a Paradigm in Liberation Theology." In *Exodus: A Lasting Paradigm,* ed. Bas van Iersel and Anton Weiler, 83-92. Edinburgh: T&T Clark, 1987.

Eagleton, Terry. *After Theory.* New York: Basic Books, 2003.

———. "Deconstruction and Human Rights." In *Freedom and Interpretation:*

The Oxford Amnesty Lectures, 1992, ed. Barbara Johnson, 121-45. New York: Basic Books, 1993.

―――. *The Illusions of Postmodernism.* Oxford: Blackwell, 1997.

Edelman, Diana, ed. *The Fabric of History: Text, Artifact, and Israel's Past.* JSOTSup 127. Sheffield: Sheffield Academic Press, 1991.

Eden, Christopher. Review of Robert B. Coote and Keith W. Whitelam, *The Emergence of Early Israel in Historical Perspective,* and Israel Finkeistein, *The Archaeology of the Israelite Settlement. AJA* 93 (1989): 289-92.

Eichrodt, Walther. "Does Old Testament Theology Still Have Independent Significance within Old Testament Scholarship?" In *The Flowering of Old Testament Theology,* ed. Ben C. Ollenburger, E. A. Martens, and Gerhard F. Hasel, 30-39.

―――. *Theology of the Old Testament.* 2 vols. OTL. Philadelphia: Westminster, 1961-67.

Eissfeldt, Otto. "The History of Israelite-Jewish Religion and Old Testament Theology." In *The Flowering of Old Testament Theology,* ed. Ben C. Ollenburger, E. A. Martens, and Gerhard F. Hasel, 20-29. Winona Lake: Eisenbrauns, 1992.

Ellis, Marc H. *Toward a Jewish Theology of Liberation.* 3rd ed. Waco: Baylor University Press, 2004.

Emerton, J. A. "New Light on Israelite Religion: The Implications of the Inscriptions from Kuntillet ʿAjrud." *ZAW* 94 (1982): 2-20.

Ermarth, Elizabeth Deeds. *Sequel to History: Postmodernism and the Crisis of Representational Time.* Princeton: Princeton University Press, 1992.

Eskenazi, Tamara Cohn. "Introduction: Facing the Text as Other: Some Implications of Lévinas's Work for Biblical Studies." In *Lévinas and Biblical Studies,* ed. Ezkenazi, Gary A. Phillips, and David Jobling, 1-16.

―――. "Love Your Neighbor as an Other: Reflections on Levinas's Ethics and the Hebrew Bible." In *Levinas and Biblical Studies,* ed. Eskenazi, Gary A. Phillips, and David Jobling, 145-57.

―――, Gary A. Phillips, and David Jobling, eds. *Levinas and Biblical Studies.* Semeia Studies 43. Atlanta: SBL, 2003.

Evans, Richard J. *In Defense of History.* New York: Norton, 1999.

Exum, J. Cheryl. *Fragmented Women: Feminist (Sub)versions of Biblical Narratives.* Valley Forge: Trinity Press International, 1993.

―――. *Plotted, Shot, and Painted: Cultural Representations of Biblical Women.* JSOTSup 215. Sheffield: Sheffield Academic, 1996.

Fewell, Danna Nolan. "Building Babel." In *Postmodern Interpretations of the Bible,* ed. A. K. M. Adam, 1-15. St. Louis: Chalice, 2001.

————, and David M. Gunn. *Gender, Power, and Promise: The Subject of the Bible's First Story.* Nashville: Abingdon, 1993.

Feyerabend, Paul. *Science in a Free Society.* London: NLB, 1978.

Finkelstein, Israel. "Archaeology and Text in the Third Millennium: A View from the Center." In *Congress Volume, Basel,* ed. André Lemaire, 323-42. VTSup 92. Leiden: Brill, 2002.

————, and Neil Asher Silberman, eds. *The Bible Unearthed: Archaeology's New Vision of Ancient Israel and the Origin of Its Sacred Texts.* New York: Free Press, 2001.

Finley, Moses I. *Ancient History: Evidence and Models.* London: Chatto and Windus, 1985.

Fisch, Harold. "Hosea: A Poetics of Violence." In *Poetry with a Purpose: Biblical Poetics and Interpretation,* 136-57. Bloomington: Indiana University Press, 1988.

Fish, Stanley. "Condemnation without Absolutes." *New York Times,* 15 October 2001, A 19.

————. *The Trouble with Principle.* Cambridge, Mass.: Harvard University Press, 1999.

Fishbane, Michael. *Biblical Myth and Rabbinic Mythmaking.* Oxford: Oxford University Press, 2003.

Fogarty, Gerald P., S.J. *American Catholic Biblical Scholarship: A History from the Early Republic to Vatican II.* San Francisco: Harper & Row, 1989.

Fontaine, Carole R. "The Abusive Bible: On the Use of Feminist Method in Pastoral Contexts." In *A Feminist Companion to Reading the Bible,* ed. Athalya Brenner and Fontaine, 84-112. Sheffield: Sheffield Academic, 1997.

————. "A Heifer from Thy Stable. On Goddesses and the Status of Women in the Ancient Near East." In *Women in the Hebrew Bible,* ed. Alice Bach, 159-78. London: Routledge, 1999.

Ford, David. *Barth and God's Story.* Frankfurt: Lang, 1981.

Foster, Benjamin R. *From Distant Days: Myths, Tales, and Poetry of Ancient Mesopotamia.* Bethesda: CDL, 1995.

Foucault, Michel. "The Ethics of a Concern for the Self as a Practice of Freedom." In *The Essential Foucault: Selections from Essential Works of Foucault, 1954-1984,* ed. Paul Rabinow and Nikolas Rose, 25-42. New York: New Press, 2003.

————. *Politics, Philosophy, Culture: Interviews and Other Writings, 1972-1977.* New York: Routledge, 1988.

Freedman, David Noel. "Yahweh of Samaria and His Asherah." *BA* 50 (1987): 241-49.

————, ed. *Anchor Bible Dictionary.* 6 vols. New York: Doubleday, 1992.

————, and Jeffrey C. Geoghegan. "'House of David' Is There." *BAR* 21/2 (1995): 78-79.

Frei, Hans. *The Eclipse of Biblical Narrative*. New Haven: Yale University Press, 1974.

Fritz, Volkmar, and Philip R. Davies, eds. *The Origins of the Ancient Israelite States*. JSOTSup 228. Sheffield: Sheffield Academic, 1996.

Frymer-Kensky, Tikva. *In the Wake of the Goddesses: Women, Culture, and the Biblical Transformation of Pagan Myth*. New York: Free Press, 1992.

————. *Reading the Women of the Bible*. New York: Schocken, 2002.

Fuchs, Esther. "The Literary Characterization of Mothers and Sexual Politics in the Hebrew Bible." In *Feminist Perspectives on Biblical Scholarship*, ed. Adela Yarbro Collins, 117-36. Chico: Scholars, 1985.

————. *Sexual Politics in the Biblical Narrative: Reading the Bible as a Woman*. JSOTSup 310. Sheffield: Sheffield Academic, 2000.

————. "Who Is Hiding the Truth? Deceptive Women and Biblical Androcentrism." In *Feminist Perspectives on Biblical Scholarship*, ed. Adela Yarbro Collins, 137-44. Chico: Scholars, 1985.

Gabler, Johann P. "An Oration on the Proper Distinction between Biblical and Dogmatic Theology and the Specific Objectives of Each." In *The Flowering of Old Testament Theology*, ed. Ben C. Ollenburger, E. A. Martens, and Gerhard F. Hasel, 489-502. Winona Lake: Eisenbrauns, 1992.

Garbini, Giovanni. *History and Ideology in Ancient Israel*. New York: Crossroad, 1988.

Garr, W. Randall. *In His Own Image and Likeness: Humanity, Divinity, and Monotheism*. CHANE 15. Leiden: Brill, 2003.

Gerstenberger, Erhard S. *Theologies of the Old Testament*. Minneapolis: Fortress, 2002.

————. *Yahweh — The Patriarch*. Minneapolis: Fortress, 1996. Originally published as *Jahwe, ein patriarchaler Gott? Traditionelles Gottesbild und feministische Theologie*. Stuttgart: Kohlhammer, 1988.

Gese, Hartmut. *Essays on Biblical Theology*. Minneapolis: Augsburg, 1981.

————. *Vom Sinai zum Zion: Alttestamentliche Beiträge zur biblischen Theologie*. BEvT 64. Munich: Kaiser, 1974.

————. *Zur biblischen Theologie*. BEvT 78. Munich: Kaiser, 1977.

Gibbs, Robert. *Correlations in Rosenzweig and Lévinas*. Princeton: Princeton University Press, 1992.

Gifford, Carolyn De Swarte. "American Women and the Bible: The Nature of Woman as a Hermeneutical Issue." In *Feminist Perspectives on Biblical Scholarship*, ed. Adela Yarbro Collins, 11-33. Chico: Scholars, 1985.

————. "Politicizing the Sacred Texts: Elizabeth Cady Stanton and *The Woman's*

Bibliography

Bible." In *Searching the Scriptures, 1: A Feminist Introduction,* ed. Elisabeth Schüssler Fiorenza, 52-63. New York: Crossroad, 1993.

Gilkey, Langdon B. "Cosmology, Ontology, and the Travail of Biblical Language." *JR* 41 (1961): 194-205.

Gilula, Mordechai. "To Yahweh Shomron and His Asherah." *Shnaton* 3 (1978-79): 129-37 [Hebrew].

Ginzburg, Carlo. "Clues: Roots of an Evidential Paradigm." In *Clues, Myths, and the Historical Method,* 96-125. Baltimore: Johns Hopkins University Press, 1989.

———. *History, Rhetoric, and Proof.* The Menahem Stern Jerusalem Lectures. Hanover: University Press of New England, 1999.

Gitin, Seymour. "Seventh Century BCE Cultic Elements at Ekron." In *Biblical Archaeology Today, 1990: Proceedings of the Second International Congress on Biblical Archaeology,* 248-58. Jerusalem: Israel Exploration Society and the Israel Academy of Sciences and Humanities, 1993.

Glock, Albert E. "Taanach." *ABD* 6:287-90.

Gnuse, Robert Karl. *No Other God's: Emergent Monotheism in Israel.* JSOTSup 261. Sheffield: Sheffield Academic, 1997.

Goss, Robert E., and Mona West, eds. *Take Back the Word: A Queer Reading of the Bible.* Cleveland: Pilgrim, 2000.

Gottwald, Norman K. *The Politics of Ancient Israel.* Louisville: Westminster John Knox, 2001.

———. "Triumphalist versus Anti-Triumphalist Versions of Early Israel: A Response to Articles by Lemche and Dever in Volume 4 (1996)." *CurBS* 5 (1997): 15-42.

Grabbe, Lester L., ed. *Can a "History of Israel" Be Written?* JSOTSup 245. Sheffield: Sheffield Academic, 1997.

———. *Did Moses Speak Attic? Jewish Historiography and Scripture in the Hellenistic Period.* JSOTSup 317. Sheffield: Sheffield Academic, 2001.

———. *Leading Captivity Captive: "The Exile" as History and Ideology.* JSOTSup 278. Sheffield: Sheffield Academic, 1998.

———. *"Like a Bird in a Cage": The Invasion of Sennacherib in 701 BCE.* JSOTSup 363. Sheffield: Sheffield Academic, 2003.

Greenberg, Moshe. "On the Political Use of the Bible in Modern Israel: An Engaged Critique." In *Pomegranates and Golden Bells: Studies in Biblical, Jewish, and Near Eastern Ritual, Law, and Literature in Honor of Jacob Milgrom,* ed. David P. Wright, David Noel Freedman, and Avi Hurvitz, 461-71. Winona Lake: Eisenbrauns, 1995.

Greenstein, Edward L. "Deconstruction and Biblical Narrative." *Prooftexts* 9 (1989): 43-71.

175

Gudorf, Christine E. "Liberation Theology's Use of Scripture: A Response to First World Critics." *Int* 41 (1987): 5-18.

Gunn, David M., and Danna Nolan Fewell. *Narrative in the Hebrew Bible*. Oxford: Oxford University Press, 1993.

Gutiérrez, Gustavo. "The Situation and Tasks of Liberation Theology Today." In *Opting for the Margins*, ed. Joerg Rieger, 89-104. Oxford: Oxford University Press, 2003.

―――. *A Theology of Liberation*. Maryknoll: Orbis, 1973.

Haag, Ernst, ed. *Gott, der Einzige: Zur Entstehung des Monotheismus in Israel*. Quaestiones disputatae 135. Freiburg: Herder. 1985.

Habel, Norman C. *The Land Is Mine: Six Biblical Land Ideologies*. OBT. Minneapolis: Fortress, 1995.

Habermas, Jürgen. *Legitimation Crisis*. Boston: Beacon, 1975.

Hadley, Judith M. "Asherah: Archaeological and Textual Evidence." In *Ein Gott allein?* ed. Walter Dietrich and Martin A. Klopfenstein, 235-68. Göttingen: Vandenhoeck & Ruprecht, 1994.

―――. "Chasing Shadows? The Quest for the Historical Goddess." In *Congress Volume Cambridge, 1995*, ed. John A. Emerton, 169-84. VTSup 66. Leiden: Brill, 1997.

―――. *The Cult of Asherah in Ancient Israel and Judah: Evidence for a Hebrew Goddess*. University of Cambridge Oriental Publications 57. Cambridge: Cambridge University Press, 2000.

Halpern, Baruch. "'Brisker Pipes than Poetry': The Development of Israelite Monotheism." In *Judaic Perspectives on Ancient Israel*, ed. Jacob Neusner, Baruch A. Levine, and Ernest S. Frerichs, 77-115. Philadelphia: Fortress, 1987.

―――. *David's Secret Demons: Messiah, Murderer, Traitor, King*. The Bible in Its World. Grand Rapids: Wm. B. Eerdmans, 2001.

―――. "Erasing History: The Minimalist Assault on Ancient Israel." In *Israel's Past in Present Research: Essays on Ancient Israelite Historiography*, ed. V. Philips Long, 415-26. Sources for Biblical and Theological Study 7. Winona Lake: Eisenbrauns, 1999.

―――. "The Exodus from Egypt: Myth or Reality?" In *The Rise of Ancient Israel*, ed. Hershel Shanks et al., 87-113. Washington: Biblical Archaeology Society, 1992.

―――. *The First Historians*. San Francisco: Harper & Row, 1988.

―――. "The Gate of Megiddo and the Debate on the 10th Century." In *Congress Volume Oslo 1998*, ed. André Lemaire and Magne Saebø, 79-121. Leiden: Brill, 2000.

Hamacher, Werner, Neil Hertz, and Thomas Keenan, eds. *Responses: On Paul de Man's Wartime Journalism*. Lincoln: University of Nebraska Press, 1989.

———. *Wartime Journalism, 1939-1943* by Paul de Man. Lincoln: University of Nebraska Press, 1988.

Handelman, Susan A. *The Slayers of Moses: The Emergence of Rabbinic Interpretation in Modern Literary Theory.* Albany: State University of New York Press, 1982.

Hanson, Paul D. *The Diversity of Scripture: A Theological Interpretation.* OBT 11. Philadelphia: Fortress, 1982.

———. "A New Challenge to Biblical Theology." *JAAR* 67 (1999): 447-59.

Harrisville, Roy A., and Walter Sundberg. *The Bible in Modern Culture: Baruch Spinoza to Brevard Childs.* 2nd ed. Grand Rapids: Wm. B. Eerdmans, 2002.

Harvey, Van A. *The Historian and the Believer.* New York: Macmillan, 1966.

Hasel, Gerhard F. *Old Testament Theology: Basic Issues in the Current Debate.* 4th ed. Grand Rapids: Wm. B. Eerdmans, 1991.

Hauerwas, Stanley. "The Church's One Foundation Is Jesus Christ Her Lord: Or in a World Without Foundations All We Have Is the Church." In *Theology Without Foundations: Religious Practice and the Future of Theological Truth,* ed. Hauerwas, Nancey Murphy, and Mark Nation, 143-62. Nashville: Abingdon, 1994.

———. *A Community of Character: Toward a Constructive Christian Social Ethic.* Notre Dame: University of Notre Dame Press, 1981.

Hayes, John H. *Dictionary of Biblical Interpretation.* 2 vols. Nashville: Abingdon, 1999.

———, and Frederick C. Prussner. *Old Testament Theology: Its History and Development.* Atlanta: John Knox, 1985.

Hendel, Ronald S. "The Exodus in Biblical Memory." *JBL* 120 (2001): 601-22.

———. *Remembering Abraham: Culture, Memory and History in the Hebrew Bible.* Oxford: Oxford University Press, 2005.

Hennessy, Scott. "Creation, Chaos, and the Shoah." In *Lévinas and Biblical Studies,* ed. Tamara Cohn Eskenazi, Gary A. Phillips, and David Jobling, 49-63. Atlanta: SBL, 2003.

van Henten, Jan Willem, and Anton Houtepen, eds. *Religious Identity and the Invention of Tradition.* Assen: van Gorcum, 2001.

Hesse, Brian, and Paula Wapnish. "Can Pig Remains Be Used for Ethnic Diagnosis in the Ancient Near East?" In *Archaeology of Israel: Constructing the Past,* ed. Neil A. Silberman and David B. Small, 238-70. JSOTSup 237. Sheffield: Sheffield Academic, 1997.

Hestrin, Ruth. "The Cult Stand from Taʿanach and Its Religious Background." In *Phoenicia and the East Mediterranean in the First Millennium B.C.,* ed. Edward Lipiński, 61-77. Studia Phoenicia 5. Louvain: Peeters, 1987.

————. "Understanding Asherah: Exploring Semitic Iconography." *BAR* 17/5 (1991): 50-59.

Higgins, Jean M. "The Myth of Eve: The Temptress." *JAAR* 44 (1976): 639-47.

Hobsbawm, Eric, and Terence Ranger. *The Invention of Tradition.* Cambridge: Cambridge University Press, 1983.

Houten, Christiana van. *The Alien in Israelite Law.* JSOTSup 107. Sheffield: JSOT, 1991.

Hurtado, Larry W. *Lord Jesus Christ: Devotion to Jesus in Earliest Christianity.* Grand Rapids: Wm. B. Eerdmans, 2003.

————. *One God, One Lord.* Philadelphia: Fortress, 1988.

Hurvitz, Avi. "The Historical Quest for 'Ancient Israel' and the Linguistic Evidence of the Hebrew Bible." *VT* 47 (1997): 307-15.

van Iersel, Bas, and Anton Weiler, eds. *Exodus: A Lasting Paradigm.* Edinburgh: T. & T. Clark, 1987.

Irigaray, L. "Questions to Levinas: On the Divinity of Love." In *Re-Reading Levinas,* ed. Robert Bernasconi and Simon Critchley, 109-18. Bloomington: Indiana University Press, 1991.

Jenkins, Keith. *On "What Is History?" From Carr and Elton to Rorty and White.* London: Routledge, 1995.

Jobling, David. "Myth and Its Limits in Genesis 2.4b–3.24." In *The Sense of Biblical Narrative: Structural Analyses in the Hebrew Bible, II,* 17-43. JSOTSup 39. Sheffield: JSOT, 1986.

Johnson, William Stacy. "Reading the Scriptures Faithfully in a Postmodern Age." In *The Art of Reading Scripture,* ed. Ellen F. Davis and Richard B. Hays, 109-24. Grand Rapids: Wm. B. Eerdmans, 2003.

Kaminsky, Joel S. "Did Election Imply the Mistreatment of Non-Israelites?" *HTR* 96 (2003): 397-425.

Kant, Immanuel. "What Is Enlightenment?" In *Critique of Practical Reason and Other Writings in Moral Philosophy,* ed. Lewis W. Beck, 286-92. Chicago: University of Chicago Press, 1949.

Katz, Claire Elisé. *Levinas, Judaism, and the Feminine: The Silent Footsteps of Rebecca.* Bloomington: Indiana University Press, 2003.

Kaufmann, Yeḥezkel. *The Religion of Israel: From Its Beginnings to the Babylonian Exile.* Chicago: University of Chicago Press, 1960.

Kearney, Richard. *Dialogues with Contemporary Continental Thinkers.* Manchester: University of Manchester Press, 1984.

Keel, Othmar, and Christoph Uehlinger. *Gods, Goddesses, and Images of God in Ancient Israel.* Minneapolis: Fortress, 1998.

Kelsey, David H. *The Uses of Scripture in Recent Theology.* Philadelphia: Fortress, 1975.

Kennedy, James M. "Peasants in Revolt: Political Allegory in Genesis 2-3." *JSOT* 47 (1990): 3-14.

King, Philip J. *Amos, Hosea, Micah: An Archaeological Commentary.* Philadelphia: Westminster John Knox, 1988.

————, and Lawrence E. Stager. *Life in Biblical Israel.* Louisville: Westminster John Knox, 2001.

Kitchen, Kenneth A. *On the Reliability of the Old Testament.* Grand Rapids: Wm. B. Eerdmans, 2003.

Kletter, Raz. *The Judean Pillar Figurines and the Archaeology of Asherah.* Oxford: BAR, 1996.

Klopfenstein, Martin A. "Auferstehung der Göttin in der spätisraelitischen Weisheit von Prov 1-9." In Walter Dietrich and Klopfenstein, eds., *Ein Gott allein?* 531-42. Göttingen: Vandenhoeck & Ruprecht, 1994.

Knauf, Ernst Axel. "From History to Interpretation." In *The Fabric of History*, ed. Diana V. Edelman, 26-64. Sheffield: Sheffield Academic, 1991.

Knierim, Rolf. "The Task of Old Testament Theology." *HBT* 6 (1984): 25-57. Repr. in *The Flowering of Old Testament Theology*, ed. Ben C. Ollenburger, E. A. Martens, and Gerhard F. Hasel. Winona Lake: Eisenbrauns, 1992.

Kraeling, Emil G. *The Old Testament since the Reformation.* New York: Harper, 1955.

Kraus, Hans-Joachim. *Die Biblische Theologie.* Neukirchen-Vluyn: Neukirchener, 1970.

Krentz, Edgar. *The Historical-Critical Method.* Philadelphia: Fortress, 1975.

Küng, Hans, and Karl-Josef Kuschel. *A Global Ethic: The Declaration of the Parliament of the World's Religions.* London: SCM, 1993.

Lakeland, Paul. *Postmodernity: Christian Identity in a Fragmented Age.* Guides to Theological Inquiry. Minneapolis: Fortress, 1997.

Lang, Bernhard. *Monotheism and the Prophetic Minority: An Essay in Biblical History and Sociology.* Sheffield: Almond, 1983.

————, ed. *Der einzige Gott: Die Geburt des biblischen Monotheismus.* Munich: Kösel, 1981.

Lanser, Susan S. "(Feminist) Criticism in the Garden: Inferring Genesis 2-3." In *Speech Act Theory and Biblical Criticism,* ed. Hugh C. White, 67-84. Semeia 41. Decatur: Scholars, 1988.

Laqueur, Thomas. *Making Sex: Body and Gender from the Greeks to Freud.* Cambridge, Mass.: Harvard University Press, 1990.

LeGoff, Jacques. *History and Memory.* New York: Columbia University Press, 1992.

Lemaire, André. "Les inscriptions de Khirbet el-Qôm et l'Ashérah de YHWH." *RB* 84 (1977): 595-608.

179

————. "The Tel Dan Stela as a Piece of Royal Historiography." *JSOT* 81 (1998): 3-14.

————. "Who or What Was Yahweh's Asherah?" *BAR* 10/6 (1984): 42-51.

————, and Magne Saebø, eds. *Congress Volume Oslo 1998.* VTSup 80. Leiden: Brill, 2000.

Lemche, Niels Peter. *The Canaanites and Their Land: The Tradition of the Canaanites.* JSOTSup 110. Sheffield: JSOT, 1991.

————. "Early Israel Revisited." *CurBS* 4 (1996): 9-34.

————. *The Israelites in History and Tradition.* Louisville: Westminster, 1998.

————. "Response to William G. Dever, 'Revisionist Israel Revisited.'" *CurBS* 5 (1997): 9-14.

Levenson, Jon D. *The Death and Resurrection of the Beloved Son.* New Haven: Yale University Press, 1993.

————. *The Hebrew Bible, the Old Testament, and Historical Criticism.* Louisville: Westminster John Knox, 1993.

————. "Liberation Theology and the Exodus." In *Jews, Christians, and the Theology of the Hebrew Scriptures,* ed. Alice Ogden Bellis and Joel S. Kaminsky, 215-30. Atlanta: SBL, 2000.

————. "The Perils of Engaged Scholarship: A Rejoinder to Jorge Pixley." In *Jews, Christians, and the Theology of the Hebrew Scriptures,* ed. Alice Ogden Bellis and Joel S. Kaminsky, 239-46. Atlanta: SBL, 2000.

Lévinas, Emanuel. *Alterity and Transcendence.* New York: Columbia University Press, 1999.

————. *Is It Righteous to Be? Interviews with Emmanuel Lévinas.* Edited by Jill Robbins. Stanford: Stanford University Press, 2001.

————. "On Jewish Philosophy." In *In the Time of the Nations,* 167-83. Bloomington: Indiana University Press, 1994.

————. "On the Jewish Reading of Scriptures." In *Lévinas and Biblical Studies,* ed. Tamara Cohn Eskenazi, Gary A. Phillips, and David Jobling, 17-31. Atlanta: SBL, 2003.

————. "Revelation in the Jewish Tradition." In *Beyond the Verse: Talmudic Readings and Lectures,* 129-50. Bloomington: Indiana University Press, 1994.

————. *Totality and Infinity: An Essay on Exteriority.* Duquesne Studies: Philosophical Series 24. Pittsburgh: Duquesne University Press, 1969.

————. "Zionisms: Assimilation and New Culture." In *The Lévinas Reader,* ed. Seán Hand, 267-88. Oxford: Blackwell, 1989.

Lewis, Theodore J. "Baal-berith." *ABD* 1:550-51.

————. "Divine Images and Aniconism in Ancient Israel." *JAOS* 118 (1998): 36-53.

Lindbeck, George. *The Nature of Doctrine: Religion and Theology in a Postliberal Age.* Philadelphia: Westminster, 1984.

———. "Toward a Postliberal Theology." In *The Return to Scripture in Judaism and Christianity: Essays in Postcritical Scriptural Interpretation,* ed. Peter Ochs, 83-103. New York: Paulist, 1993.

Lipiński, Edward. "The Goddess Atirat in Ancient Arabia, in Babylon, and in Ugarit." *Orientalia Lovaniensia Periodica* 3 (1972): 101-19.

Lohfink, Norbert F., S.J. *Option for the Poor: The Basic Principle of Liberation Theology in the Light of the Bible.* Berkeley: BIBAL, 1987.

———. "Zur Geschichte der Diskussion über den Monotheismus im Alten Israel." In *Gott, der Einzige,* ed. Ernst Haag, 9-25. Freiburg: Herder, 1985.

Long, Burke O. *Planting and Reaping Albright: Politics, Ideology, and Interpreting the Bible.* University Park: Penn State University Press, 1997.

Louis, C., O.S.B., ed. *Rome and the Study of the Scriptures: A Collection of Papal Enactments on the Study of Holy Scripture together with the Decisions of the Biblical Commission.* 7th ed. St. Meinrad: Grail, 1962.

Lüdemann, Gerd. *The Unholy in Scripture: The Dark Side of the Bible.* Louisville: Westminster John Knox, 1997.

Lyotard, Jean-François. *The Postmodern Condition: A Report on Knowledge.* Theory and History of Literature 10. Minneapolis: University of Minnesota Press, 1984.

McCarter, P. Kyle, Jr. "Aspects of the Religion of the Israelite Monarchy: Biblical and Epigraphic Data." In *Ancient Israelite Religion,* ed. Patrick D. Miller, Paul D. Hanson, and S. Dean McBride, 137-55. Philadelphia: Fortress, 1987.

McCarthy, Brian Rice. "Response: Brueggemann and Hanson on God in the Hebrew Scriptures." *JAAR* 68 (2000): 615-20.

Machinist, Peter. "The Question of Distinctiveness in Ancient Israel." In *Ah, Assyria — : Studies in Assyrian History and Ancient Near Eastern Historiography Presented to Hayim Tadmor,* ed. Mordechai Cogan and Israel Eph'al, 196-212. Scripta Hierosolymitana 33. Jerusalem: Magnes, 1991.

MacIntyre, Alasdair. *After Virtue: A Study in Moral Theory.* Notre Dame: University of Notre Dame Press, 1981.

———. *Whose Justice? Which Rationality?* Notre Dame: University of Notre Dame Press, 1988.

McKenzie, Steven L., and Stephen R. Haynes, eds. *To Each Its Own Meaning: An Introduction to Biblical Criticisms and Their Application.* Louisville: Westminster John Knox, 1993.

Margalit, Baruch. "The Meaning and Significance of Asherah." *VT* 40 (1990): 257-97.

Marsden, George M. *Fundamentalism and American Culture: The Shaping of*

Twentieth-Century Evangelicalism, 1870-1925. New York: Oxford University Press, 1980.

Meshel, Ze'ev. "Did Yahweh Have a Consort?" *BAR* 5 (1979): 24-35.

———. "Kuntillet 'Ajrud." *ABD* 4:103-9.

———. *Kuntillet 'Ajrud: A Religious Centre from the Time of the Judean Monarchy on the Border of Sinai.* Jerusalem: Israel Museum, 1978.

Meyers, Carol L. *Discovering Eve: Ancient Israelite Women in Context.* New York: Oxford University Press, 1988.

———. *Households and Holiness: The Religion Culture of Israelite Women.* Facets. Minneapolis: Fortress, 2005.

Míguéz-Bonino, Jose, Solomon Avotri, and Choan-Seng Song. "Genesis 11:1-9: A Latin-American Perspective." In *Return to Babel: Global Perspectives on the Bible,* ed. Priscilla Pope-Levison and John R. Levison, 13-33. Louisville: Westminster John Knox, 1999.

Milbank, John. "The Midwinter Sacrifice." In *The Blackwell Companion to Postmodern Theology,* ed. Graham Ward, 107-30. Oxford: Blackwell, 2001.

Miller, J. Hillis. "An Open Letter to Professor Jon Wiener." In *Responses,* ed. Werner Hamacher, Neil Hertz, and Thomas Keenan, 334-42. Lincoln: University of Nebraska Press, 1989.

Miller, J. Maxwell, and John H. Hayes. *A History of Ancient Israel and Judah.* Philadelphia: Westminster, 1986.

Miller, Patrick D. *The Religion of Ancient Israel.* Louisville: Westminster John Knox, 2000.

———, Paul D. Hanson, and S. Dean McBride, eds. *Ancient Israelite Religion: Essays in Honor of Frank Moore Cross.* Philadelphia: Fortress, 1987.

Milne, Pamela. "No Promised Land: Rejecting the Authority of the Bible." In *Feminist Approaches to the Bible: Symposium at the Smithsonian Institution,* ed. Hershel Shanks, 47-73. Washington: Biblical Archaeological Society, 1995.

———. "Toward Feminist Companionship: The Future of Feminist Biblical Studies and Feminism." In *A Feminist Companion to Reading the Bible,* ed. Athalya Brenner and Carole Fontaine, 39-60. Sheffield: Sheffield Academic, 1997.

Moghadam, Valentine M., ed. *Identity Politics and Women: Cultural Reassertions and Feminisms in International Perspective.* Boulder: Westview, 1994.

Momigliano, Arnaldo. "Considerations on History in an Age of Ideologies." In *Sèttimo Contributo alla Storia degli Studi Classici e del Mondo Antico,* 253-69. Storia e Letteratura. Raccòlta di Studi e Tèsti 161. Rome: Edizioni di Storia e Letteratura, 1984.

———. "The Rhetoric of History and the History of Rhetoric: On Hayden

White's *Tropes.*" In *Sèttimo Contributo alla Storia degli Studi Classici e del Mondo Antico*, 49-59.

Moore, Stephen D. *God's Beauty Parlor and Other Queer Spaces in and around the Bible.* Stanford: Stanford University Press, 2001.

————. *God's Gym: Divine Male Bodies of the Bible.* New York: Routledge, 1996.

————. *Poststructuralism and the New Testament: Derrida and Foucault at the Foot of the Cross.* Minneapolis: Fortress, 1994.

Morgan, Robert, with John Barton. *Biblical Interpretation.* Oxford: Oxford University Press, 1988.

Mosala, Itumeleng J. *Biblical Hermeneutics and Black Theology in South Africa.* Grand Rapids: Wm. B. Eerdmans, 1989.

Mulder, Martin J. "Baal-Berith." *DDD*, 141-44.

Munz, Peter. *The Shapes of Time: A New Look at the Philosophy of History.* Middletown: Wesleyan University Press, 1977.

Na'aman, Nadav. "Cow Town or Royal Capital? Evidence for Iron Age Jerusalem." *BAR* 23/4 (1997): 43-47, 67.

Newman, Carey C., James R. Davila, and Gladys S. Lewis, eds. *The Jewish Roots of Christological Monotheism.* JSJSup 63. Leiden: Brill, 1999.

Newsom, Carol A. "Bakhtin, the Bible, and Dialogic Truth." *JR* 76 (1996): 290-306.

————. *The Book of Job: A Contest of Moral Imaginations.* Oxford: Oxford University Press, 2003.

Nicholson, Ernest W. *The Pentateuch in the Twentieth Century: The Legacy of Julius Wellhausen.* Oxford: Clarendon, 1998.

————. "Story and History in the Old Testament." In *Language, Theology and the Bible: Essays in Honour of James Barr,* ed. Samuel E. Balentine and John Barton, 135-50. Oxford: Clarendon, 1994.

Niditch, Susan. "Historiography, 'Hazards,' and the Study of Ancient Israel." *Int* 57 (2003): 138-50.

Nissen, Andreas. *Gott und der nächste im antiken Judentum.* WUNT 15. Tübingen: Mohr Siebeck, 1974.

Nissinen, Martti, ed. *Prophecy in Its Ancient Near Eastern Context: Mesopotamian, Biblical, and Arabian Perspectives.* SBLSymS 13. Atlanta: SBL, 2000.

North, Robert. "Ezra." *ABD* 2:726-28.

Noth, Martin. *Exodus.* OTL. Philadelphia: Westminster, 1962.

————. *The History of Israel.* New York: Harper & Row, 1960.

Novick, Peter. *That Noble Dream: The "Objectivity Question" and the American Historical Profession.* Cambridge: Cambridge University Press, 1988.

Ollenburger, Ben C. "From Timeless Ideas to the Essence of Religion: Method in

Old Testament Theology before 1930." In *The Flowering of Old Testament Theology*, ed. Ollenburger, E. A. Martens, and Gerhard F. Hasel, 3-19.

———, E. A. Martens, and Gerhard F. Hasel, eds. *The Flowering of Old Testament Theology: A Reader in Twentieth-Century Old Testament Theology, 1930-1990.* Winona Lake: Eisenbrauns, 1992.

Olyan, Saul M. *Asherah and the Cult of Yahweh in Israel.* SBLMS 34. Atlanta: Scholars, 1988.

Oppenheim, A. Leo. *Ancient Mesopotamia: Portrait of a Dead Civilization.* Chicago: University of Chicago Press, 1964.

Osborne, Peter. *The Politics of Time.* London: Verso, 1995.

Osiek, Carolyn. "The Feminist and the Bible: Hermeneutical Alternatives." In *Feminist Perspectives on Biblical Scholarship*, ed. Adela Yarbro Collins, 93-105. Chico: Scholars, 1985.

Palmer, Bryan D. *Descent into Discourse: The Reification of Language and the Writing of Social History.* Philadelphia: Temple University Press, 1990.

Pannenberg, Wolfhart. "Problems in a Theology of (Only) the Old Testament." In *Problems in Biblical Theology*, ed. Henry T. C. Sun and Keith L. Eades, 274-80. Grand Rapids: Wm. B. Eerdmans, 1997.

Patai, Raphael. *The Jewish Mind.* New York: Scribner, 1977.

Patte, Daniel. *The Ethics of Biblical Interpretation: A Reevaluation.* Louisville: Westminster John Knox, 1995.

Penchansky, David. *The Politics of Biblical Theology: A Postmodern Reading.* Macon: Macon University Press, 1995

———. *Twilight of the Gods: Polytheism in the Hebrew Bible.* Louisville: Westminster John Knox, 2005.

Perdue, Leo G. *The Collapse of History.* OBT. Minneapolis: Fortress, 1994.

———. *Reconstructing Old Testament Theology after the Collapse of History.* OBT. Minneapolis: Fortress, 2005.

———. *Wisdom and Creation: The Theology of Wisdom Literature.* Nashville: Abingdon, 1994.

Phillips, Gary A. "The Ethics of Reading Deconstructively, or Speaking Face to Face: The Samaritan Woman Meets Derrida at the Well." In *The New Literary Criticism and the New Testament*, ed. Edgar V. McKnight and Elizabeth Struther Malbon, 283-325. JSNTSup 109. Sheffield: Sheffield Academic, 1994.

Pleins, J. David. *The Social Visions of the Hebrew Bible: A Theological Introduction.* Louisville: Westminster John Knox, 2001.

Porten, Bezalel. "The Jews in Egypt." In *The Cambridge History of Judaism*, 1: *Introduction; The Persian Period*, ed. W. D. Davies and Louis Finkelstein, 372-400. Cambridge: Cambridge University Press, 1984.

Preuss, Horst Dietrich. *Old Testament Theology*. 2 vols. Louisville: Westminster, 1995-96. German original, Stuttgart: Kohlhammer, 1991.

Prior, Michael. *The Bible and Colonialism*. Biblical Seminar 48. Sheffield: Sheffield Academic, 1997.

Provan, Iain W. "Ideologies, Literary and Critical: Reflections on Recent Writing on the History of Israel." *JBL* 114 (1995): 585-606.

————. "In the Stable with the Dwarves: Testimony, Interpretation, Faith and the History of Israel." In *Congress Volume Oslo,* ed. André Lemaire and Magne Saebø, 281-319. Leiden: Brill, 2000. Repr. in *Windows into Old Testament History,* ed. V. Philips Long, David W. Baker, and Gordon J. Wenham, 161-97. Grand Rapids: Wm. B. Eerdmans, 2002.

————, V. Phillips Long, and Tremper Longman III. *A Biblical History of Israel*. Louisville: Westminster John Knox, 2003.

Pui Lan, Kwok. "Discovering the Bible in the Non-Biblical World." In *Interpretation for Liberation,* ed. Katie G. Cannon and Elisabeth Schüssler Fiorenza, 25-42. Semeia 47. Atlanta: Scholars, 1989.

————. *Postcolonial Imagination and Feminist Theology*. Louisville: Westminster John Knox, 2005.

von Rad, Gerhard. "Offene Fragen im Umkreis einer Theologie des Alten Testaments." *ThLZ* 88 (1963): 401-16. Repr. in *Gesammelte Studien zum Alten Testament*. ThB 48. Munich: Kaiser, 1973.

————. *Old Testament Theology*. 2 vols. New York: Harper & Row, 1962.

Rainey, Anson. "The 'House of David' and the House of the Deconstructionists." *BAR* 20/6 (1994): 47.

Rapaport, Herman. *The Theory Mess: Deconstruction in Eclipse*. New York: Columbia University Press, 2001.

Rendtorff, Rolf. "Approaches to Old Testament Theology." In *Problems in Biblical Theology,* ed. Henry T. C. Sun and Keith L. Eades, 13-26. Grand Rapids: Wm. B. Eerdmans, 1997.

Rieger, Joerg, ed. *Opting for the Margins: Postmodernity and Liberation in Christian Theology*. Oxford: Oxford University Press, 2003.

Röllig, W. "Bethel." *DDD,* 173-75.

Rogers, Max G. "Briggs, Charles Augustus (1841-1913)." In *Dictionary of Biblical Interpretation,* ed. John H. Hayes, 1:138-39. Nashville: Abingdon, 1999.

Rogerson, John W. *The Bible and Criticism in Victorian Britain: Profiles of F. D. Maurice and William Robertson Smith*. JSOTSup 201. Sheffield: Sheffield Academic, 1995.

————. "Smith, William Robertson (1846-94)." In *Dictionary of Biblical Interpretation,* ed. John H. Hayes, 2:477-78. Nashville: Abingdon, 1999.

Rorty, Richard. *Consequences of Pragmatism.* Minneapolis: University of Minnesota Press, 1982.

————. *Contingency, Irony, and Solidarity.* Cambridge: Cambridge University Press, 1989.

————. *Philosophy and the Mirror of Nature.* Princeton: Princeton University Press, 1979.

————. "Pragmatism, Relativism, and Irrationalism." *Proceedings and Addresses of the American Philosophical Association* 53 (1980): 719-38.

Rowlett, Lori L. *Joshua and the Rhetoric of Violence: A New Historicist Analysis.* JSOTSup 226. Sheffield: Sheffield Academic, 1996.

Russell, Letty M. "Authority and the Challenge of Feminist Interpretation." In *Feminist Interpretation of the Bible,* 137-46. Philadelphia: Westminster, 1985.

Rutledge, David. *Reading Marginally: Feminism, Deconstruction, and the Bible.* Biblical Interpretation 21. Leiden: Brill, 1996.

Said, Edward W. *Culture and Imperialism.* New York: Vintage, 1994.

————. "Michael Walzer's 'Exodus and Revolutions,' A Canaanite Reading." *Grand Street* 5 (Winter 1986): 86-106.

————. *Orientalism.* New York: Vintage, 1979.

Sakenfeld, Katherine Doob. "Feminist Biblical Interpretation." *Theology Today* 46 (1989): 154-68.

————. "Feminist Perspectives on Bible and Theology: An Introduction to Selected Issues and Literature." *Int* 42 (1988): 5-18.

Sanders, James A. "Adaptable for Life: The Nature and Function of Canon." In *Magnalia Dei: The Mighty Acts of God: Essays on the Bible and Archaeology in Memory of George Ernest Wright,* ed. Frank Moore Cross, Werner E. Lemke, and Patrick D. Miller, 531-60. Garden City: Doubleday, 1976.

Sandys-Wunsch, John, and Laurence Eldredge. "J. P. Gabler and the Distinction between Biblical and Dogmatic Theology: Translation, Commentary, and Discussion of His Originality." *SJT* 33 (1980): 133-58.

Schmidt, Brian B. "The Iron Age *Pithoi* Drawings from Horvat Teman or Kuntillet 'Ajrud: Some New Proposals." *JANER* 2 (2002): 91-125.

Schmidt, Werner H. "'Jahwe und . . .': Anmerkungen zur sog. Monotheismus-Debatte." In *Die Hebräische Bibel und ihre zweifache Nachgeschichte: Festschrift für Rolf Rendtorff zum 65. Geburtstag,* ed. Erhard Blum, Christian Macholz, and Ekkehard W. Stegemann, 425-48. Neukirchen-Vluyn: Neukirchener, 1990.

Schroer, Silvia. *In Israel gab es Bilder?* OBO 74. Göttingen: Vandenhoeck & Ruprecht, 1987.

Schüssler Fiorenza, Elisabeth. *But She Said: Feminist Practices of Biblical Interpretation.* Boston: Beacon, 1992.

———. "The Ethics of Biblical Interpretation: De-Centering Biblical Scholarship." *JBL* 107 (1988): 3-17.

———. "Feminist Hermeneutics." *ABD* 2:783-91.

———. *In Memory of Her: A Feminist Theological Reconstruction of Christian Origins.* New York: Crossroad, 1983.

———. *Jesus and the Politics of Interpretation.* New York: Continuum, 2000.

———. "Remembering the Past in Creating the Future: Historical-Critical Scholarship and Feminist Biblical Interpretation." In *Feminist Perspectives on Biblical Scholarship,* ed. Adela Yarbro Collins, 43-64. Chico: Scholars, 1985.

———. *Rhetoric and Ethic: The Politics of Biblical Studies.* Minneapolis: Fortress, 1999.

Schwartz, Regina M. *The Curse of Cain: The Violent Legacy of Monotheism.* Chicago: University of Chicago Press, 1997.

Schweiker, William. Review of Daniel Patte, *The Ethics of Biblical Interpretation: A Reevaluation. JR* 76 (1996): 355-57.

Scott, James C. *Domination and the Arts of Resistance: Hidden Transcripts.* New Haven: Yale University Press, 1990.

Scott, Joan Wallach. *Gender and the Politics of History.* New York: Columbia University Press, 1988.

Segal, Robert A., ed. *The Myth and Ritual Theory.* Oxford: Blackwell, 1998.

Shanks, Hershel, "In This Corner: William Dever and Israel Finkelstein Debate the Early History of Israel." *BAR* 30/6 (2004): 42-45.

———. "Where is the Tenth Century?" *BAR* 24/2 (1998): 56-61.

———, and Jack Meinhardt, eds. *Aspects of Monotheism: How God Is One.* Washington: Biblical Archeology Society, 1997.

Shapiro, Susan E. "'And God Created Woman': Reading the Bible Otherwise." In *Levinas and Biblical Studies,* ed. Tamara Cohn Eskenazi, Gary A. Phillips, and David Jobling, 159-95. Atlanta: SBL, 2003.

Sherwood, Yvonne. *A Biblical Text and Its Afterlives: The Survival of Jonah in Western Culture.* Cambridge: Cambridge University Press, 2000.

———. *The Prostitute and the Prophet: Hosea's Marriage in Literary-Theoretical Perspective.* JSOTSup 212. Sheffield: Sheffield Academic, 1996.

———, ed. *Derrida's Bible: Reading a Page of Scripture with a Little Help from Derrida.* New York: Palgrave Macmillan, 2004.

———, and Kevin Hart, ed. *Derrida and Religion: Other Testaments.* New York: Routledge, 2005.

Smend, Rudolf. "Julius Wellhausen and his *Prolegomena to the History of Israel.*" *Semeia* 25 (1982): 1-20.

Smith, Daniel L. "The Politics of Ezra: Sociological Indicators of Postexilic

Judaean Society." In *Second Temple Studies, 1: Persian Period,* ed. Philip R. Davies, 73-97. JSOTSup 117. Sheffield: JSOT, 1991.

Smith, Mark S. *The Early History of God.* 2nd ed. Biblical Resource Series. Grand Rapids: Wm. B. Eerdmans and Livonia: Dove, 2002.

———. *The Origins of Biblical Monotheism: Israel's Polytheistic Background and the Ugaritic Texts.* New York: Oxford University Press, 2001.

———. "Remembering God: Collective Memory in Israelite Religion." *CBQ* 64 (2002): 631-51.

Smith, Morton. *Palestinian Parties and Politics That Shaped the Old Testament.* New York: Columbia University Press, 1971.

Smith, W. Robertson. *The Religion of the Semites.* London: Black, 1894. Repr. New Brunswick: Transaction, 2002.

Smith-Christopher, Daniel L. "The Book of Daniel." NIB 7: 17-151.

Soggin, J. Alberto. *A History of Ancient Israel.* Philadelphia: Westminster, 1985.

Sommer, Benjamin D. "Unity and Plurality in Jewish Canons: The Case of the Oral and Written Torahs." In *One Scripture or Many? Canon from Biblical, Theological, and Philosophical Perspectives,* ed. Christine Helmer and Christoph Landmesser, 108-50. Oxford: Oxford University Press, 2004.

Spivak, Gayatri Chakravorty. "Can the Subaltern Speak?" In *Marxism and the Interpretation of Culture,* ed. Cary Nelson and Lawrence Grossberg, 271-313. Urbana: University of Illinois Press, 1988.

Stager, Lawrence E. "Forging an Identity." In *The Oxford History of the Biblical World,* ed. Michael D. Coogan, 123-75. New York: Oxford University Press 1998.

Stanton, Elizabeth Cady, ed. *The Woman's Bible.* New York: European, 1895. Repr. Mineola, N.Y.: Dover, 2002.

Stendahl, Krister. "Biblical Theology, Contemporary." *IDB* 418-32.

Stone, Ken. "The Garden of Eden and the Heterosexual Contract." In *Take Back the Word,* ed. Robert E. Goss and Mona West, 57-70. Cleveland: Pilgrim, 2000.

———, ed. *Queer Commentary and the Hebrew Bible.* JSOTSup 334. Cleveland: Pilgrim, 2001.

Stout, Jeffrey. *Ethics after Babel: The Languages of Morals and Their Discontents.* Boston: Beacon, 1988.

Sugirtharajah, R. S. *Postcolonial Criticism and Biblical Interpretation.* Oxford: Oxford University Press, 2002.

Sullivan, Nikki. *A Critical Introduction to Queer Theory* (New York: New York University Press, 2003).

Sullivan, William M. "After Foundationalism: The Return to Practical Philosophy." In *Anti-Foundationalism and Practical Reasoning,* ed. Evan Simpson, 21-44. Edmonton: Academic, 1987.

Sun, Henry T. C., and Keith L. Eades, eds. *Problems in Biblical Theology: Essays in Honor of Rolf Knierim.* Grand Rapids: Wm. B. Eerdmans, 1997.

Tadmor, Miriam. "Female Cult Figurines in Late Canaan and Early Israel: Archaeological Evidence." In *Studies in the Period of David and Solomon and Other Essays,* ed. Tomoo Ishida, 139-73. Winona Lake: Eisenbrauns, 1982.

Talmon, Shemaryahu. "The Desert Motif." In *Biblical Motifs,* ed. Alexander Altmann, 31-63. Cambridge, Mass.: Harvard University Press, 1966.

Taylor, Charles. *Sources of the Self: The Making of the Modern Identity.* Cambridge, Mass.: Harvard University Press, 1989.

Taylor, J. Glenn. *Yahweh and the Sun: Biblical and Archaeological Evidence for Sun Worship in Ancient Israel.* JSOTSup 111. Sheffield: JSOT, 1993.

Thiel, John E. *Nonfoundationalism.* Guides to Theological Inquiry. Minneapolis: Fortress, 1994.

Thompson, Thomas L. *Early History of the Israelite People from the Written and Archaeological Sources.* SHANE 4. Leiden: Brill, 1992.

———. *The Historicity of the Patriarchal Narratives.* BZAW 133. Berlin: de Gruyter, 1974.

———. "'House of David': An Eponymic Referent to Yahweh as Godfather." *SJOT* 9 (1995): 59-74.

———. *The Mythic Past: Biblical Archaeology and the Myth of Israel.* New York: Basic Books, 1999.

———. "A Neo-Albrightean School in History and Biblical Scholarship?" *JBL* 114 (1995): 683-98.

Tigay, Jeffrey II. "Israclite Religion: The Onomastic and Epigraphic Evidence." In *Ancient Israelite Religion,* ed. Patrick D. Miller, Paul D. Hanson, and S. Dean McBride, 157-94. Philadelphia: Fortress, 1987.

———. *You Shall Have No Other Gods: Israelite Religion in the Light of Hebrew Inscriptions.* HSS 31. Atlanta: Scholars, 1986.

Tolbert, Mary Ann. "Defining the Problem: The Bible and Feminist Hermeneutics." In *The Bible and Feminist Hermeneutics,* 113-26. Semeia 28. Chico: Scholars, 1983.

Tombs, David. *Latin American Liberation Theology.* Leiden: Brill, 2002.

van der Toorn, Karel. "Anat-Yahu, Some Other Deities, and the Jews of Elephantine." *Numen* 39 (1992): 80-101.

———. "The Exodus as Charter Myth." In *Religious Identity and the Invention of Tradition,* ed. Jan Willem van Henten and Anton Houtepen, 113-27. Assen: van Gorcum, 2001.

Tracy, David. *The Analogical Imagination.* New York: Crossroad, 1981.

———. "Exodus: Theological Reflection." In *Exodus: A Lasting Paradigm*, ed. Bas van Iersel and Anton Weiler, 118-24. Edinburgh: T&T Clark, 1987.

Trible, Phyllis. "Depatriarchalizing in Biblical Interpretation." *JAAR* 41 (1973): 30-48.

———. "Eve and Adam: Genesis 2–3 Reread." *Andover Newton Quarterly* 13 (1973): 251-58.

———. *God and the Rhetoric of Sexuality*. OBT 2. Philadelphia: Fortress, 1978.

———. *Texts of Terror: Literary-Feminist Readings of Biblical Narratives*. OBT 13. Philadelphia: Fortress, 1984.

Troeltsch, Ernst. "Historiography." In *Encyclopedia of Religion and Ethics* 6, ed. James Hastings, 716-23. New York: Scribner, 1914.

———. "Über historische und dogmatische Methode in der Theologie." *Gesammelte Schriften*, vol. 2, 729-53. Tübingen: Mohr, 1913.

Tutu, Desmond. *The Rainbow People of God: The Making of a Peaceful Revolution*. New York: Doubleday, 1994.

de Vaux, Roland. "Is It Possible to Write a 'Theology of the Old Testament'?" In *The Bible and the Ancient Near East*, 49-62. Garden City: Doubleday, 1971.

de Vries, Hent. *Philosophy and the Turn to Religion*. Baltimore: Johns Hopkins University Press, 1999.

Wacker, Marie-Theres. "Historical, Hermeneutical, and Methodological Foundations." In *Feminist Interpretation: The Bible in Women's Perspective*, ed. Luise Schottroff, Silvia Schroer, and Wacker, 3-35. Minneapolis: Fortress, 1998.

———, and Erich Zenger, eds. *Der Eine Gott und die Göttin: Gottesvorstellungen des biblischen Israel im Horizont feministischer Theologie*. Quaestiones disputatae 135. Freiburg: Herder, 1991.

Walhout, Mark. "The Intifada of the Intellectuals: An Ecumenical Perspective on the Walzer-Said Exchange." In *Postcolonial Literature and the Biblical Call for Justice*, ed. Susan VanZanten Gallagher, 198-217. Jackson: University of Mississippi Press, 1994.

Walls, Neal H. *The Goddess Anat in Ugaritic Myth*. SBLDS 135. Atlanta: Scholars, 1992.

Walsh, Carey Ellen. *Exquisite Desire: Religion, the Erotic, and the Song of Songs*. Minneapolis: Fortress, 2000.

Walzer, Michael. *Exodus and Revolution*. New York: Basic Books, 1985.

———, and Edward W. Said. "An Exchange." *Grand Street* 5 (Summer, 1986): 246-59.

Warrior, Robert Allen. "Canaanites, Cowboys, and Indians: Deliverance, Conquest, and Liberation Theology Today." *Christianity and Crisis* 49 (1989): 261-65.

Watson, Francis. *Text and Truth: Redefining Biblical Theology.* Grand Rapids: Wm. B. Eerdmans, 1997.

Weems, Renita. "Gomer: Victim of Violence or Victim of Metaphor?" In *Interpretation for Liberation,* ed. Katie G. Cannon and Elisabeth Schüssler Fiorenza, 87-104. Atlanta: Scholars, 1989.

―――. "Reading Her Way through the Struggle: African American Women and the Bible." In *Stony the Road We Trod: African American Biblical Interpretation,* ed. Cain Hope Felder, 57-77. Minneapolis: Fortress, 1991.

Weinfeld, Moshe. *Deuteronomy and the Deuteronomic School.* Oxford: Clarendon, 1972. Repr. Winona Lake: Eisenbrauns, 1992.

―――. *Social Justice in Ancient Israel and in the Ancient Near East.* Minneapolis: Fortress, 1995.

Wellhausen, Julius. *Die kleinen Propheten.* 3rd ed. Berlin: Reimer, 1898.

Wessels, Anton. "Biblical Presuppositions for and against Syncretism." In *Dialogue and Syncretism: An Interdisciplinary Approach,* ed. Jerold Gort, Hendrik Vroom, Rein Ferhout, and Wessels, 52-65. Grand Rapids: Wm. B. Eerdmans, 1989.

West, Gerald O. *Biblical Hermeneutics of Liberation: Modes of Reading the Bible in the South African Context.* 2nd ed. Maryknoll: Orbis, 1991.

Westermann, Claus. *Genesis 1–11.* CC. Minneapolis: Augsburg, 1984.

White, Hayden. *Metahistory: The Historical Imagination in Nineteenth-Century Europe.* Baltimore: Johns Hopkins University Press, 1973.

―――. "New Historicism: A Comment." In *The New Historicism,* ed. H. Aram Veeser, 293-302. London: Routledge, 1989.

―――. *Tropics of Discourse.* Baltimore: Johns Hopkins University Press, 1978.

Whitelam, Keith. *The Invention of Ancient Israel: The Silencing of Palestinian History.* London: Routledge, 1996.

Wiggins, Steve A. *A Reassessment of "Asherah": A Study According to the Textual Sources of the First Two Millennia B.C.E.* AOAT 235. Neukirchen-Vluyn: Neukirchener, 1993.

Wilson, Norman J. *History in Crisis? Recent Directions in Historiography.* Upper Saddle River: Prentice Hall, 1999.

Wilson, Veronica. "The Iconography of Bes with Particular Reference to the Cypriot Evidence." *Levant* 7 (1975): 77-103.

Wittgenstein, Ludwig. *Philosophical Investigations.* 3rd ed. Oxford: Blackwell, 1968.

von Wolde, Ellen. "The Tower of Babel as Lookout over Genesis 1–11." In *Words Become Worlds: Semantic Studies of Genesis 11:1-9,* 84-109. Biblical Interpretation 6. Leiden: Brill, 1994.

Wright, G. Ernest. *God Who Acts: Biblical Theology as Recital.* SBT 8. London: SCM, 1952.

——. *The Old Testament Against Its Environment.* SBT 2. London: SCM, 1950.

——, and Reginald H. Fuller. *The Book of the Acts of God: Christian Scholarship Interprets the Bible.* Garden City: Doubleday, 1957.

Wyatt, Nicholas. "Asherah." *DDD,* 99-105.

Wyschogrod, Edith. *Emmanuel Lévinas: The Problem of Ethical Metaphysics.* 2nd ed. New York: Fordham University Press, 2000.

Yadin, Yigael. "Hazor, Gezer and Megiddo in Solomon's Time." In *The Kingdoms of Israel and Judah,* ed. Abraham Malamat, 66-109. Jerusalem: Israel Exploration Society, 1961.

Yarbro Collins, Adela, ed. *Feminist Perspectives on Biblical Scholarship.* SBLBSNA 10. Chico: Scholars, 1985.

——, and John J. Collins. "The Book of Truth: Daniel as Reliable Witness to Past and Future in the United States of America." In *Europa, Tausendjähriges Reich und Neue Welt: Zwei Jahrtausende Geschichte und Utopie in der Rezeption des Danielbuches,* ed. M. Delgado, K. Koch, and E. Marsch, 385-404. Stuttgart: Kohlhammer, 2003.

Yee, Gale A. *Poor Banished Children of Eve: Woman as Evil in the Hebrew Bible.* Minneapolis: Fortress, 2005.

Yoder, John Howard. "Probing the Meaning of Liberation." *Sojourners* 5/7 (1976): 26-29.

Young, Robert J. C. *Postcolonialism: An Historical Introduction.* Oxford: Blackwell, 2001.

Zenger, Erich. "Das jahwistische Werk: Ein Wegbereiter des jahwistischen Monotheismus?" In *Gott der Einzige,* ed. Ernst Haag, 26-53. Freiburg: Herder, 1985.

Zevit, Ziony. *The Religions of Ancient Israel: A Synthesis of Parallactic Approaches.* New York: Continuum, 2000.

Index of Names

Index of Ancient Literature